SWAMI VIVEKANANDA

Swami Vivekananda

SWAMI VIVEKANANDA

A Reassessment

Narasingha P. Sil

SUP

Selinsgrove: Susquehanna University Press
London: Associated University Presses

Associated University Presses
440 Forsgate Drive
Cranbury, NJ 08512

Associated University Presses
16 Barter Street
London WC1A 2AH, England

Associated University Presses
P.O. Box 338, Port Credit
Mississauga, Ontario
Canada L5G 4L8

The paper used in this publication meets the requirements of the American National Standard for Permanence of Paper for Printed Library Materials Z39.48–1984.

Library of Congress Cataloging-in-Publication Data

Sil, Narasingha Prosad (date)
  Swami Vivekananda : a reassessment / Narasingha P. Sil.
     p.   cm.
  Includes bibliographical references and index.
  ISBN 0-945636-97-0 (alk. paper)
  1. Vivekananda, Swami, 1863–1902. 2. Ramakrishna Mission—
Biography. 3. Hindus—India—Biography. I. Title.
BL1280.292.V58S55   1997
294.5′55′092—dc20
[B]   96-29425
                                                           CIP

PRINTED IN THE UNITED STATES OF AMERICA

For *Sati*

Contents

Abbreviations

B.E.   Bengali Era, that is, the Bengali calendar, which precedes the Gregorian calendar by 593 years, 3 months, and 14 days in reckoning time. For example, 1401 B.E. coincides with A.D. 1994.

CB   Shailendranath Dhar, *A Comprehensive Biography of Swami Vivekananda,* 2 vols.

CW   *The Complete Works of Swami Vivekananda,* 8 vols.

DBN   Lizelle Reymond, *The Dedicated: A Biography of Nivedita*

KM   Mahendranath Gupta (ŚrīM), *Śrīśrīramakrishnakathāmṛta,* 5 *bhāgas* [parts].

KSV   Mahendranath Datta, *Kāśīdhāme Swami Vivekananda*

LoSV   Mahendranath Datta, *Londone Swami Vivekananda,* 3 vols. in 2 pts.

LP   Svami Saradananda, *Śrīśrīramakrishnalīlāprasaṅga,* 5 pts. in 2 vols.

LSN   *Letters of Sister Nivedita,* 2 vols.

LSV   His Eastern & Western Disciples, *The Life of Swami Vivekananda,* 2 vols.

LV   *Letters of Swami Vivekananda*

MJD   Dr. Abhaychandra Bhattacharya, *ŚrīMar Jīvan Darśan*

NWV   Sister Nivedita, *Notes of Some Wanderings with the Swami Vivekananda*

PAT   Svami Vivekananda, *Patrāvalī*

RBM   Svami Gambhirananda, *Śrīramakrishna Bhaktamālikā,* 2 vols.

REM   His Eastern & Western Admirers, *Reminiscences of Swami Vivekananda*

RPP   Narasingha P. Sil, *Rāmakṛṣṇa Paramahaṁsa: A Psychological Profile*

SAS   Swami Purnatmananda, *Smṛtir Āloy Swamiji*

SPP   Swami Abjajananda, *Swamijīr Padaprānte (Swami Vivekanander Sannyāsī-Śiṣyaganer Jīvancarit)*

SSS   Saracchandra Chakravarti, *Swami Śiṣya Saṁvād*

SVV   Mahendranath Datta, *Swami Vivekanander Vālyajīvanī*

VAC   Niranjan Dhar, *Vivekananda Anya Cokhe*

VIN   Sankari P. Basu and Sunil B. Ghosh, eds. *Vivekananda in Indian Newspapers, 1893–1902*

VJG   Mahendranath Datta, *Śrīmat Vivekananda Swamijīr Jīvaner Ghatanāvalī*, 3 vols.

VUG   Romain Rolland, *Life of Swami Vivekananda and the Universal Gospel*

Preface

THE reputation of Swami Vivekananda (monastic name of Narendra-nath Datta), Ramakrishna Paramahamsa's most famous and favorite disciple, as the spiritual ambassador of India to the West has been established since his celebrated address to the World's Parliament of Religions in Chicago in September 1893. Within India the Swami has been a most powerful inspiration behind the country's successful nationalist struggle and her subsequent development. Above all Swa-miji's has been the most authoritative voice of Hindu India, which owes its prominence in the comity of nations to the resounding roars of this Vedantic lion in the West a century ago.

Such an august personality has been the subject of a powerful my-thology started by his admirers, devotees, and disciples and perpetu-ated by the Ramakrishna Order which he founded. He is seen not just as a patriot-prophet of resurgent India but much more—an incar-nation of Shiva, Buddha, and Jesus. His magnificent portrait as a handsome, gorgeously attired heroic monk has become a national icon—at once a Hindu messiah, a socialist thinker and worker of the highest caliber and perspicacity, a modern educationist, an emancipa-tor of the poor, the high priest of women's liberation and regencra-tion, a great patriot, and a most astute observer of international politics of his time—in short, a veritable *Übermensch* of Friedrich Nietzsche's idea.[1] To this day the great Swami continues to command universal ovation and obeisance from pupils, pundits, and politicians alike. Even marxist and socialist activists of recent times have engaged in serious polemics on their right to quote from Vivekananda's ser-mons and writings in their ideological battles.[2] On the occasion of the birth anniversary of India's late Prime Minister Rajeev Gandhi a few years ago, his huge cardboard cutout showed him in turbans in order to give it "the Swami Vivekananda" look.[3] The Swami's ubiqui-tous influence on modern India has been most succinctly recognized by a scholar-politician of independent India, who declared: "We . . . owe everything to Swami Vivekananda."[4]

It has at once been an exciting and exasperating experience to write a critical evaluation of such a historical figure. Sifting the chaf from the grain in almost all the sources for his life and *logia,* the author

11

has risked resentment of friends, fellow-scholars, and, of course, the devotees of Swamiji in this country as well as in India. Yet his overriding concern has been to pay heed to the scholarly warnings against apologetic writings on Indian saints and prophets. Professor White reminded us long ago that "there is little biographical material that one can be certain of, while the tradition concerning their lives . . . achieve [a] kind of stylization."[5] My earlier psychohistorical study of Ramakrishna has been a response to this admonition against hagiography.[6] Centuries ago St. Augustine said something that still remains valid for the world of scholars: *Audi partem alteram*—"Hear the other side."

It is absolutely essential that Vivekananda's achievements be assessed after a careful perusal of all the extant sources, especially those in Bengali. As I have demonstrated in my biography of Ramakrishna, any uncritical reliance on the existing translations is bound to be precarious, because most often those authorized by the Ramakrishna Order have been doctored or censored. As a native Bengali, I propose to offer my own translation of all the vernacular sources on the Swami. My translation of the passages from *Śrīśrīramakrishnakathāmṛta* has shown how the *Thākur*'s (that is, "Master's"—Ramakrishna's popular prefix) speech and behavior as recorded by the complier of this monumental diary were altered by the translator, Swami Nikhilananda, who claimed "to have made a literal translation omitting only a few pages of no particular interest to English-speaking readers."[7]

Although I appreciate, as has been pointed out by a friendly critic of an earlier draft of my proposal for this book, the need to distinguish between the Swami's personal failure and his cultural success,[8] I have chosen not to rehash what has been discussed in numerous tomes on the latter theme but instead to focus mainly on the man by evaluating his career and character on the basis mostly of his own conversations, missives, and ministrations. In this connection let me point out that an *imprimatur* for such an exercise has been provided by none other than a monk of the Ramakrishna Order itself, who has written: "Biography should be true. Otherwise we may fall into the difficulty of confusing the readers, should others write opposite facts."[9]

Several individuals, in addition to my wife Sati—who has always been a willing and smiling companion in all my scholarly pursuits since my graduate days—have provided substantial help. The Ramakrishna scholar Jeffrey Kripal of Westminster College has helped edit and improve the manuscript. The Kamalakanta scholar Rachel McDermott of Barnard College, not only rescued me from the harangues of monks and devotees at the Twenty-seventh Bengal Studies Conference at Old Westbury (May 27–29, 1994) with her superb leadership as the Chair of the session on Vivekananda in which I was a discussant but has also provided a thoughtful and helpful critique of an earlier draft of the chapter on the Swami and his women devotees. Dr. Rajagopal Chattopadhyaya of Bose Institute, Calcutta, whose reappraisal of Sister Gargi's voluminous *Swami Vivekananda in the West: New Discoveries* was published in 1994 and *World's Parliament of Religions, 1893* in 1995 in Calcutta, has been generous with his encouragement and advice during my last visit to India. He has also helped me contact the Brahmo scholar, Professor Surath Chakravarti, whose several papers in Bengali on Vivekananda at the World's Parliament of Religions have been extremely helpful, to say the least. Similarly thanks to Chattopadhyaya, I have benefited from my contact with the members of *Utsa Mānus,* an organization of progressive and enlightened professionals of Calcutta. I thank them all, though I remain, as always, solely responsible for the contents of my book.

Although I do not wish to minimize Sati's contributions by a formal acknowledgment with the customary "thank you" note, the least I can do by way of showing my gratitude and appreciation is to dedicate this work to her.

Acknowledgments

I thank the office of the Provost, Western Oregon State College, for having provided development funds in 1991 and in 1995 for acquiring primary sources in English available in the United States. My colleagues in the Social Science and the Humanities Divisions very patiently and kindly listened to my lectures on Vivekananda at the Social Science Faculty Seminar in early May 1994. Later that month, I presented a summary of the main arguments put forward in my book to the Twenty-seventh Bengal Studies Conference at the State University of New York, College at Old Westbury. I thank my audience for their enthusiasm, support, and constructive criticism. I also spoke on my research project for this book at the Salt Lake Seminar in September 1994 during my last visit to Calcutta. I thank Professor Surath Chakravarti for chairing the session and Dr. Rajagopal Chattopadhyaya for making the initial arrangements. Thanks are also due to the organizers of the Conference on Enriching the Curriculum: Understanding and Teaching Asian Studies at the College of DuPage, Westmont, Illinois, where I presented a paper on Vivekananda on 1 April 1995. I am grateful to Professors Ralph Nicholas and Clinton Seely for inviting me to present a paper on Vivekananda to the Thirtieth Anniversary Bengal Studies Conference at the University of Chicago on 29 April 1995. Above all I am, as always, deeply indebted to the Western Library, especially to Carolyn Hall and Lori Black, for their uniformly excellent and timely help in procuring numerous obscure titles used in my research. Finally I thank Swami Satyavratananda of Udbodhan Office and Swami Bodhasarananda of Advaita Ashrama, Dr. Ashoke Bandyopadhyay of Utsa Mānus, Devkumar Mukherjee of the Mahendra Publishing Committee, and K. P. Shivkumar of Vivekananda Kendra Prakashan for giving their permission to cite from a number of titles published by them. Likewise, I thank the editor of *Numen* for his permission to use my article "Vivekānanda's Rāmakṛṣṇa: An Untold Story of Mythmaking and Propaganda" (vol. 40, 1993) in chapter 8 of this book. It is, of course, understood that their permission to use their publications does not in any way constitute their endorsement of my interpretation of the life and teaching of Swami Vivekananda.

A Note on Bengali Orthography and Source Citations

ALL quotations from Bengali sources appear in my translation. Except those Bengali words and names too familiar in their conventional spelling to change or the *tatsama* (Sanskritized) Bengali words, I have avoided the use of "a" at the end of most Bengali terms because Bengalis do not generally pronounce the short "a" at the end of syllables. Also I have avoided the use of the Sanskritized "v" for the soft "b" appropriate for Bengali pronunciation in respect of *only* a few words. I have not used diacritics on proper nouns designating names of persons and, very sparingly, of places and also on the familiar religious terms and names of popular gods and goddesses.

SWAMI
VIVEKANANDA

Introduction

I

"... A young man exceptionally handsome and with features that would command attention anywhere"—reported the *Chicago Times* on 12 September 1893. On the same day another paper, the *Chicago Advocate* wrote: "In certain respects the most fascinating personality was the Brahmin [*sic*] monk, Swami Vivekananda with his flowing orange robe, saffron turban, smooth shaven, shapely, handsome face, large dark subtle penetrating eye, and with the air of one being inly-pleased with the consciousness of being easily master of his situation."[1] To A. Srinivasa Pai, "no photograph or description can give a correct idea of the power of his eyes. They were wonderful. Like the 'Ancient Mariner' in [Samuel T.] Coleridge's famous poem he 'held you by the eye.'"[2] A teacher of German in a Detroit high school was "so aware of his greatness and holiness that ... [she] couldn't bear to wash ... [her] hand for three days" after she shook hands with the fiery speaker with an unforgettable "searching look."[3] The prima donna of the French opera, Emma Calvé, felt her brain emptied "of all its feverish complexities" after the Swami told her to "become gay and happy" and transmute her emotions "into some form of external expression."[4] On meeting him for the first time, Edith Allan "kept on weeping as though the floodgates had been opened," and when she finally took leave of him, she had all her problems solved.[5] The young Harinath Waddedar was beside himself on beholding the Swami's countenance in Benares in 1902. As he confessed:

My mind was swayed simultaneously by the conflicting currents of titillation and terror. Sometimes I looked upon Swamiji and his companions. Sometimes I felt everything around me crumbling into nothing—a grand void. I felt I was on a flight to nowhere—without a body or the mind, devoid of thoughts. I was unable to linger in that silent space and I felt I was descending like someone awakened after slumber, and looking at the former spot and its people vaguely, as if half-awake.[6]

Martha Fincke was simply "fascinated by his turban."[7]

The *Boston Evening Transcript* of 30 September 1893 described the

21

young monk as a "large well-built man, with the superb carriage of the Hindustanis, his face clean-shaven, squarely molded regular features, white teeth, and with well-chiselled lips that are usually parted in a benevolent smile."[8] Swami Atulananda saw Vivekananda in New York in 1899 and did not at first consider his appearance as remarkable. However he was startled when he saw the Swami standing on the platform before beginning his lecture:

> What a giant, what strength, what manliness, what a personality! Everyone near him looks so insignificant in comparison. . . . What was it that gave Swamiji his distinction? Was it his height? No, there were gentlemen there taller than he was. Was it his build? No, there were near him some very fine specimens of American manhood. It seemed to be more in the expression of the face than anything else. Was it his purity? What was it? . . . I remembered what had been said of Lord Buddha—"a lion amongst men."[9]

Christina Greenstidel recalled her first impression of the Swami: "A sickly saint everyone understands, but who ever heard of a powerful saint? . . . What was it which emanated from him which all felt and none could explain? Was it the *ojas* of which he spoke, that mysterious power which comes when the physical forces of the body are transmuted into spiritual power?"[10] "[He] seemed to me so big," Mrs. Allan wrote, "as though he towered above ordinary mortals. The people on the street looked like pygmies and he had such a majestic presence that people stepped aside to let him pass by."[11] To her husband, Thomas J. Allan, the Swami appeared as a forty-foot giant.[12] He not only seemed taller than others and possessed "of a color calculated to make artists of fish wives," but, to Blanche Partington, he seemed "a Buddha come to judgment."[13]

Such was the impression created by Narendranath Datta in the West as well as in his own country. To almost everybody he appeared as the quintessential heroic monk (*vīra sannyāsī*). The journalists of Detroit called him "the cyclonic Hindu" for his fiery sermons. Indeed it was his handsome features, expressive eyes, and rich baritone voice, together with his colorful robe and turban, that made the young man from Calcutta the center of attention of the Americans, and especially American women, who simply found him enchanting, mysterious, and utterly irresistible. The reporter of a midwestern newspaper observed:

> When in certain emotional situations, he hisses out his iteration upon the *meddlesome* but intended kindness of other nations, one thought, O Vivekananda, were it possible for you to be a lover of women, what a

magnificent Othello you might make! but alas, this man of superb beauty is a Brahman Monk and therefore he may never marry.[14]

He not only appeared to many "as handsome as a god of classic sculpture,"[15] or as "someone out of the Bible,"[16] his sheer presence was believed to have exuded vibrations that affected even animals. As Sister Devamata recalled, "Even my dog—an Irish setter—felt this. He would stand perfectly still and a quiver would run through his body whenever Swamiji would lay his hand on his head and tell him he was a true *yogi*."[17] Perhaps the most eloquent description of Vivekananda's stature in the eyes of his devotees and admirers comes from Josephine MacLeod, who wrote: "The thing that held me in Swamiji is his *unlimitedness*. I never could touch the bottom—or top—or sides. The amazing size of him!"[18]

II

Like his spiritual mentor Ramakrishna, the Swami became a celebrity and a legendary figure during his lifetime. Hence it is not an easy task to see the historical and human Narendranath through the hagiographical halo that surrounds the personality of Swami Vivekananda. The problem is compounded further by a paucity of critical analyses of his character and career. All the existing biographies of the Swami, including Sister Gargi's monumental six–volume *New Discoveries* on Vivekananda's activities in the West, reaffirm the larger-than-life stature of a princely, handsome, erudite, and eloquent young man—the roaring Vedantic lion of fin de siècle India. Even the three most recent anthologies, based on the researches of leading Indian scholars, regard Swamiji as a hypercosmological and ultramundane *sannyāsī*, who was also a profoundly original thinker and social reformer—the patriot-prophet of modern India.[19]

In the entire *Thesaurus Vivekanandi*, the works of three scholars stand out for their critical stance. George Williams sought to "penetrate through dual consideration of the hero legend created by well-meaning followers, and of the camouflaging effect created by Vivekananda himself as he changed his patterns of ultimate concern during his lifetime."[20] His object was to rescue the historical Vivekananda from the "archetype of the spiritual hero" with a view toward discerning "the human quest for meaning and purpose" of life. Williams's study reveals how a restless young man, buffeted by the crosscurrents of family tradition, political trends, and the Brahmo Samaj,[21] was transformed into a Hindu revivalist under Ramakrishna's influence.

Williams also shows how Vivekananda resolved his spiritual/existential angst after he had discovered in the Advaita Vedanta the basis of a universal religion which he preached in the West. "It is in the calm with which he faced death," concludes Williams, "that one sees no evidence of his wrenching, lifelong doubts."[22] Williams constructed the profile of a sensitive and intelligent religious leader whose travails and tribulations remind one of the famous early modern Christian reformer, Martin Luther.[23]

Professor Niranjan Dhar's two brief but incisive chapters (VII: "Feudal Background of the Ramakrishna Movement" and VIII: "A Prophet under Duress") in his *Vedanta and Bengal Renaissance* bring out a lot of contradictions and discrepancies in the Swami's career and character and provide a refreshingly new and credible perspective to his sanitized and deified image. More recently Dhar's six essays published in the radical Bengali journal *Utsa Mānuṣ* (October 1983– June 1984) have taken a hard, critical look at Vivekananda's reputation for austerity and renunciation; his social, political, and humanitarian thoughts; and his actual achievements at the World's Parliament of Religions.[24] Dhar's rejoinder to a searching critique by an admirer of the Swami demonstrates the force of his arguments, as well as the justification for a continued critical examination of the Vivekananda phenomenon. The exchange between Dhar and his critic Aratikumar Basu, published in the *Utsa Mānuṣ* serially, has now been reprinted as a booklet; it makes fascinating reading.[25]

Professor Surath Chakravarti has extensively researched the Brahmo antecedents of Swami Vivekananda's Vedantic vocation. Chakravarti's various articles have sought to rescue Protap Mozoomdar, who had preached the essence of Vedanta in the United States a decade before Vivekananda's debut in Chicago, from the obscurity to which the Swami and his monastic brethren had relegated him— a trend that has continued with the monastic and academic exponents of Vivekananda's Vedantization of the world. Chakravarti has discovered numerous distortions and deliberate suppression of facts in the writings, especially of the most popular Vivekananda scholar in India at the moment, Professor Sankari Prasad Basu.[26] Chakravarti, who has published in such Brahmo journals as *Tattvakaumudī* and *Dharmatattva*, has been spared the fate of Professor Dhar, whose articles in the *Utsa Mānuṣ* have elicited adverse reader response.[27] Dhar's and Chakravarti's excellent scholarship seems to have left out of discussion Swamiji's various pronouncements on the situation of the women and the poor, especially his odyssey with his women disciples. And, of course, their work, which is written mainly in Bengali, remains inaccessible to scholars and researchers without the necessary language competence.

III

My study seeks, inter alia, to find answers to a number of questions: Was Narendranath really inclined spiritually since his childhood as maintained by all his biographers? How and when did he study the Hindu scriptures he taught in the West? What were the contents and interpretations of Hindu religion and culture he propagated abroad? What was his real attitude to women in general, and what were his experiences with some of his women devotees and disciples? And finally how should a historical evaluation of his achievements be reconciled with his colossal image in the studies that are extant? The editors' preface to *Vivekananda Anya Cokhe* aspires "to look at the human Vivekananda with the eyes of a rationalist and remove the halo of divinity surrounding his personality . . . [and] say those things that have hitherto remained unspoken." In similar spirit I attempt to uncover (or discover) the human Vivekananda behind the mask of an all-conquering *karmayogī* of the Orient. My study reveals the striving of an ambitious, idealistic, impulsive, and imaginative militant monk who envisioned, rather naively, a global spiritualization in the manner of a Napoleonic conquest.[28]

Sadly enough the restless Hindu missionary fell victim to his naïveté and nonchalance in respect to women. Vivekananda's monastic training repudiated woman as a sexual being while elevating her to the status of a dehumanized deity or a de-erotized mother and sister. With little experience of the world of man and woman, the Swami confronted a severe emotional crisis arising from his relationship with his Anglo-Irish disciple Margaret Noble. Bred in the Hindu middle-class culture of the Bengali *bhadralok,* he could never transcend its masculine worldview, which made it somewhat easy for him to renounce the company of a sexually mature woman or *kāminī.* However, his contact with Western women in general, and with Miss Noble in particular, brought about a profound psychic revolution at a time when he was troubled by his terminal illness—a compound of diabetes, heart disease, and asthma. His dual struggle against failing health and crumbling monastic indifference to *kāminī-kāñcana* contributed to a sense of utter nothingness and extinction. In the end his fantastic vision of Hindu India bearing the beacon of spiritual light to the world never materialized. The impossibility and impracticability of such a monumental undertaking finds a pathetic expression in his final confession of failure at the end of his diseased, tumultuous, and troubled life, which lasted less than four decades. He died a totally frustrated *sannyāsī*, disavowing his much vaunted conviction in the success of his exertions for the uplifting of the socially and economically deprived Indians, and, contrary to his reputation for militant activism, he recoiled in mystical isolationism and quiescence toward the end of his short life.

1

Narendranath's Childhood and Education

I

NARENDRANATH was born on 12 January 1863 in the Datta family of Simulia (or Simla), north Calcutta. The Dattas hailed from Daria-tona (or Dereton) village in Burdwan, West Bengal. The story of his remarkable birth, childhood, and adolescence follows closely that of his guru Ramakrishna (monastic name of Gadadhar Chattopadhyay, alias Gadai), a priest of the Kali temple at Dakshineshwar. This highly stylized biography duplicates for the little Biley (shorter form of Vireshwar, Narendranath's name at birth) the child Gadai's manner-isms, interests, and inclinations. Thus we are told that both were hyperactive and highly intelligent kids.[1] It is said that Gadai was a divine child, indeed, an incarnation. His father Kshudiram Chatto-padhyay had dreamed that Lord Vishnu would be born to his wife Chandra. She claimed that she was impregnated by a divine ray ema-nating from the Shiva *lingam* and penetrating her body with a terrific force.[2] Prior to his birth, Naren's mother Bhuvaneshwari had made supplications to Vireshwar Shiva in Benares and even dreamt that God "rouse Himself from His meditation and take the form of a male child who was to be her son."[3] Hence the child was named Vireshwar. While a toddler, he was recognized by Shibi Ghataki, an old brahmin woman from the neighborhood, to be divine.[4] The divine child's great aunt, however, felt that he was in fact a reincarnation of his grandfather Durgaprasad.[5] Durgaprasad "had such a strong leaning towards monastic life that after the birth of a son in 1835 [Vishwa-nath, Naren's father] he renounced the world becoming a monk at the age of twenty-five." Hence claim Swamiji's disciple biographers, "Vivekananda's pronounced tendency towards the monastic life was 'in his blood.'"[6]

Recounting his childhood to Margaret Noble, Vivekananda claimed that he began meditating from the age of seven and even experienced *samādhi* at eight.[7] We learn that his meditation as a child was so intense that he remained perfectly calm and still even in the close proximity of a cobra. Later while at college, he was approached momentarily by the Buddha during meditation. "He gazed at me for some time, and seemed as if to address me," the Swami reported. "I too gazed at him in speechless wonder. . . . It was the Lord Buddha whom I saw."[8] Reportedly he was also fond of worshipping the image of Shiva, the divine ascetic, and harbored a special fascination for the mendicants. It was while holding Shiva's image in one hand that the child Biley, reportedly, pulled his playmate to safety from an imminent fatal accident on the street.[9] Once he even gave away the clothing he was wearing to a beggar monk.[10] He also loved to playact *vairāgī* (mendicant) with the syce (coachman's assistant) of his father's cab-driver. Reportedly he learned to despise and dread women under the influence of the syce, who had "for some reasons turned a woman-basher."[11]

All these behaviors of the child Biley were an echo of those of the child Gadai, who had experienced *samādhi* at the age of six, who was drawn to the company of the roving *sādhus,* and who once discarded his own outfit to wear just a *kaupīna* (loincloth of a monk) like them.[12] Both Gadai and Biley exhibited precocious intelligence. While at school the latter astounded Bhutnath Dey, a veteran lawyer, with his scholarship.[13] Similarly Ramakrishna's biographers often refer to his native cunning and forensic skill which surprised even some *paṇḍits*.[14] Both also had a penchant for acting. Although Biley loved to play the part of a king, Gadai earned celebrity by acting the part of Shiva in his village *yātrā*. Additionally Gadai also loved to dress up and act like a girl.[15] In fact both have been credited with organizing a drama club. Naren's amateur theatrical party was organized at his home, whereas Gadadhar had formed a *yātrā* group in the mango grove of the local worthy Manikraja.[16] While at college Narendranath "was one of the actors on the stage which was erected at the home of . . . Keshub Chunder Sen to represent religious drama."[17]

II

Naren often engaged in soliloquies with a strange, twisted facial expression, which always revealed a sense of dissatisfaction or disgust. Mahendranath writes that since his childhood, Naren could hardly ever stay still but used to fidget all the time as if he had to do something. He would often speak to himself: "I will be king," "I shall do this or that," or "Look, this has got to be done, done now." Often he would engage in loud soliloquies and his mood would change.

When the spell was over, he would be terribly self-conscious and would pucker his face and blink or crinkle his cheeks. Sometimes he would chuckle and pull his nostrils upward.[18] He also blinked, puckered his nose, and stretched his gaze upward whenever he saw a pigeon fly or had an unpleasant thought. His habits are said to have been a typical trait of his family for generations.[19] Not surprisingly he earned the sobriquet of "nutty Biley" among his schoolmates, who used to say: "Biley is a nice chap, but he is a bit cranky and babbles like a madcap sometimes."[20] His penchant for the dramatic often amused as well as amazed his monastic brethren. Sometime in 1887 after Ramakrishna's death, he dressed himself up as a *vairāgī* one day and caricatured the *vairāgīs'* prayers and songs. Suddenly he yelled the name of "Hari" and began to dance wildly. This created such an uproar that soon people from the neighborhood crowded around the young man, singing and dancing with uncontrollable force.[21]

As Swami Vivekananda in the West, Narendranath's personality had undergone a profound change. Mahendranath noticed in London how his famous brother exuded the personality of a "very powerful man of authority" with deliberate movement of his left hand while expressing a thought and with a "hushing commanding voice."[22] He even demonstrated (rather enacted) *samādhi* on the stage in front of an audience gathered to hear his lecture, and he stayed in that state—like a "still, motionless living doll of flesh."[23]

III

Vivekananda's much acclaimed and publicized scholarship and thirst for knowledge contrasts sharply with Ramakrishna's apathy, even contempt, for what he called book learning.[24] The master's attitude in this regard has been explained away as his disenchantment with the materialism of the scholars.[25] Yet his intelligence and interests in religious literature have often been emphasized.[26] The Swami's biographers agree that Naren had a colorful and eventful early youth. He learned how to ride, swim, row (at the Hedua Swimming Club), wrestle and practice gymnastics (at the gymnasium of Yogen Pal, Nabagopal Mitra, and Ambu Guha), and fight with stick and sword. Additionally he learned classical Indian music from a number of masters (*ustād*) such as Beni Adhikari, Ahmad Khan, and Jwalaprasad in vocal music and from percussionists such as Kashinath Ghosal (*tablā*) and Murari Gupta (*pākhwāj*). He even authored a handbook of the popular north Indian percussion instrument *tabla* and coedited a booklet titled *Saṅgītakalpataru*.[27]

He earned a reputation as a prodigy at school and college. Rev. William Hastie, the principal of General Assembly's Institution (later renamed as Scottish Church College), where he studied during 1881–84, reportedly observed: "Narendra is really a genius. I have travelled far and wide but have never come across a lad of his talents and possibilities, even in German universities, among philosophical students."[28] Naren is also reported to have completely subdued Dr. Mahendralal Sarkar in an informal discussion of a certain philosophical work. The veteran doctor had to confess: "I could never have thought that such a young boy had read so much!"[29]

Apparently Narendranath studied the writings of David Hume, Immanuel Kant, Johann Gottlieb Fichte, Baruch Spinoza, Georg W. F. Hegel, Arthur Schopenhauer, Auguste Comte, Herbert Spencer, John Stuart Mill, and Charles Darwin, among others. According to Shailendranath Dhar, "among philosophers . . . Herbert Spencer was perhaps the greatest favourite."[30] Dhar also informs us that Narendranath "did not probably study the actual works of the philosophers even in translations" though whatever his source, he did "read and actually grasp a lot."[31] Further Narendra read some classics in Sanskrit, Bengali, and English. His expertise in Sanskrit—not known to his associates and acquaintances, who had a high opinion of his facility with English—was so thorough that he astounded Yajneshwar Bhattacharya by teaching him Kalidasa's *Abhijñānaśakuntalam*.[32]

During his Himalayan travels in 1889–90, he occupied himself with the study of the Upanishads and the *Brahmasūtras*. During his peregrinations of 1891–92, he studied Sanskrit grammar in Jaipur, Jain, and Muslim culture in Ahmedabad and Christian theology in Goa. He proudly referred to his power of comprehension of sophisticated literature from an early age. In a sermon on the *Bhāgavadgītā* in San Francisco on 29 May 1900, he claimed that he had read John Milton's *Paradise Lost* as a boy and admired Satan as a saint possessing a "soul that never weakens, faces everything, and determines to die game,"[33] most probably echoing the interpretation of Satan by one of the greatest intellectuals and poets of Vivekananda's days, Michael Madhusudan Dutt of Calcutta.[34]

According to some, he was a *śrutidhar*—possessed of prodigious memory.[35] He boasted of his skill as a rapid reader. He demonstrated it to a librarian in Meerut by repeating the contents of a book he had read in a couple of days.[36] He reportedly committed to memory all the volumes of Edward Gibbon's *Decline and Fall of the Roman Empire* in the course of three days.[37] He tried to impress the famous Vedanta scholar of Europe, Paul Deussen, with the power of his memory. While the learned German tried to describe his somewhat unpleasant experiences in India to the young Indian monk, the latter began to read a book of poetry and then "recited from memory long passages from whatever he had been reading" and thus "astounded" the professor.[38]

Vivekananda was quick to learn from scholars such as Pramadadas Mitra of Benares, Pandit Narayan Das and Pandit Sunderlal Ojha of Khetri, and Pandit Shankar Pandurang of Porbandar. In particular Pandit Pandurang not only taught him Sanskrit grammar and let him study a variety of subjects in his personal library but also suggested to him the idea that he should preach the Hindu *sanātana dharma* and Vedic learning to westerners. The Pandit's help and encouragement instilled so much confidence in the Swami that he unhesitatingly told his *gurubhāi* Swami Trigunatitananda: "Really, there is so much power in me that I feel as though I could revolutionize the world."[39] He was similarly helped by the Barrister Chhabildas of Bombay in Vedanta studies and told Abhedananda in 1892: "Kali, I have acquired so much power that I fear I will explode one day."[40] Likewise, some of his brother monks and devotees, such as Alasinga, Abhedananda, Akhandananda, and Sturdy, procured a number of books for him at his request.

IV

We must note that information on Vivekananda's childhood, early youth, and education comes mostly from his devotees and admirers to whom the Swami had described his experiences. Therefore no one has ever attempted to examine it critically or objectively. Rev. Hastie's admiring comments were loving exaggerations at best. Hastie hated Hinduism and Hindus—witness his diatribes against both in his controversy with Bankimchandra Chattopadhyay.[41] His comparing his favorite student with the best of the German philosophers is too frivolous to merit attention. Similarly one need not take seriously the observation made by John Henry Wright of Harvard that Vivekananda's learning "matched that of all of the professors of his university put together."[42] An expert in the Classics, with a two-year study of Sanskrit in Leipzig, Wright was unlikely to have fathomed the Swami's erudition in the Hindu scriptures and philosophy, though he undoubtedly was charmed by his eloquence and facility with the English language. It should also be borne in mind that he was perhaps driven to exaggeration for the sake of writing an effective recommendation for the young monk who had come all the way from India to participate in the World's Parliament of Religions without any credentials and a letter of invitation from the organizers.

In spite of being an intelligent individual, Naren was neither a brilliant student nor an accomplished scholar. He had to take a transfer from the Presidency College, the leading institution of higher learning in India in his day, where he had enrolled after high school, and actually passed his First Arts and B.A. examinations from the General Assembly's Institution, both in the moderate second division. His poor performance in examinations might very well have been an outcome of his rapid reading habits (which could be skimpy reading), causing facile generalizations and simplifications with which he could possibly have astounded his admirers in a public lecture or his acquaintances in informal conversation, but which could, upon critical perusal, prove to be unsatisfactory, even unacceptable, scholarship.[43]

Nagendranath Gupta has written that Naren "was an average student with no promise of brilliance, because he was not destined to win any prize of the learned or unlearned professions."[44] Swamiji's biographer has observed: "Naren did not win any laurels at the university examinations, though during his four years at college, he acquired a considerable scholarship, for which and for his other qualities of head and heart he was admired by his fellow-students and the teachers."[45] A scholar has recently argued that the Swami's poor performances in examinations "testify to a disinterest in the formal aspects of Western education."[46] Vivekananda's admirer and a senior college mate, Brajendranath Seal, commented on his "ardent and pure nature" and sociability and recognized his musical and forensic talents but remained silent on his academic accomplishments. In Seal's language Narendranath was "an inspired Bohemian . . . possessing . . . an iron will." He did refer to Naren's spiritual angst, the *Sturm und Drang* of his soul, and the "hour of the darkest trial." However, Seal's reminiscences, published in the *Prabuddha Bharata* (a journal begun by Swami Vivekananda in Madras) in 1907, were most certainly an encomium for his erstwhile college mate who had died in 1902 an international celebrity.[47] Chandicharan Bandyopadhyay questioned Seal's suppression of Vivekananda's early life and its multiple crises and his highlighting the "calm-moonlit" profile of the Swami.[48]

The Swami, however, thought of himself primarily as an intellectual. As he claimed: "I was born for the life of a scholar—retired, quiet, poring over my books. But the Mother dispenses otherwise— yet the tendency is there."[49] Years earlier he had boasted to Haramohan Mitra: "See, Haramohan, the philosophical books are all within my grasp. Even the Western philosophers are on my lips. Do you have any idea what class of men are we? We belong to the class of teachers. We come to this world to give it a new thought."[50] He also told Mary Hale that his "nature is the retirement of a scholar."[51] There is little doubt that he was quick on the uptake of controversial issues; that his trenchant critique of Christian evangelism in India was sincere, though not quite fair or accurate; and that his generalizations on the history and culture of India and Europe, though not wholly credible, were yet presented with a flair for the sensational.

Undeniably as Professor Raychaudhuri has demonstrated recently, Narendranath was brought up in a fairly cosmopolitan environment of Indo-Islamic culture at home. His father was an admirer of Urdu literature and learning; classical Indian music, "the most syncretic element in Indian culture"; delighted in Mughal food; socialized with Muslim friends and clients; and revered the Muslim *pīrs*. Young Naren thus imbibed his father's love of Islamic culture and cultivated an interest in classical music, gourmet Muslim cuisine, and Mughal architecture. He was also frankly partial to Islamic science and, as Raychudhuri argues, to Islamic mysticism with its simple *fiducia* and directness to the divine.[52] However, as we shall see, his youthful eclecticism and cosmopolitanism would decline toward the end of his life.

2

Narendranath and Ramakrishna

I

VIVEKANANDA did not seem much inclined to spiritualism, mysticism, or devotionalism. His early connection with the Brahmo Samaj—which contributed immensely to his intellectual growth—was really not prompted by spiritual curiosity or concern, even though he claimed that he was attracted to the Samaj because of its message of social reform.[1] He was led to the Samaj because of his musical expertise. He chose to affiliate himself with the Sadharan Brahmo Samaj rather than the Adi Brahmo Samaj of Devendranath Tagore, even though he had been personally known to the Tagores, especially to Maharṣi Devendranath. His choice was made because he found a better scope for personal advancement and prominence as the principal singer at the Sadharan Samaj, whereas he would have to face competition at the Adi Samaj where the pride of place went to the well-known singer Vishnuchandra Chakravarti.[2]

He was similarly brought to the notice of the Paramahamsa ("Supreme Swan," meaning the great discriminator—Ramakrishna's famous appellation) as a singer at the residence of Surendranath (alias Sureshchandra) Mitra and not as a seeker after spiritual wisdom, as he later told Nivedita. In a public lecture in Bombay delivered after Vivekananda's death, the Sister declared that the Swami's intellectual faculties were fully developed in his early teens, and he "began to wander in the woods and jungles to search for the great Hanuman to find out the truth. Time after time he returned disconsolate, for no Hanuman was there." "Then there came a day when," she went on, "while he was rambling in the garden of the great temple, on the banks of a river he met one, who answered his question 'Have you seen God?' That person was Shri Ram Krishna Paramahounsa."[3]

There are actually two stories about Narendra's coming in contact with the saint of Dakshineshwar. The most popular one is the account given in his official biography, according to which his college principal

Sri Ramakrishna Paramahamsa

Hastie advised him and his classmates to visit Ramakrishna to get a firsthand experience of *samādhi* and thus appreciate the trances of English poets like William Wordsworth. The other story, not quite popular with Vivekananda scholars, comes from his younger brother Mahendranath. According to him Narendra's elder cousin Ramchandra Datta, who had become a devotee of Ramakrishna, persuaded him to visit Dakshineshwar and meet the saint who "was very nice" and whose "talks were very sweet." A subscriber to Brahmo faith at the time, Narendranath objected: "He is a worshipper of idols and so how could he be a nice fellow?"[4] He even said that the Paramahamsa, an illiterate fellow, could not possibly possess any knowledge to teach someone like himself who had read the philosophies of Mill, Hamilton, and Locke. "What does he know?" Narendranath inquired of his cousin and declared: "If he could feed me *rasagollā*, well and good, otherwise I'll fix that ignorant bum by boxing his ears."[5] Ultimately Ram had to promise his cousin brother a feast of *rasagollā* before the latter could agree to accompany him to Dakshineshwar.[6]

II

Narendranath met Ramakrishna for the first time in November 1881 at Mitra's home. The Paramahamsa was absolutely enchanted by the personality and performance of the young man with large eyes. It was love at first sight, so to speak. Saradananda has written about the "indescribable" attraction of the Master for Narendra and his "intense and engrossing love" for the young college sophomore.[7] Ramakrishna felt much disturbed and distressed if he could not see Narendra for some days, and one night he even begged his devotees, Ramdayal Chakravarti and Baburam Ghosh, to fetch the young man to Dakshineshwar. At another time he wept profusely and confessed to his devotees: "I am hurting badly for not being able to see him. The inside of my heart is being wrenched, as it were, but he does not seem to understand the vehemence of my attraction for him."[8] ŚrīM noted how "the Master kept on staring hard at Narendra."[9] Saradananda writes: "On sighting him from afar the inner soul of the Master would rush out of his body with terrific force to be locked in love-embrace with him. It is impossible to say how many times we noticed the Master become ecstatic uttering 'There's Na——, there's Na.'"[10] Ramakrishna's infatuation for Naren was expressed frequently in petting the young man's face and body, shedding tears on seeing him, staring at him intently for a long stretch of time, and above all becoming rigid in *samādhi* while listening to his songs and touching him.[11] Once he mounted on Naren's back and went into *samādhi*.[12] At the home of his lay devotee, Balaram Basu, Ramakrishna crawled stealthily toward Narendranath who was asleep on the same mat with his back turned toward him. According to an eyewitness account, at the Master's "touch," the startled devotee cried out *in English* (!): "Lo! the man is entering into me!" Ramakrishna is said to have retorted: "You wretch! [*Sālā!*] You think I can't make out your prattles in English! You said I was entering into you!"[13]

Ramakrishna once confided, in his characteristic manner, some secret (*guhyakathā*) to his intimate (*antaraṅga*) devotees: "Let me say something very secret. Why do I love Purna [Purnachandra Ghosh], Narendra, and others so much? While trying to embrace Lord Jagannath in *madhur*, I broke my arm. The Lord commanded: 'You have assumed a human body, you must establish intimate relations with human beings.'" Ramakrishna's divine mandate to substitute his *madhur* relationship with God by close intimacy with men suggests his feminine attitude to male. In fact he told Narendra: "Look! In you is Shiva! In me is Shakti! And these two are One." Saradananda reports that Ramakrishna used to say that "Narendra is, as it were, my counterpart—the Principle that resides within this (showing himself) is female and that which is within him (showing Narendranath) is male." In a similar tone he had earlier entreated Narendranath: "Look here, come a little more often. It's because you are a newcomer. After the first acquaintance all newcomers pay frequent visits as is the case with a new male lover. You will come, o.k.?" The metaphors used by the Master in respect of his favorite disciple had deep sexual overtones. He compared the young man to a "thousand-petalled" lotus, a "jar of water," "Haldarpukur," "a huge red-eyed carp," "a very big receptacle," and "a big bamboo with holes." Above all "he is like a male pigeon." Ramakrishna succeeded in implanting his feminine image in Naren's psyche. One night the young man dreamed his older admirer said to him: "Come, I will show you Gopi Radha!" Following Ramakrishna's footsteps in the dream, he saw the Master turning to him saying: "Where else will you go?" Saying this Ramakrishna "transformed himself into the beautiful personality and exquisite form of Radha herself."[14]

No doubt the aging mystic was fully aware of public reaction to his apparent homoeroticism and is reported to have confessed: "I am such an old fart [*buḍo minse*]! What will people say if they see me restless and weeping for him? . . . But I can't control myself."[15] In fact he was once reprimanded (though to little effect) by his dauntless devotee, the insufferable Pratapchandra Hazra. As Ramakrishna himself reported, "Hazra took me to task because I was anxious to see

the boys. He asked 'When do you think of God?'"[16] Hazra is also
reported to have observed that the saint was especially fond of good-
looking and wealthy boys.[17] Needless to mention Narendranath, a
college student with some acquaintance with Western rationalism and
enlightened Brahmo views, felt scandalized by the bizarre behavior
of the famous mystic of Dakshineshwar, whom he thought of as somewhat weird, even insane.[18] He was eventually tamed by Ramakrishna's
constant adulation and admiration for the young man. Naren was
compared to everything and every being that could be imagined or
described in superlatives. He was called one of the *saptarṣi*—the seven
magis—and was feasted and feted by his adoring mentor.[19]

III

Such attention and adoration as well as the *ambiance* of Dakshineshwar's erotic community naturally worked on the teenager. Yet Naren
was not quite sure of the ways of the "crazy brahmin," and one day
sometime in 1882, he even inquired of Latu (nickname of Swami
Adbhutananda) whether the Paramahamsa passed his nights in ecstasy
without sleep. He must have felt comfortable with his new older
acquaintance after Latu had told him about "Kiṅśhubbābu's" (Keshabchandra Sen) visit with the master who had profusely praised the
young man to his great Brahmo visitor.[20] More important this outburst of infatuation was especially comfortable to the restless and
hapless youth after his father's untimely death in 1884 which had
importuned his entire family, for the spendthrift Vishwanath passed
away leaving his family nearly bankrupt. Sudden confrontation with
the harsh realities of life was quite upsetting, almost traumatic, for
the inexperienced and easygoing Narendranath. In spite of his reputation at college for his eloquence, erudition, and leadership qualities
and the fact that his lawyer father had connections in influential cir-
cles, Naren never did manage to procure a suitable employment except for a short stint as a school teacher. We have a graphic account
of his personal predicament: "I had to look for job even before the
period of mourning was over. I went from office to office barefoot
and hungry, carrying an application for a job. . . . But I was unsuc-
cessful everywhere."[21]

Unable to cope with abject poverty, the shocked college graduate
naturally wondered: "Does God really exist? And if so, does He ever
hear the piteous supplications of the humanity? . . . Where has so
much evil come from in the world of a just God?"[22] Henceforth he
became a regular visitor to Dakshineshwar, most probably, inter alia,

to benefit from Ramakrishna's contact with the elites of Calcutta. In fact on his own admission, he accidentally met the Paramahamsa in Calcutta the night before he decided to leave home to become a monk and was persuaded to accompany him to Dakshineshwar. He stayed there for the night, and there the saint suddenly came near him, took his hand, and sang a song in tears. Having renewed his contact with Ramakrishna, one day Naren begged the saint to pray to the Goddess Kali for his financial welfare.[23] We also have Vivekananda's report on his being despatched to the temple of the goddess by Ramakrishna to pray for his material well-being and his inability to ask the Divine Mother for anything other than power of discrimination, renunciation, knowledge, and devotion.[24] We have, however, Mahendranath's description of the dismal condition of his tottering home at this time: "There are no signs of the earlier state of the house, except a broken bunk bed, a rolled up mat, a torn mattress (with its cotton fillings oozing out) on the bed, a couple of shredded pillows, and a dirty mosquito curtain hanging on a nail on the western wall. A torn tussle from the hand-operated fan was hanging from the ceiling."[25] Ramakrishna did sympathize with Narendra's financial predicaments after his father's death. "His household is starving and though he has been trying his best to get employed, he can't find a job," the master remarked during a conversation with his devotees. "See what he has been reduced to doing!" he added despondently.[26] Indeed the young man's situation was quite precarious. As Ramakrishna observed: "He can't even afford salt to eat his banana roast with!"[27] He even asked Annada Guha, an acquaintance, to help Naren. Although Naren did not quite like the idea of soliciting Guha for help, his Master wept and told him that he was even prepared to beg for him from door to door.[28]

IV

It is quite likely that Narendranath's acquaintance with the Master at such a moment of torment and doubt proved to be especially helpful. Ramakrishna had not forgotten the memories of his own childhood trauma after his father's death and later after the death of his fatherlike elder brother, Ramkumar. Indeed the little Gadai had become listless, lonely, and somewhat scared of the uncertainties of life, and thus he was drawn more to making clay images of gods and to the company of roving monks. Similarly after his brother's demise, he became a reluctant priest at Dakshineshwar Kali temple and engaged in an intense and quite unconventional exercise to confront the Mother Goddess in a real-life situation and even, reportedly, attempted to kill himself but desisted from this act of suicide when she did actually reveal herself to him.[29] Thus the Master sympathized and came up with a powerful justification for Naren's present tribulations. One night he told the distraught young man: "I know that you have come [to this world] to do Mother's work. You will never be able to stay in the family. But remain there as long as I live."[30]

There may be some substance in the popular claim that it was Ramakrishna who was responsible for Narendra's spiritual transformation.[31] It is most certainly a fact that he provided a deep psychological support to the flamboyant but flabbergasted young man facing a crisis of career and family responsibility. Indeed as Dr. Kakar has written, Narendra was under intense mental strain, highly vulnerable and suggestible when he came close to the Master, and the "mighty mentor" stepped into the void of his would-be disciple's life which had been rendered utterly chaotic after his father's death. Thus there might have developed a "quasi-therapeutic relationship" between Ramakrishna and Narendranath.[32] We must, however, recognize that all speculations—psychological or otherwise—about the Ramakrishna-Vivekananda relationship are based solely on the Swami's own reminiscences and depositions. Anybody familiar with his writings must admit that he had a penchant for the dramatic and the dithyramb. His recorded conversations with his devotees, disciples, admirers, and visitors are replete with his fantastic spiritual claims and descriptions of himself and his activities in superlatives.

3

From Narendranath to Vivekananda

I

VIVEKANANDA'S reputation as a spiritual leader of immense proportions so gripped the imagination of his admiring contemporaries and adoring posterity that he has been regarded as a fully realized *ṛṣi* (saint) whom his Master had seen, in one of his ecstatic moods, drop from the heavens.[1] Naturally no biographer—hagiographical or historical—has even bothered to investigate the transition of a college student with Anglicized education and Brahmo affiliation having little interest in Hindu philosophy or spirituality into a Vedantic monk of world stature. Even an academic historian like Shailendranath Dhar, who, on his own account, attempted "to give an objective narrative—explain natural events by natural circumstances and conform to the standards that are usually insisted upon in historical works," confessed that "it must for ever remain a mystery how a young College lad like Narendra developed into Swami Vivekananda."[2]

We have, however, some idea of the chronology of this process. Since his chance encounter with Ramakrishna in November 1881 at the home of Surendranath Mitra and subsequently his personal encounter with the saint at Dakshineshwar the following month, Narendranath had found a father figure who came to fill the void left by the sudden demise of his own father Vishwanath on 25 February 1884 and who launched the young man's boat of life "on a voyage in a limitless ocean," with himself "at the helm of the vessel."[3] According to the author of *Ghaṭanāvalī*, Naren's career as a monk proper began from the time when Ramakrishna's throat cancer, detected since August 1885, became aggravated, and he had to be relocated from Dakshineshwar to Calcutta for better medical care, first to a rented home in Shyambazar on 2 October and subsequently to another house in Cossipore on 11 December.[4] Here, as Dhar writes, Narendra "could easily see that the Helmsman's post was ere long to pass into his unwilling hands and he intensified his sadhanas which were crowned with the achievement of *nirvikalpa samādhi*."[5]

41

We need to look closely into the available information of his *sādha-nās*. First we must identify the various spiritual training he allegedly had received at Dakshineshwar from 1882 through 2 October 1885, when the ailing Master finally left his abode of Dakshineshwar. During this three year period, we know that his meetings with Ramakrishna were fairly irregular because he had not been able to fathom the saint's infatuation with him and also because he had been preoccupied with college friends and examinations. Then his father's sudden death on 23 February 1884 came as a rude shock to him and his family. Vishwanath, though a lawyer with good briefs, was nevertheless a spendthrift, and he had left his family nearly bankrupt. Narendra was caught unaware by this exigency as he was thoroughly unprepared to shoulder the responsibilities of his family as the eldest surviving son. He could not procure a steady job and consequently faced the prospect of utter starvation. He ultimately found a temporary job as a high school teacher. Under the circumstances his visits to Dakshineshwar had become quite infrequent—most probably he could not afford the expenses of the long trip.[6]

It is difficult to surmise any occasion for his training by the Master at this time. On the other hand, he seemed to have reached enlightenment on his own. Reportedly one day he experienced extreme fatigue and hunger "but almost instantly . . . felt that his soul was freed of all burdens."[7] He therefore decided to renounce the world and sought his Master's blessings at the home of Suresh sometime in August 1884. Ramakrishna was delighted and coaxed him to accompany him back to Dakshineshwar to spend the night with him, and there, in front of his other devotees and admirers, sang a song, locked up in embrace with the young man, while profusely shedding tears. This was an erotic *bhakti* number supposed to have been sung by Radha (alias Rai) for Krishna, which goes something like this: "*Kathā kahite darāi, nā kahite darāi; (āmār) mane sanda hoi—bujhi tomāy hārāi—Hā—Rāi*" ("I dare not to speak though I am scared to remain silent; I have a feeling that I might lose you—alas, O Rāi!").[8]

The story of Naren's *kathor tapasyā* (severe penance) at Dakshineshwar is apochryphal at best, most probably fabricated by Swamiji himself for his admirers and devotees and perpetuated by the Ramakrishna Order that he founded. As we learn partly from the *Kathāmṛta*, he was constantly flattered and petted by his frankly enchanted homoerotic mentor, fed adoringly by him, made to sing songs on a fairly regular basis for the Master's mystical merriment, and told by the older man that he was a *dhyānasiddha* (realized individual through his meditations), *nityasiddha* (eternally realized person), and an *īśvarakoṭi*—free from the lure of *kāminī-kāñcan* (woman and wealth).[9] He, however, cultivated the friendship of Ramakrishna's acquaintance from a neighboring village in the Hooghly District, and a friendly critic, the intelligent and somewhat skeptical Pratap Chandra Hazra. Naren would enjoy sharing a smoke or a joke, or just conversing, with Pratap whom he regarded as a "swell guy" (*khub lok*), but the Master was apprehensive of the young man's growing intimacy with this insufferable character from Mahmudpur, who could never look on Ramakrishna's obsession with young boys with equanimity.[10] Similarly the Master did not quite like Naren's intimacy with the unpredictable and impetuous Girish Ghosh.

The most persistent and apparently quite effective "spiritual" ministration of the master for his beloved "Laren" (a rustic corruption of Naren) consisted in his admonition against active heterosexual life. As Saradananda informs us, Ramakrishna often suggested to Narendranath that "a man's vein of intelligence in the brain [*medhānāḍī*] opened up after an unbroken continence of twelve years and acquired the wisdom to comprehend the most subtle entities and see God face to face [*pratyakṣa*]."[11] At Dakshineshwar, Narendra's spiritual exercises, if any, consisted in meditating for hours at the Panchavati and then climbing the trees, swinging from the creepers, and holding merry picnics. "Sri Ramakrishna often joined them in their rompings, and partook of the food that Narendra cooked."[12] The example of his "scaling higher and higher cliffs in the realm of the spirit" is furnished by his singing some devotional numbers one night and then remaining calm and silent. That same night he, reportedly, felt that he was being awakened by the Master, and he had a long chat with an apparition. Another night he dreamed his guru transformed himself into the beautiful Radha and beckoned him. He also began to see his "double" following him after he meditated. All these visions and voices are regarded by numerous writers and biographers as spiritual par excellence.[13]

We read in Swamiji's official biography about Narendra's imbibing the ultimate spiritual truth from his Master through some kind of osmosis. He had, of course, become Ramakrishna's disciple, "from a mystical point of view," when the Master "touched his heart" and had thus "taken possession of him." Then he had to be intellectually convinced before becoming the Paramahamsa's "conscious" disciple.[14] However, we never get to see the operation of this process. We hear of his conversion to Mother Kali when he gloriously failed to ask for mundane comforts from the goddess even though, reportedly, he had gone to Dakshineshwar to make a supplication through Ramakrishna but was forced to do it himself. He now prayed, apparently in ecstasy, for the faculty of discrimination (*vivek*), in front of the image. His failure so delighted his Master that he was in a transport. He sat on the young aspirant's lap, telling him that both of them had been united as one (earlier Ramakrishna had designated Narendra as the male Shiva and himself the female Shakti[15]) and shared a smoke together from the same hookah. According to an eyewitness account, the Master was ecstatic for having sucked smoke from the same bowl Narendra had touched with his lips. The reporter was "surprised to see Shri Ramakrishna, who could not take any food if a part of it had already been offered to somebody else, making this remarkable exception in the case of Narendranath."[16]

We are told further that "to Shri Ramakrishna Naren was indebted for his understanding of Hinduism. This understanding was gained by watching the Master engaged in worship, in teaching [though virtually nothing is said in this regard], and absorbed in ecstasy."[17] He also learned that God is both Personal and Impersonal and that "he is not to be found between the covers of a book or within the walls of a temple. . . . Intense longing was the one thing needful."[18] He likewise imbibed the essence of Vedanta crystallized in Ramakrishna's expression of cosmic compassion—*jīve dayā, jīve dayā* ("compassion for living beings")—through an enlightened understanding.[19]

II

In respect of Narendranath's accomplishments as a *sādhak,* he had begun to linger at Cossipore longer than before, especially after he had lost his month-long stint as a high school teacher, apparently upon complaints from the upper-class boys that he did not know how to teach properly. At first he tried to prepare himself for the law school finals (he had enrolled at the Metropolitan Institution, which was later renamed Vidyasagar College), but he gave up his law studies. His explanation for his change of mind was that he was very concerned when his guru told him that he could not drink water out of a lawyer's hand.[20] As Swami Prabhananda claims, Narendranath was consumed, as it were, by his master, who truly was the prince of renouncers.[21] Narendranath began to nurse the ailing Master in earnest and at the same time practice severe austerity with Rakhalchandra Ghosh, Sharatchandra Chakravarti, Shashibhusan Chakravarti, Gangadhar Gangopadhyay, Kaliprasad Chandra, Gopal Ghosh ("Buḍo" or "Huṭko" Gopal), Saradaprasanna Mitra, Yogendranath Raychaudhuri, Taraknath Ghosal, and Nityaniranjan Ghosh—all the *antaraṅga* disciples of the Great Master—who would form a monastic brotherhood.[22]

Examples of this austerity include, as per Huṭko Gopal's testimony, Narendra's meditation for several days by smearing his body with ashes and carrying a pair of tongs like a real life *sannyāsī;* his being possessed by the spirit of Mahāvīra—the divine monkey, factotum of Lord Rama—and rushing out of the Cossipore home yelling, "Victory to Rama," which even upset his guru.[23] Ramakrishna also worried on 19 January 1886 over the wearing of ochre-colored (*geruā*) clothes on the part of Naren and a few others, when these were presented to them by Huṭko Gopal.[24] The master did not wish him to become a *sannyāsī* during the lifetime of his mother. Naren also said that one day, while he was meditating, his *gurubhāi* Kaliprasad touched him and received a "shock."[25] Further he startled his friend Girishchandra Ghosh during a meditative session under a mango tree by sitting still even after having been stung by mosquitos. Nityaniranjan Ghosh once found Narendra unconscious, and his body was ice cold while he was meditating. Having regained consciousness Narendra reportedly cried out: "Where is my body? Where is it?" Upon hearing the incident, the Master hinted that this state of the young ascetic approximated *nirvikalpa samādhi.*[26] Naren even exhibited unusual compassion for a mentally disturbed woman who visited Cossipore and for someone reportedly "inflicted with cancer due to starvation"(!)[27]

III

Narendranath began to sing *kīrtan* wildly every night ever since his guru's condition turned worse, beyond all hope of recovery. Sometime during 1 to 9 April he suddenly left for Bodhgaya with Tarak and Kali, attired as *sannyāsīs,* after he had read some Buddhist literature at Cossipore. Upon his return to Calcutta a few days later, he began to read the Bible. Gradually his personality underwent a change. He seemed to be engrossed in a mysterious mood all the time. Its outward manifestation included shaking his head from time to time, keeping his eyes half-closed or wide open at times, raising and lowering his voice occasionally, and sometimes laughing loudly by himself, apparently for no reason.[28] At last as Baikunthanath Sanyal writes, Naren asked his guru to channel some of his "special powers" into him, and reportedly, the Master obliged him in private.[29] We are told that just three or four days before his death, Ramakrishna summoned Narendranath into his room and went into *samādhi.* At that time the disciple "felt that a subtle powerful ray was penetrating his body like an electric shock, as it were, and he gradually lost con-

sciousness." When he came to, he saw Ramakrishna awakened from
his trance, in tears. When he asked his Master the reason for his grief,
the latter said: "I have become bankrupt today after I have transferred
to you whatever I had. You will do a lot of work for the world with
the help of this power. And you will go back after you have done
your work." Again Ramakrishna told Naren two days before his
death: "Naren, I am leaving them [devotees and disciples] in your
care because you are extremely intelligent and resourceful. You shall
make arrangements for their spiritual exercises lovingly so that they
do not have to return to their families."[30] The most popular and
powerful hagiographical explanation goes as follows:

> Naren had suddenly become the possessor of the spiritual wealth of his
> Guru, acquired by years of superhuman effort and by means of the stern-
> est austerities. Shri Ramakrishna willingly deprived himself of his powers
> in order that Naren might be endowed with spiritual omnipotence. When
> that which was Ramakrishna had completed its task in its human manifes-
> tation, it gave itself wholly to Naren, for the good of the world.[31]

There is also the Paramahamsa's own note scribbled on a piece of
paper that Naren will teach the world (ghare bāire). Even though this
note probably means nothing more than the Master's loving regard
for the young man's erudition, several writers consider this document
as a definitive proof of Ramakrishna's mandate to Narendranath.[32]
Quite expectedly Narendranath became the leader of his gurubhāis
after Ramakrishna's death.

IV

The Master's flock soon faced a terrible financial situation. After
he had passed away (16 August 1886), his devotees and admirers,
who had undertaken to maintain his Cossipore establishment,
stopped supplying funds. Consequently the rent for the home remained unpaid. Ram Datta suggested that the boys who had left their
families to nurse their guru now return home, and Suresh Mitra,
one of the rasaddārs (suppliers of victuals), concurred. Suresh even
promised to find employment for Huṭko Gopal and requested Narendra to return home and resume his legal studies. Naren and the other
young ascetics wished to build a temple at Cossipore for worshiping
the ashes of their late guru, which were kept in the room where he
died. Naren was thus quite reluctant to quit the rented house at
Cossipore, and he even ordered Rakhal to approach a Marwari busi-

nessman, who had been a devotee of the late Paramahamsa, for funds. Rakhal, however, felt too embarrassed to ask for money from the Marwari, although their tenure at the Cossipore home was about to terminate by the end of August 1886 because rents had been paid up to that period.

Ramakrishna's householder disciples, such as Ram Datta, Devendranath Majumdar, and Nityagopal Goswami, also demanded the ashes of their late Master be buried ceremonially in Ram's retreat at Kankurgachhi. The ascetics refused to comply and guarded the pot zealously. In fact Shashi had already transferred a substantial amount of bones and ashes from this pot to another one.[33] Subsequently Narendranath emerged as the mediator and directed that half of the ashes and bones of the deceased be transferred to Kankurgachhi. Reportedly "Narendra and his brother-disciples each swallowed a minute portion of the ashes and as a result had deep meditation that night."[34] The other half of the sacred relic, intended for the Ramakrishna temple, was transferred to the home of Balaram Basu.

A few days before the ashes for Kankurgachhi were transferred, Naren had a vision of a luminous figure at Cossipore that "left a profound impression" on him. However the holy ash was duly carried to Ram's place on 23 August, the day of Janmastami (birthday of Lord Krishna). Thereafter Narendra and his cohorts were at a loss as to how to start a monastery at Cossipore, where they had hoped to construct their dream temple. Ram and other householder disciples maintained that the Master never intended to create a monastic order. But as Gambhirananda informs us, Ramakrishna had in fact initiated his *antaranga* disciples into *sannyas* secretly, without informing his householder disciples.[35] The split of the holy ash thus also represented a split between the householder and the renouncer disciples of the Master.

Meanwhile following the ceremonial dedication of Ramakrishna's remains at Kankurgachhi, the plight of the hapless and homeless renouncers was mitigated by the timely generosity of Suresh Mitra, who had been concerned about the fate of three disciples—Latu, who had been a domestic servant at Ram's home before coming to Dakshineshwar to serve the Master; Budo Gopal, whose family was extinct and who thus had nowhere to go; and Tarak, who also could not return to his family. Therefore to provide a shelter for them and also for the other renouncers and reportedly to create a retreat for his pastime with friends after office hours, Mitra offered to help with funds.[36] Eventually Narendranath took the responsibility for locating a shelter and found one on 19 October—a deserted, dilapidated, and reputedly haunted house at 125/1 Pramanick Ghat Road, Baranagore, near the Hooghly River, which once belonged to the secretary (*munsī*) of the landlords of Taki. The rent was cheap (Rs. 11.00 a month), so that Mitra even employed Shashi Ganguly as a cook for the comfort of the ascetics.

V

This is the genesis of the Baranagore Math. The young renouncers used to procure their victuals by *mādhukarī*, that is, holy begging, quite an acceptable and respectable ascetic vocation in Hindu culture. They ate their simple meals in a communal dinner and smoked hookah from the same bowl. There was a single latrine which they took turns entering. While waiting outside to take his turn, each one would smoke and discuss the Vedanta and other scriptures. They went naked and appeared to have had fun in their joint living, free from the hassles of the world of work. Mahendranath has described the innocent but sincere quest for spiritual wisdom and insight on the part of these naive and not very educated young men and their camaraderie and closeness to each other.

Naren's austerity was caused more by his pecuniary difficulties than by any deliberate renunciation of the world for spiritual quest. Mahendranath has written about hunger, sleeeplessness, and lack of clothes and even beds for the young renouncers at Baranagar. On top of that, Naren's problems, in particular, were compounded because of the dire poverty of his family members as well as by litigations with his kinsmen. Hence he and his cohorts had to beg for a living. In fact he suffered from severe stomach trouble due to eating foods procured by *mādhukarī*; he recovered after Balaram Basu supplied him with a healthy diet and after Balaram's maid had cooked his favorite *chāpāṭi* and a spicey preparation of pumpkin.[37] Naren acquired a reputation for demonstrable "flaming renunciation" (*jvalanta vairāgya*) and was considered by the people of the neighborhood to have gone off his rocker. They complained that he and his gang were all vagabonds who avoided work and responsibility, were parasites on benefactors, and talked endlessly and aimlessly of the Vedanta, Advaita, and the like.[38] In fact the Math was an adult male haven, a counterculture community of freedom-seeking youths on the fringe of society and the city. It was also a kind of Bengali counterpart of the Greek gymnasium, albeit a less elegant one.[39]

Even though the Baranagore home housed a band of young men, some of whom—Naren, in particular—were raucous and unpredictable in their habits (witness, for example, Naren's wild yelling in the

name of Hari ["*Haribol*"] all of a sudden one evening and starting a
frenzied *kīrtan* on the street, which created enough commotion to
gather a large crowd), in reality that home was converted into a
monastery after Narendra and some of his close cohorts had made a
trip to Baburam's parental home at Antpur in the Hooghly district,
some twenty miles from Calcutta, and pledged themselves "to a life
of renunciation."[40] Naren initiated all his *gurubhāis* into *sannyās* by
performing *Virajā Hom* sometime in the third week of January
1887.[41] He now took a monastic name and emerged as the leader of
a monastic brotherhood. He would, however, change his monastic
name at least twice. During his south Indian travels and his first visit
(June 1891) to Khetri in Rajasthan, he would be known as Swami
Sachchidananda. Most probably his name Vivekananda was chosen
by his royal disciple, Raja Ajit Singh of Khetri, during the Swami's
second visit there (April 1893).[42]

The Math relocated to 95 Deshbandhu Road, Alambazar, in February 1892. It was a two-storey home with two sections—outer and
inner—and its rent was quite affordable (Rs. 10.00 per month). The
Math once again moved, on 13 February 1898, following the damage
in the building of the Alambazar monastery caused by an earthquake
on 12 June 1897, to Nilambar Mukhopadhyay's retreat at 48 Lala-
babu Shrine Road, Belur, across the Hooghly River. The land adja-
cent to this building was purchased on 4 March 1898 for Rs.
39,000.00, which was contributed to by Henrietta Müller. The Belur
Math was built on this plot of land, and it was consecrated by Vivekananda on 9 December 1898. It finally opened on 2 January 1899.

VI

The popular belief that Swami Vivekananda was literally "made"
by Ramakrishna and that he was endowed with a natural flair for the
life of a monk calls for a critical examination. Surath Chakravarti has
studied Vivekananda's mental/intellectual evolution in five stages.
First during 1863–83, he grew up in the liberal atmosphere of his
family, studying Western history and philosophy and coming in contact with the Brahmø Samaj. He came close to Brahmo stalwarts,
such as Maharṣi Devendranath, Keshab Sen, Protap Mozoomdar, and
Shivanath Shastri. He even became a member of the Sadharan
Brahmo Samaj and identified himself as a Brahmo. Then during
1883–86, he came under the influence of Ramakrishna Paramahamsa,
whose spiritual teachings had been publicized by Sen and Mozoomdar
both in India and abroad. Next during 1886–92, he began his pere-

grination of India following Ramakrishna's death, and he came in contact not only with the masses throughout the length and breadth of the country but also with the feudal chiefs and petty princelings. The fourth stage covers the period 1893–97, when he visited the West with the help of his princely devotees, as well as of some of his south Indian disciples, and he preached Vedanta in that part of the world. He returned home in 1897, and in the next five years (1897–1902), he became busy with the inauguration of the Ramakrishna Mission and with the task of national regeneration on the basis of the ideals he had preached until his death in Belur on 4 July 1902.

Devotees and admirers of the Swami have deemphasized the first stage of his life with a view to underscoring the paramount influence of the second.[43] As we have already seen, contrary to his and his associates' proclamation that Ramakrishna had shown Naren the way to God realization, the latter despaired of any success in this regard even a year after his master's death.[44] Narendranath was even mildly admonished by Saradaprasanna, who commented on his singing "O Lord, I am your slave" and his insistence that God did not exist. "Sometimes you say that there is no God," complained Sarada to Narendra, "and now you are saying all this. You really are not consistent in what you say because you often change your mind."[45]

As a matter of fact, Narendranath's intellectual interests had been greatly influenced by the enlightened social and spiritual gospels of the Brahmo Samaj. As early as 1819, the founder of the Brahmo movement, Raja (king, or prince—title for a native chief) Rammohan Roy, had translated *Kaṭhopaniṣad* into English—a work that he claimed was "intended to assist the European community in forming their opinion respecting Hindu theology." He had emphatically declared that "by a reference to history it may be proved that the world was indebted to our ancestry for the first dawns of knowledge which sprang in the East."[46] The Raja seems to have been a pioneering voice from India in the West. Adrienne Moore has observed that "previous to New England's knowledge of Rammohun Roy, there was no sign of any influences of oriental thought on the American mind."[47]

Maharṣi Devendranath had the Hindu scriptures reinterpreted with a view to examining the reputed absolute correctness or rightness of the Vedic and Upanisadic treatises and proclaimed the efficacy of pure heart enlightened by a knowledge of the self as the basis of religion. Yet his Brahmo community never debunked the Hindu scriptures but continued to study the Vedas and the Upanisads; for example, see the series of translations from these sources published in the Brahmo journal *Tattvabodhini* during 1848–71. In 1863 Keshab declared in a speech titled "The Brahmo Samaj Vindicated" that the Brahmo scriptures were grounded in the Vedantic truths predicated on natural reasoning. He declared in Bath, England, on 15 April 1870 that he could "never look upon the redeeming features of India in past history without feeling a thrill of patriotic feeling."[48] When the social worker Pandita Ramabai met with him and discussed her project of female regeneration, Sen presented her with a copy of the Vedas so that she would act in consonance with the cultural traditions of India.

Nineteen years before the Chicago Parliament of Religions, Protap Mozoomdar told his audience in England that the Brahmos worshiped the same Supreme Person (*Parampurus*) upon whom the ancient Indian sages meditated. On 26 September 1883, he explained Hindu theology in the United States. "In every school of Hinduism," declared Protap, "you will find the essence of true religion to lie in a sense of union between the soul and the super soul . . . the religion in India means absorption in God, oneness of the human spirit with the spirit of the Divine Being." The Sadharan Brahmo Samaj produced a host of scholars such as Shivanath Shastri, Nagendranath Chattopadhyay, Sitanath Tattvabhusan, Bipinchandra Pal, Dhirendrachandra Vedantabagish, Pratulchandra Som, Hemchandra Sarkar, and others who agreed with Shastri's view that "the Theistic Church [Brahmo Church] of India is not un-Hindu, but something more than Hindu."[49]

VII

As David Kopf observed, "at the close of the nineteenth century . . . [dharma] was a moral principle which operated in all aspects of man's life, directing the whole and integrating all the noble functions of humanity. It was motivated by love of God, a love manifested in one's view of all other men in whom God resided."[50] This interpretation of dharma in the spirit of universalism was the achievement of thinkers like Rammohan Roy and Bankimchandra Chatopadhyay. Keshab's New Dispensation (*Navavidhān*) Brahmo movement consciously preached this universalism since 1866 (when he founded the Bhāratvarṣīya Brahmo Samaj), especially from 1882 with the annunciation of his New Dispensation (*Navavidhān*). Vijaykrishna Goswami, a former Brahmo missionary under Sen, sought to infuse this spirit into a new Vaishnavism.[51] Prior to meeting the Paramahamsa of Dakshineshwar, young Narendranath had come in contact with this intellectual world of the Calcutta Brahmos. That he was deeply influenced by the Vedanta is attested to by his senior college mate Seal.[52] Even Nivedita has reported Swamiji's acknowledgment of

Rammohan's acceptance of the Vedanta, propagation of patriotism, and acceptance of a harmony between the Hindus and the Muslims. She even wrote that Vivekananda never forgot that his critical understanding of the religious problems of his country had begun in his Brahmo days. He of course preached mainly Advaita Vedanta, based on the Vedas and the Upanishads, in the West. Yet his discourse was grounded primarily in Brahmo universalism with which he had been acquainted during his association with Keshabchandra Sen's Samaj. The publication of the Sadharan Brahmo Samaj, *Sañjīvanī*, reported that Vivekananda, who had once been a singer of the society, did not preach Hinduism in Chicago but Brahmoism.[53] The Swami's religious/spiritual ideas were thus a culmination of a trend and the product of a heritage of an earlier generation.

4

Vivekananda the Worldly Monk

I

As we noted in chapter 2, Narendranath's career as the great peripatetic Hindu missionary was chosen by default—when the life of a common householder with a normal secular profession seemed impossible. Fond of foods from early childhood, he had even organized an association of gluttons—Greedy Club, as it was called. His preference for gourmet cuisine and other creature comforts of life persisted throughout his monastic career. When his disciple Chakravarti asked his opinion about consuming nonvegetarian foods, the Swami ordered him to eat fish and meat as much as possible to become healthy and courageous. He once proudly recalled the ancient Hindu society of beef-eating Brahmins and advised the youths of India to "be strong" so that they could "understand the Gita better with . . . biceps."[1] "The entire country has become crowded with sickly, dyspeptic, vegetarian ascetics. They do not bear the signs of *sattva* but mirror the shadow of terrible *tamas*—the shadow of death," he lamented to Chakravarti and told him: "I want *rajas*. . . . Can't you see that the country is enveloped in *tamas*? Now we have to make our countrymen enterprising by feeding them fish and meat. . . . That is why I was telling you to eat plenty fish and meat."[2] In fact John Barrows reportedly observed that in the United States, Vivekananda used to devour beef somewhat ostensibly.[3]

On a Sunday sometime in 1901, Chakravarti brought a huge fish to Belur to offer to the temple of Ramakrishna. Vivekananda, though suffering from an aggravated diabetic condition, lost no time in getting up from his sickbed to have a look at the succulent *bhog* (sacred food dedicated to gods). Quite expectedly he was delighted and told his *gurubhāi* Premananda to cook and prepare the fish for offering to the Master. On being told that no fish could be offered in ritual worship to Ramakrishna on a Sunday because the Master himself never ate fish or meat on that day, Swamiji ruled that it was unnecessary to follow conventions with respect to sacred foods brought by a devotee. And defying his indisposition, he even cooked the fish English style with milk, yogurt, and dried vermicelli he had brought with him from London.[4] He in fact told Chakravarti, by way of complimenting him on his cooking a feast of fish preparations for the Swami, that one could not be a good *sādhu* unless one knew how to cook well because good cooking called for purity of the mind.[5] "You seem to me a queer sort of saint," the famous German Sanskrit scholar Paul Deussen had told Vivekananda frankly in Amsterdam in 1896. "You eat well, you drink well, you smoke all day, and you deprive yourself of nothing."[6]

Swamiji's so-called *pravrajyā* in India was not really the austere travels of an aspiring ascetic who desired to get firsthand knowledge of the material and moral condition of his countrymen. It was, on the other hand, some kind of holy hitchhiking, consisting mainly of long distance travels, mostly by train (and often in the first class). Travel expenses were usually borne by his aristocratic and middle-class acquaintances in northern and southern India, who later became his devotees. Dr. Chattopadhyaya's forthcoming book, *Swami Vivekananda in India,* documents the Swami's travels in India with startling effect.[7] Mahendranath provides fascinating and insightful snippets from his elder brother's experiences as a *parivrājak*; the central theme is always the latter's pangs of hunger and penchant for eating chilies and smoking *chillums*.[8] Vivekananda once responded to a visitor's questioning his consumption of chilies in a language that is characteristically his own. "Look here, Mr.," the irate renouncer retorted, "I have wandered about in the road my whole life and eaten rice licking my fingers. Chilies constituted my only possession and they are my only friend. Nowadays I get to eat a few stuff, but I have suffered starvation most often."[9] Once somewhere in the Himalayas, Vivekananda, together with a few friends, including Vaikunthanath Sanyal, confronted a snowstorm and feared imminent death. They entered a grotto and began to meditate for the last time. Ultimately Sanyal took out some black peppercorns from his bag and distributed the "life savers" to everybody to warm themselves by chewing the hot stuff, and he "somehow saved their life that night."[10] In fact the college graduate *bhadralok* of Calcutta could not withstand extreme climate. He was extremely reluctant to travel to Rajputana in summer even though he needed to go there to meet his benefactor, the Raja of Khetri, regarding his proposed trip to the United States. As the Swami wrote to Alasinga from the home of his Bengali host (Madhusudan Chattopadhyaya) in Hyderabad:

I am very sorry to tell you that I cannot go back at present to Rajputana. It is so very dreadfully hot here [Hyderabad] already. I do not know how hot it would be at Rajputana, and I cannot bear heat at all. So the next thing, I would do, would be to go back to Bangalore and then to Ootacamund to pass the summer there. My brain boils in heat.[11]

One of the most effective instances of Swamiji's severe penance was his startling a young girl with his booming voice by uttering "Narayan Hari." She had brought some alms for the ascetic with "grave countenance and shining eyes" but bolted in fear after having been startled by his yelling the name of God.[12]

II

Early in life the young Biley had exhibited his fondness for tobacco. As a child he used to suck the pipe from the water bowl of the hookah.[13] As a boy he would secretly smoke from the hookah his lawyer father had set aside for the entertainment of his Muslim clients.[14] Saradananda was appalled to hear the comments of a neighbor on young Naren's rude behavior and haughty attitude, which included his walking "in the street smoking a cheroot even in the presence of the elders of the neighborhood."[15] Vivekananda's admirer and devotee Sara Bull once warned him against his chronic smoking habit and his having "at luncheons and dinners a few times tasted wine," as well as his "impulsive and combative nature."[16] His extravagant eating and smoking astounded the women of the Home of Truths in Alameda and Los Angeles, where the Swami stayed for some time during his second and last visit to the United States. They "were of the firm opinion that a spiritual person seldom ate—certainly *never* ate meat—never smoked, and never became ill. It was clear to them that Swamiji was not a spiritual person."[17]

Saradananda once narrated to Mahendranath the amusing story of Vivekananda's determination to quit smoking and then importuning him to prepare a smoke for him even with the tobacco leafs Saradananda had used to wrap his swollen foot. He observed that "Vivekananda renounced everything but tobacco" and teased Mahendranath: "Really you folks are a family of tobacco addicts."[18] Vivekananda complained to Alasinga of his expenses in the United States and of his diminishing funds. His daily pocket expenses of one pound included his favorite cigars.[19] Indeed the Swami was terribly upset with his English devotee, Edward Sturdy, who had procured cheap tobacco for Vivekananda, which could not be lit easily. "I have to toil the whole day, talk to people, and think. And I can't even have a little smoke!" he complained to his other English devotee, Josiah J. Goodwin.[20] Sturdy, in fact, was highly critical of the Swami's smoking habit.[21] Vivekananda, on his part, remained absolutely impervious to any criticism of his habits. He regarded his critics as fanatics and in fact gave a lecture "On Fanaticism" in which he declared: "Some people are wine fanatics and cigar fanatics. Some think that if men gave up smoking cigars, the world would arrive at the millennium. Women are generally amongst these fanatics."[22] With respect to his addiction to tobacco, he confessed to his utter helplessness: "It . . . seems . . . my smoking is sinful . . . but I am what I am."[23] His pangs of hunger, coupled with his fondness for green chilies, led him to accept a meal of *chāpāti* and chili from the keeper of a wealthy man's stable, and this snacking resulted in his heartburn and stomach cramp later.[24]

III

A self-made monk, Vivekananda admitted with disarming candor in 1900 that he did not believe in monasticism.[25] He in fact blamed his aggravated diabetic condition and lumbago on his austere monastic life. He wrote to Edward Sturdy on 2 September 1899: "In India the moment I landed, they made me shave my head, and wear 'Kaupin' . . . with the result I got diabetes, etc."[26] He thought his lumbago was caused by his sleeping on a wet floor during his travels as a monk.[27] He told his disciple Chakravarti that "one could never extinguish desires for comfort and enjoyment by just becoming a monk."[28] He had declared a few years earlier that asceticism was "fiendish" and that "to laugh is better than to pray."[29] Shortly afterward in a private conversation in London, he confessed to the extreme hardships of the life of an Indian *sannyāsī* who had to beg for food and sleep on damp floors, risking muscular disorder. Mahendranath, the reporter of this conversation, writes how Swamiji, a patient of lumbago, "lamented over the miseries of a *sādhu's* career."[30] Complaining of the discomforts of his *gurubhāis* in London, Vivekananda wrote to Sturdy that "no Sannyasin should unnecessarily throw away his life or *undertake unnecessary hardship*."[31] He confessed to Sturdy that he felt extremely depressed during his early renouncer life at Baranagar for having persuaded his *bhadralok* friends to leave their comfortable homes for the uncertain and degrading life of a street beggar.[32] He advised young Virajananda: "Do not spoil your health on hard (*kaṭhor*) austerity. See, how we have broken our body by *kaṭhor tapa-*

syā. What good is there in it? Learn from our experience."[33] The primary reason for founding a monastery at Belur was, as he is reported to have said, the following: "I have realized how painful is hunger. That is why I have founded the Math. More boys will join afterwards. They will at least get something to eat here."[34]

Toward the end of his life, Vivekananda expressed his earnest desire to give up his monastic career and return home. On 17 January 1900, he wrote to Sara Bull from California: "It is becoming clearer to me that I lay down all the concerns of the Math and for a time go back to my mother. She has suffered much through me. I must try to smooth her last days."[35] In another letter he even provided Mrs. Bull with a detailed financial arrangement he had made for his family, and he reiterated his desire: "As for my mother, I am going back to her—for my last days and hers."[36]

It ought to be noted in this connection that the financial problems of Swamiji's family had been solved somewhat satisfactorily by 1888. Early in 1887 his mother had been embroiled in a court case concerning her share of the property of her late husband Vishwanath; she won the case on 10 November of the same year. For a time Narendranath, as her eldest son, had to be involved in this litigation and even stood as a witness on 8 March. However, following a ruling of the High Court of Calcutta, his mother recovered her portion of the property in question, and "from that moment Naren was freed from his responsibility and all his worries regarding property and patrimony came to an end."[37]

Yet the Swami told Josephine MacLeod a couple of months before his death: "I have nothing in the world. I haven't a penny to myself for I have given away everything that has ever been given to me." When his beloved "friend" Jo Jo promised to provide him with a pension of $50 a month as long as he lived, he wondered: "Can I live on that?"[38] He continued to receive an allowance of Rs. 100 every month from Raja Ajit Singh since June 1893.[39] Additionally, he had received a onetime donation of Rs. 8000 from his English disciple, Captain James H. Sevier.[40] He also requested Mrs. Bull to procure funds in addition to the $1,000 promised by Francis Leggett to finance his final return to India.[41]

He once tried to recover the huge landed property bought by his father in his name, the so-called Vireshwar's Estate (*Vireśvarer ābād*), which he never inherited due to family litigations. On his return from the West, Swamiji told Brahmananda: "Rakhal, you just recover my 'Vireśvar's Estate.' Your father was a landlord and you have inherited a property holder's cunning. Please get my landed property back through a court case."[42] Niranjan Dhar has observed that for the

Swami "his monastic career was but an interim period of his life. Just before death he wished to return to the same family he had left to become a monk and he was troubled by the frequent shadows of his cherished householder past cast on his monastic life."[43] Indeed the Swami confessed to Nivedita that he wanted "to do something for his relatives" because he felt that "it was Mother's wish." He wrote, "I am happy to shoulder [the burden of] what I had abandoned two decades ago."[44]

IV

The normal aspiration for an affluent life did affect Narendranath's mind. As he confessed to Saradananda, since his early youth he had been assailed by two images of his future at bedtime. One was the vision of a prosperous and socially influential career fortified with the conviction in his ability to realize it. "But the next moment I would see myself sleeping under a tree, wearing a loin cloth, and eating foods acquired by chance, and surviving by the grace of God," he continued. "I used to feel that I was able to lead a saint's life, if I wished. Thus this twin vision of two modes of life would flash before my mind's eye and the latter would possess my soul," the Swami concluded.[45]

Vivekananda's onetime admirer, the French poet Jules Bois, provides an interesting description of the Swami's monastic life in India. When he arrived at the Belur Math, Vivekananda stood on the threshold of the main door. His first words were: "I am free, my friend, free again. I have given away everything. In the poorest country of the world, I am the poorest man." But when Bois saw the hermit's cell, he was surprised to see that the poorest man on earth yet retained some American furniture, including a rocking chair. He was probably even more surprised when he heard his host proclaim:

What you others call a dream is for us the only reality. Cities, luxuries, the marvels of material science—we have awakened from that brutal dream by which you are still entranced. We close our eyes, we hold our breath, we sit under the kindly shade of a tree before the primitive fire, and the Infinite opens its doors to us and we enter into the inner world which is the real one.[46]

Mahendranath provides a graphic but sincere description of what one might consider the daily habits of his saintly brother, who made his admiring English devotee Goodwin his factotum, or worse, a veritable slave. Once at the Müller residence in London, while eating his dinner, Vivekananda asked Goodwin to look into his diary to find out if there were any engagements for him that evening. On being reminded that the Swami indeed had an appointment at a duke's residence in Park Lane and that he had just ten minutes until the appointment, Vivekananda left the dinner half finished, dressed up, and ordered Goodwin (who hadn't finished his meal) to tie the laces of his boots, fetch his hat and walking stick, prepare a cigarette for him (and had it lit by his devotee), and finally get a hansom and pay the coachman the required fare. As Datta writes: "All this took two to three minutes. Goodwin performed his chore in minute detail even within this short time. He moved like a machine, as it were. He joined others to finish the dinner after Swamiji had left."[47]

Long after he had graduated into *sannyās* and become a spiritual celebrity, the thirty-five-year-old Swami encouraged his favorite *bāṅgāl* (mildly pejorative term for a native of eastern Bengal considered to be bucolic by the Bengalis of Calcutta) disciple, Sharat Chakravarti, to quit teaching and start a small business of his own in the United States. "Remaining a teacher for too long perverts intelligence. You can't gain real knowledge. . . . Do not teach any more," he counseled. "If you really want a householder's life and earn money, then go to the States. I shall give you business tips. You would see what an enormous amount of money you could make in five years." Vivekananda even suggested selling silk saris from Benares to the Americans and assured Chakravarti of help in the United States through his local contacts. When the disciple remained lukewarm at his guru's materialist exhortation, he was asked to choose between a commercial and an ascetic life, though in the end he recommended the latter because "this is surely the best life, what will one gain by being in the world? After all everything is ephemeral."[48] Even after he had earned worldwide fame as a colossal renouncer—indeed a *mahāyogī*—Vivekananda could never resolve his deep-seated ambivalence toward a secular and a saintly life! As he had opted, rather listlessly, for the life of a monk in his youth, so he decided, not quite spiritedly, in favor of a renouncer's career for his disciple. Never really a spiritually inclined man, all hagiographical insistence notwithstanding, Narendranath had taken to cowl to escape from the hunger and deprivation of his impoverished home to lead the carefree life of a monk with his cohorts without social or financial hassle or responsibility. As he confided to Pramadadas Mitra, he wholeheartedly wished to get out of the terribly indigent and inhospitable family environment and to go far away from it, never to return.[49] He appears to be what Niranjan Dhar has said is an *abhāv-sannyāsī* (monk due to distress) rather than a *svabhāv-sannyāsī* (monk by inclination).[50]

5

Vivekananda on Hinduism and the Hindus

I

In the United States, Swami Vivekananda wished to rescue Hinduism from the quagmire of Oriental esoterism to which some Christian missionaries had relegated it and to proclaim vocally its anteriority and superiority vis-à-vis all other religions of the world. His strategy was first to establish his credibility and goodwill by praising Jesus and yet admonishing the Christians for not following Christ's precepts. "I tell you . . . you are not like your Christ, whom we honour and reverence," the Swami thundered in the Chicago Parliament of Religions.[1] "We want missionaries of Christ," he declared in Detroit in February 1894. "Let such come to India by the hundreds and thousands. Bring Christ's life to us and let it permeate the very core of society. Let him be preached in every village and corner of India."[2] He was of course influenced by the ideas of his Brahmo mentor Keshab Sen, who had written about Christ a generation earlier: "I have always regarded the cross as a beautiful emblem of self-sacrifice into the glory of God . . . one which is calculated to quicken the higher feelings and aspirations of the heart, and to purify the soul."[3]

His real intention, however, was to render Christ somewhat unoriginal and proclaim the ultimate primacy of Hinduism. On 12 August at Greenacre, Maine, he preached:

> The divine ones of God are all my Masters. I learn of your Christ in learning of Krishna, of Buddha, in learning of Mohamet. I worship God alone . . . I learn from all that is called evil or good. The nation and all such nonsense may go. It is love, love, love God and my brother.[4]

A few months earlier, he had hinted that "there is the same beauty in the character of Christ and the character of Buddah [sic]."[5] A year later in 1895, he observed in his address to the Brooklyn Ethical Association that "Christianity is founded in Buddhism."[6] While traveling from England to India in January 1897, on board the ship

60

Prinz-Regent Luitpold, he told Nivedita about his dream of an old bearded man named Therapeutae (Theraputra—son [*putra*] of an old monk [*thera*]) and observed that "no such person as Jesus Christ ever existed and that the truths and ideals of the Therapeutaes' creed were given out by the Christians as having been taught by Jesus."[7] Almost a year earlier, Vivekananda had told a member of the audience at the Graduate Philosophical Society of Harvard University, where he had been invited to deliver a lecture on the Vedanta, that "Buddha was one of the Sannyasins of the Vedanta. . . . The ideas which now are called Buddhism were not his. They were much more ancient."[8] Even Zoroaster was, according to the Swami, "a reformer of some old religion which must have been Vedantic."[9] Thus through his various sermons, Vivekananda made the point that Christianity really was not different but in fact was derived from the Hindu Vedanta. He further claimed that Sanskrit, a language of the Hindus, was "the foundation of all European languages which are nothing but jargonized Sanskrit."[10]

Having "proved" the anteriority of the Vedanta, that is, of Hinduism, he then made a number of quite unfounded generalizations on the superiority of the Aryans. He declared in Boston that "nearly all civilizations that the world has today have come from that one peculiar race of mankind, the Aryans. Civilization has been of three types: the Roman [imperial and organizational], the Greek [aesthetic and immoral], the Hindoo [metaphysical and spiritual]."[11] In Detroit he expatiated on the character and countenance of the Indian Aryans.

> To the great tablelands of the high Himalaya mountains first came the Aryans, and there to this day abides the pure type of Brahman, a people which [the Westerners] can but dream of. Pure in thought, deed and action, so honest that a bag of gold left in a public place would be found unharmed twenty years after; so beautiful that . . . "to see a girl in the fields is to pause and marvel that God could make anything so exquisite." Their features are regular, their eyes and hair dark, and their skin the color of which would be produced by the drops which fell from a pricked finger into a glass of milk. These are the Hindus in their pure type, untainted and untrammeled.[12]

He was to write in 1897 in a fantastic essay titled "The East and the West" (*Prācya O Pāścātya*] that "of all the nations of the world, the Hindus are the handsomest and finest in feature." He even reminded his readers: "I am not bragging nor saying anything in exaggeration because they belong to my own nationality, but this fact is known all over the world."[13] He claimed that the Greek traveler Megasthenes had spoken of the "white Indians" and that their fair complexion darkened due to the intermixture of many racial stocks, especially the Tartars, following the spread of Buddhism.[14] Vivekananda, Farquhar has observed astutely, "appealed to history without possessing a historical conscience."[15]

The Swami was not only proud of how the Hindu looked, he even found his habits and character most exemplary. In response to a Boston woman's protest against his calling the city uncivilized when he was heckled by some youngsters in the street because of his strange garment, Vivekananda unhesitatingly posited: "with us it is unpardonable to show even polite curiosity to the stranger within our gates, and *never* open hostility."[16] Of course according to him, "the Aryans are lovers of peace, cultivators of soil, and are quite happy and contented if they can only rear their families undisturbed. In such a life they have ample leisure, and therefore greater opportunity of being thoughtful and civilised."[17] The Swami presented a quasi-fantastic and overly idealistic image of the Hindus to the Americans during his second visit there. The Hindus "are [of a] poetic nature," he declared in San Francisco. "They go crazy over poetry. Their philosophy is poetry. . . . All [high thought] in the Sanskrit is written in poetry. Metaphysics, astronomy—all in poetry."[18] This obsession with the beauty and quality of his own race did not square very well with the Swami's admonition to Nivedita: "All that I want you to see is that most people's actions are the expression of self-interest, and you constantly oppose to this the idea that a certain race are all angels. Ignorance so determined is wickedness."[19] However, we must also note that the Swami's assertions often were more rhetorical than substantial, and often were made intentionally to impress a select group of audience. For example he wanted his Indian audience to recognize the virtues of the Westerners so as not to be complacent about Hindu traditions and mores, which he critiqued. Thus in a conversation with Shachindranath Basu at Belur, he brutally attacked the traditions and morals of his fellow Indians and praised the West:

> . . . there isn't this much brutality in their country. How childish you are! Tell me which country is better. . . . please keep your mouth shut and you'll see everything is o.k. Damn it, you have howled enough in the name of chastity and have roasted thousands of widows on bamboo planks. . . . Chastity! Chastity is nothing but "The wife is my object of pleasure . . . I shall enjoy her the way I like"![20]

II

The Swami waxed eloquent on the virtues of the Hindus in the West. He contrasted the beauty and beatitude of the Hindus with the

cruelty and crudity of the Europeans: "You look about India, what
has the Hindoo left? Wonderful temples, everywhere. What has the
Mohammedan left? Beautiful palaces. What has the Englishman left?
Nothing but mounds of brandy bottles!"[21] He also went so far as to
assert that "there are hundreds of churches that have been erected
with the assistance of the Hindoos, but no Hindoo temples for which
a Christian has given a penny."[22] "Morally," declared the ebullient
Swami, "India is head and shoulders above the United States or any
other country on the globe."[23] He almost hurt himself by hitting his
knuckles angrily on the table while trying to drive home the distinction between Hindu chastity and English laxity to a Californian
woman: "No, madam, the relationship in which children creep into
life amidst lust and in darkness, does not exist in India."[24] With a
view to asserting India's moral superiority over England, he provided
his special brand of proof: "in England one in every 400 is a drunkard,
while in India the proportion is one to every million."[25] As Bishop
W. X. Ninde, who had welcomed Vivekananda to speak at the Unitarian Church in Detroit, later remarked, this was truly the Swami's
"rose-colored exhibits of Hindoo morality." The bishop had firsthand
knowledge of India, and he pointed out that "the drinking habit had
become quite recently so rife among the natives in a portion of western India that a firm of Hindoo merchants in Bombay engaged one
of our unemployed missionaries to go through the country with a
Brahman to lecture on temperance."[26] As a matter of fact, the neighborhood of Swamiji's ancestral home had acquired a reputation for
being a veritable haven for drunkards and *tāntriks*. As Mahendranath
Datta informs us, the district of Simulia in northern Calcutta was
nicknamed as the hangout of eight Basus, boozers from the influential
Basu household, who used to sleep in the streetside sewers every
Sunday night following a drinking spree at the local tavern. Mahendranath observes that the educated *bhadralok* of Calcutta were habit-
ual drunkards.[27]

Vivekananda made further outlandish claims on behalf of Hindu
cleanliness. As he wrote in *The East and the West,*

No nation in the world is cleanly in the body as the Hindu, who uses
water very freely. Taking a plunge bath is wellnigh scarce in other nations,
with a few exceptions. The English have introduced it into their country
after coming in contact with India. . . . When the Westerners bathe—and
that is once a week—they change their inner clothing. . . . Imagine their
eating of garlic in abundance, profuse perspiration day and night, and yet
no bath! Ghosts must surely run away from them, what to say of men![28]

He also wrote about an unbelievable handicap of a most luxurious hotel in Paris, the city he considered to be: "the capital of modern civilization . . . the heaven of luxury, fashion, and merriment on earth—the centre of arts and sciences." He wrote that as a guest of his millionaire friend, Francis Leggett, he was sent to "a huge palatial hotel" where he suffered because it had no bathrooms! Twelve other hotels were contacted, but none had bathroom facilities. Vivekananda also chanced on a local newspaper that reported "that an old lady entered into the bath-tub and died then and there!" He thought that "perhaps that was the first occasion in her life to come in contact with so much water, and the frame collapsed by the sudden shock!"[29]

He also unleashed his venom against the English at the home of Professor Wright:

> Ah, the English, only just a little while ago they were savages, . . . the vermin crawled on the ladies' bodices, . . . and they scented themselves to disguise the abominable odor of their persons. . . . Most hor-r-ible. Even now, they are barely emerging from barbarism. . . . They are quite savage. The frightful cold, the want and privation of their northern climate has made them *wild*. They only think to kill.[30]

A few years later, he was to write to Mary Hale that "English soldiers are killing our men and outraging our women—only to be sent home with passage and pension at our expense. . . . Heathen-murdering is only a legitimate pastime for the Christians."[31] His accusation was based on the report of a gang rape of a woman and the death of a native cook at the hands of two soldiers of a British cavalry regiment.[32] The English did not kill just heathens at random. Even worse they killed Vedantic monks. Sister Nivedita writes, apparently on the authority of the Swami himself, that "his personal ideal was that sannyasin of the Mutiny, who was stabbed by an English soldier, and broke the silence of fifteen years to say to his murderer—'And thou also art He'!"[33] "You come," Vivekananda cried, waving his arms and foaming at the mouth, "with the Bible in one hand and the conqueror's sword in the other. . . . You trample on us. . . . You destroy precious life in animals. You are *carnevores* [sic]. You degrade our people with drink. You insult our women."[34]

The Swami's vilification of the Christians was little better than what he regarded as slander on Indian customs and behaviors by the missionaries. He was perhaps uninformed or deliberately unmindful of the fact that some of the missionaries had already written extremely critical accounts of the profanity and perversity of the Europeans as well as the native converts of Bengal.[35] Moreover if he faulted them for making gross generalizations about the Hindus, he, too, was a master generalizer given to purposive flattery for political reasons or quite insensitive to others' feelings to make a point regardless of propriety or truth. For example as a newcomer to the United States trying to make a favorable impression on the Americans, the Swami concluded his paper on "Hinduism as a Religion" with a rather irrelevant and patently false but quite effective hyperbole praising the Americans: "Hail, Columbia, motherland of liberty! It has been given to thee, who never dipped her hand in her neighbour's blood, who never found out that the shortest way of becoming rich was by robbing one's neighbours, it has been given to thee to march on at the vanguard of civilisation with the flag of harmony."[36] Commenting on his lectures on Hinduism, a correspondent of the *Indian Social Reformer* noted: "The pure and undefiled Hinduism which the Swami preached has no existence to-day, has not had existence for centuries, and is at the present moment only an affair of books and not of life, a thing, therefore, of merely abstract interest."[37] Dinanath Ganguli of Halishahar commented on Vivekananda's nonchalant and defiant attitude and warned that "he *must* care for the results of his words, expressive of his feelings towards his opponents."[38] Gyanchandra Banerji observed: "when we go through his Epistles we find aspersions, angry words, and abuses hurled against those whose ideas differed from him, those who could not do what he wanted, or who did not recognise him as a spiritual guide."[39] A correspondent of the *Indian Mirror* commented on Vivekananda's Madras address following his return from the West: "I have read Swami Vivekananda's first lecture in Madras and it has never been my lot to see a more sickening twaddle put down in black and white. From one end to the other, the speech is characterised by a rigmarole of arrant nonsense and vituperative fustian."[40] In the same address, the Swami executed a volte-face in his attitude to India. "I will be the last man to claim perfection for the Hindu society," he declared, thus contradicting his many assertions in the West glorifying his country.[41] The reporter's comment on his lecture on Hinduism in the Drake University monthly magazine, *The Delphic,* appears to be right on the mark: "His lectures will not bear too close scrutiny, not because the man is unable, but because underlying the whole is a false unreal basis."[42] In any case his boasts with regard to the Indians' hospitality to and respect for strangers in their midst were rudely shattered by the horrendous experience of Nivedita, Josephine, and Sara at Naini Tal, where their escort, Swamiji, was worshiped by the local people but they were greeted with a shout from the crowd: "Unclean women, be off with you!"[43] Similarly when Vivekananda was being "worshiped . . . as God Himself" at Colombo on 15 January 1897 and escorted into a temple with the cry "Jai Jai Mahādeva," his English devotee Josiah Goodwin, being a *mleccha,* was not allowed entry into the shrine—a discrimination that disheartened the once-enthusiastic young follower of the Swami.[44]

III

The Swami's deliberate glorification of Hindu civilization called for explaining away the caste system and the deplorable status of women—the two most familiar and notorious features of Hindu society. He rose to the occasion with his characteristic dithyramb and braggadocio. He translated the term caste as *jāti* and said that it is "the first idea of creation." Creation connotes variation or diversity (*vicitratā*), and "Jati means creation." According to him, "the original idea of Jati was . . . freedom of the individual to express his nature, his Prakriti, his Jati, his caste." Such was the case with Hindu society for millennia, and the system worked. India's bane was "the giving up of this idea of caste. The present caste is not the real Jati, but a hindrance to its progress. It really has prevented the free action of Jati, i.e., caste or variation." Influenced in his early youth by the Brahmo endorsement of the Hindu caste system, the Swami posited that caste, properly speaking, conduced individuality and variety and hence fostered prosperity, but unfortunately, it was replaced by "hereditary class" that thwarted caste or *jāti.*[45] He also justified caste on nationalistic grounds. As he declared:

> It is owing to caste that three hundred millions [*sic*] of people [presumably this figure was used by Swamiji to denote India's total population which, according to him, had been "living for years upon wild flowers"[46]] can find a piece of bread to eat yet. It is an imperfect institution, no doubt. But if it had not been for caste, you would have had no Sanskrit books to study. This caste made walls, around which all sorts of invasions rolled and surged, but found it impossible to break through. That necessity has not gone yet; so caste remains.[47]

His other argument in defense of the caste system was that it was a more civilized way of dealing with the inferior or conquered people than simply killing them off, as the Westerners did in Australia, New Zealand, South Africa, the Americas, and the Pacific Islands. "Wherever you have found weaker races, you have exterminated them by the roots, as it were," Vivekananda thundered against the Western world. By contrast he claimed,

. . . India has never done that. Aryans were kind and generous . . . and . . . would there have been this institution of Varnashrama if the Aryans had exterminated the aborigines in order to settle their lands? . . . The means of European civilization is the sword; of the Aryans, the division into different Varnas. This system of division into different Varnas is the stepping stone to civilization, making one rise higher and higher in proportion to one's learning and culture.[48]

However, the Swami declared that

. . . the caste system is opposed to the religion of the Vedanta. Caste is a social custom, and all our great preachers have tried to break it down. . . . Caste is simply the outgrowth of political institution of India; it is a hereditary trade guild. Trade competition with Europe has broken caste more than any teaching.[49]

Sometimes the Swami would be carried away by his own rhetoric and would unconsciously give away his caste bias while trying to reinforce his argument or rebut that of his challenger. By way of criticizing the Western authors of Indian social and cultural life, he said that "the people who write books on India came only into contact with the . . . Pariahs [who] . . . did all the menial work, ate carrion and were scavengers." He claimed that these people were not "genuine Hindus."[50] In fact his love for the Kshatriya caste was quite explicit in his deliberate public falsification of his own caste. He claimed that he belonged to the Kshatriya caste whereas he really was a Kayastha, a caste below the Kshatriya.[51] He praised the Khsatriyas of India in his Harvard lecture: "Most of our great teachers throughout India have been Kshatriyas, and were always universal in their teachings. . . . Rama, Krishna, and Buddha—worshipped as Incarnations of God—were Kshatriyas."[52] At another time when some brahmins of Madras wanted to know his caste, he replied: "I belong to the king maker's caste. The brahmins were silenced."[53] When he had to acknowledge his real Kayastha caste, he elevated it, claiming a divine origin for it, descending from Chitragupta, clerk of Dharmaraja Yama, the God of Death, and producing geniuses for India. He asked his audience in Madras:

If my caste is left out of consideration, what will there be left of the present-day civilisation of India? In Bengal also, my blood has furnished them with their greatest philosopher, the greatest poet, the greatest historian, the greatest archaeologist, the greatest religious preacher [note here how the force of his rhetoric has led the speaker to deny his guru Ramakrishna who was a caste brahmin and whose message he was spreading in the world]; my blood has furnished India with the greatest of her modern scientists.[54]

Vivekananda's exposition and explanation of the Hindu caste system was idiosyncratic at best and simply incorrect at worst.[55] Having declared on various occasions that Vedanta was India's pristine religion and the caste system the upholder of Aryan civilization, he lectured on the incompatibility between the Vedanta and caste. His thesis that trade with the West has led to the dismantling of Indian caste system was not quite true. According to a recent study, the caste system of Bengal had already been on the wane at least among certain radical sections of the Hindu society, for example, the Young Bengal group led by Henry Louis Vivian Derozio, a teacher of the Hindu (later named Presidency) College of Calcutta. Dr. Dutta has observed: "The decline was mainly due to the diffusion of rationalist western ideas into Bengal in the nineteenth century." "It was also due," Dutta continues, "to the phenomenon of social mobility among various caste orders . . . [and to the] Christian missionary endeavours to bring knowledge to the minds of the degraded female population in Bengal in the nineteenth century."[56]

The Swami's claims for compassion and tolerance of the Hindu Aryans toward the non-Aryans through the social device of caste defy all Puranic and scriptural stories of clashes between the Devas (Aryans) and the Asuras, Rākṣasas, and Dānavas (non-Aryans). Also the story of the Brahmanic holocaust of the Kshatriyas, as illustrated in the *Mahābhārata* story of Ashvatthama, provide an embarrassing anomaly of intra-Aryan viciousness and violence. Then his deliberate confusion of the Vaisya (of which the Kayasthas form a subcaste) and the Kshatriya castes and his claim that he belonged to the latter were not only inaccurate, they also were, as one contemporary critic pointed out, quite contrary to monastic ideals. Commenting on Vivekananda's claim that he was a Kshatriya, an anonymous correspondent to the *Indian Mirror* (2 March 1897) wondered "what he will do with the empty title of Kshatriya. He is a devotee, he has cut off all connection with the world, yet he claims the Kshatriya title."[57]

The Swami frankly was quite contemptuous of the low-caste people. He thought that they were lowly because they had failed to imbibe the Sanskrit culture of the Brahmins, the men of God.[58] He also regarded them as ugly in appearance. He once teasingly told a young girl from the neighborhood that her face was as ugly as a *dom*'s.[59] He was of course quite aware of the cultural inadequacies of the low-caste people. While prophesying the advent of the Shudra regime in the world, which would be accompanied by wide distribution of material comforts in society, he was quick to point out that "its disadvantages (perhaps) . . . [were] the lowering of culture." No doubt the Shudra period will witness "a great distribution of ordinary education, but extraordinary geniuses will be less and less."[60] It is not surprising that he had little hesitation calling his opponents pariahs to insult them.[61] His elite consciousness was quite explicit in his somewhat idiosyncratic prescriptions for solving the caste problem:

> The solution of the caste problem in India, . . . assumes this form, not to degrade the higher castes, not to crush out the Brahmins. The Brahminhood is the ideal of humanity in India . . . .This Brahmin . . . must remain; he must not go. . . . The solution is not by bringing down the higher, but by raising the lower up to the level of the higher.[62]

This process was to be gradual. As he said, "now as to the details, they of course have to be worked out through generations." He regretted the fact that "in modern times there should be so much dissension between the castes. This must stop." His admonition in this regard was clear: "To the non-Brahmin castes I say, wait, be not in a hurry."[63]

IV

Vivekananda made a number of claims with respect to the status of women in Hindu society. In Detroit, "he stated that in India the woman was the visible manifestation of God and that her whole life was given up to the thought that she was a mother, and to be perfect mother she must be chaste." He even went to the length of asserting that "the girls of India would die if they like American girls, were obliged to expose half their bodies to the vulgar gaze of young men."[64] He in fact claimed that "Hindu women are very spiritual and very religious, perhaps more so than any other women in the world."[65] It is precisely because the Indian women are so exemplary and held in high esteem by the society that they had to be kept in seclusion.[66]

He further declared that Hinduism considers "drinking wine, killing a woman, and killing a Brahmin" as "the highest crimes," and the Hindu scriptures are the only one of their kind in the whole world to praise women.[67] The Swami spoke of a veteran of the Sepoy Mutiny of 1857, who declared: "Kill a woman! You know we could not do that." Thus Vivekananda informed his American audience that it was probably the Muslims who had been responsible for the slaughter of British women and children in Delhi and Kanpur during the Mutiny.[68] He disposed of the embarrassing reputation of the Hindus for burning their widows. First he flatly denied that child widows were abused in society. "I have travelled all over India, but failed to see a case of the ill-treatment," reported the Vedantic *parivrājak*. Then he explained the custom of sati by observing that those widows who immolated themselves in the funeral pyres of their husbands were "fanatics" and that the Hindus never believed in widow burning even though they permitted the custom.[69] On another occasion, however, he said that "the Hindu widow went to her death agony amid feasting and song, arrayed in her costliest garments and believing for the most part that such an act meant the glories of Paradise for herself and family. She was worshipped as a martyr and her name was enshrined among the family records."[70] The Swami's sanitized rendering of the Hindu society upholding the dignity of widows' needs to be contrasted with what seems to be a realistic account of the Presbyterian missionary, Rev. Dr. Thackwell, who had lived and worked in India for nearly half a century. According to the Reverend,

> some people may come over as did Kananda [*sic*], and say that the widow's position is improved, but if it is true then the word of all returned missionaries is untrue. The widow is stripped of her jewels and her finery and a coarse garment placed upon her and she is the Cinderella of the family. The belief in regard to their being burned was that the gods were displeased and to insure the husband's salvation his widow must die.[71]

To establish himself as an authentic Hindu in this regard, Vivekananda made a couple of unfounded claims. He said that *he had seen* his guru Ramakrishna "taking little girls by the hands, placing them in a chair and actually worshiping them, placing flowers at their feet and prostrating himself before these little children because they represented the mother God."[72] He obviously drew on the Master's reminiscences on 4 June 1883 and on 5 April 1884 of his spiritual exercises during the days of his divine madness, in the course of which he had told his devotees about his worshiping virgin teenagers as part of the *tāntrik* ritual of *soḍaṣī pūjā* (virgin worship).[73] He did not worship little girls on chairs. Most importantly there is no evidence that he did so at any time in the 1880s or in front of Narendranath or any other disciple. Vivekananda also declared: "Whatever I know of religion I learned from my master, and he learned of a woman."[74] It is, however, known that Ramakrishna learned Tantra from his female mentor, the *Bhairavī* Yogeshwari. And on his own admission, he learned Vedanta—the religion Vivekananda was preaching in the West—from a man, Totapuri the *nyaṅgtā* ("naked": member of a particular sect of all-renouncing monks).[75] According to an admiring scholar, such dissimulation of truths is justifiable manipulation of a "hierarchy of truths" for a religious leader with an impeccable personal moral integrity and a clear spiritual vision. "Vivekananda," he goes on to claim, "certainly believed that his life and vision qualified for this special dispensation."[76]

In an eloquent essay, Vivekananda reminded his countrymen: "O India! Forget not that the ideal of thy womanhood is Sita, Savitri, Damayanti."[77] He categorically asserted that "the women of India must grow and develop in the footprints of Sita, and that is the only way."[78] Indeed for him the ideal of Hindu womanhood remained, as these names make manifestly clear, chastity and loyalty to the husband. He of course maintained that the quintessential femininity consisted in motherhood. "The ideal of womanhood in India is motherhood—that marvellous, unselfish, all-suffering, ever-forgiving mother," the Swami announced in California.[79] The mother "deserved worship" because she "was a saint in bringing . . . [her child] into the world," by keeping "her body pure, her mind pure, her food pure, her clothes pure, her imagination pure, for years" in expectation of becoming a mother.[80] The other ideal role for women, according to Swamiji, was to be a *sannyāsinī*—dedicated to the welfare of humanity—a role he thrust on Margaret Noble.

Yet he was capable of making some very reasonable comments on the debased condition of Hindu women. The tragic death by suicide of his younger sister Yogendrabala[81] as well as his experience with Western women had made him conscious of the tribulation and degradation of Indian women. He told Brahmananda on 6 November 1898 at Balaram Basu's home that the relationship between Indian men and women was based on the latter's servitude and as such it was not good at all. "Can a race that accords no liberty to its women ever prosper?" the Swami asked his *gurubhāi*. In a conversation with a visitor at the Belur Math, he burst out: "All laws, customs [*smṛti*], and the canons of love [*bhālobāsā*] are meant to keep women subdued. Oh, I shudder to say that this country of ours has humiliated the Mother of the Universe [*Jagadambā*] for two millennia and is paying for its sins and yet hasn't come to its senses. . . . [You] hypocrites and selfish to the bone!. . . . quit humiliating the Mother of Universe and you will see how quickly the country prospers."[82] However, for him women had no identity as sexual beings. Niranjan Dhar astutely observes that Vivekananda's ideal women were all chaste wives who had been loyal to their spouses without demur. But the Swami did not bother to adduce the example of independent-minded women such as Draupadi of the *Mahābhārata*.[83]

Then even though women had exhibited "spiritual genius and great strength of mind" in the past, the Swami found contemporary women a decadent lot, who think of "nothing but eating and drinking, gossip and scandal."[84] He therefore prescribed education for Indian women with a view toward creating "great fearless women—women worthy to continue the traditions of Sanghamitra, Lila, Ahalya Bai, and Mira Bai—women fit to be mothers of heroes."[85] Though Vivekananda has been seen by the women scholars of modern India as one who harbored "great confidence in women"[86] and who "had charted the path to women's emancipation on the basis of . . . the Vedanta,"[87] he really had nothing to say with respect to developing the manifold possibilities of women in the larger arena of life.[88] Above all the volatile Vivekananda would have few qualms changing his mind. His letter to his disciples of Madras unmistakably reveals his reprioritized social agenda: "With the question whether caste shall go or come I have nothing to do. . . . Whether there should be caste or not, whether women should be perfectly free or not, does not concern me."[89]

6

Vivekananda's Humanitarian and Social Thought

I

As with his sermons and writings on the Hindu caste system and women, Vivekananda showed equal disregard for reality in his sermons on the Indian poor—his much proclaimed *gananārāyaṇ* or *daridranārāyaṇ*, that is, "God as the masses" or "God as the poor and oppressed." He has been universally acknowledged, especially in India, even by scholars and researchers, as a sharp critic of India's exploitative social system and as a militant monk who struggled to arouse the conscience of the rich and the consciousness of the masses.[1] Consequently he has been hailed as a socialist thinker and activist. In fact it was Dr. Bhupendranath Datta who first attempted to make a socialist out of his "patriot-prophet" elder brother.[2] Datta's passionate enterprise has been continued in a recent tendentious treatment by an erstwhile professor of economics of a Calcutta college.[3]

Admittedly Vivekananda's Vedantic social thought was owed to his experiences in the United States or rather to his contact with the Christian world. Since the late eighteenth century, the Christian church of Europe had become a collaborator of the rising capitalist classes in exploiting and oppressing the masses. Socialists such as Karl Marx or Ludwig Feuerbach mounted a vigorous attack on the church from outside, whereas from within the church there developed what later came to be called the critique in the form of Christian Socialism or the Social Gospel Movement, based primarily on the humanitarian and egalitarian messages of Jesus. The Social Gospel Movement, led by Washington Gladden and Walter Rauschenbusch, had reached a climax in the United States by the time Vivekananda arrived. The 1890s were a decade of economic depression in America, and the church leaders with Christian Socialist orientation were busy providing relief to scores of the homeless and jobless in society. Swamiji came in close contact with a number of social activists such as Charles Pankhurst, Benjamin Mills, and the Vrooman brothers (Walter, Hiram, and Carl); he saw social action firsthand while reading a variety of articles on the subject.

It is a fact that since its inception at Baranagore, the residents of the Ramakrishna Math exerted themselves for spiritual work only, and even Vivekananda does not seem to have been conscious of the efficacy of *jīvasevā* (service to humanity) prior to his Western travels. On the other hand, one notes the Swami's eagerness to proclaim the virtues of Vedantic Socialism at Pambam on landing there from the West in 1897 and, subsequently, his efforts at founding the Ramakrishna Mission in Calcutta even in the face of severe criticisms from some of the Master's monastic and householder disciples. The Ramakrishna Order would have met with an inevitable split had not the Swami, riding high on his newfound celebrity and backed by the promise of financial help from his wealthy admirers, both in India and the West, threatened to sever all connections with the Math— thereby disowning Ramakrishna as his guru and discontinuing financial support for the Math (something he had already hinted at a year ago in anticipation of any opposition to his plans).[4]

The transformation of the Order from a primarily spiritual to a mainly social organization was not really predicated on the Paramahamsa's prescriptions, as Vivekananda insisted time and again. The Master had recognized the supremacy of Advaita Vedanta as the vehicle of the *jñānī*, though he preferred, and indeed prescribed, *bhakti*, Dualism (Dvaita), or Pantheism as the practicable path for the people, leading to the same goal: *Brahmajñāna* (knowledge of the Brahman).[5] At the same time, toward the fag end of his life, Ramakrishna counseled extreme detachment of the Advaita Vedanta that had little regard for living beings and even condoned murder committed in the Advaita state.[6] He of course had contemptuously rejected the idea of social service as an impediment to the spiritual goal of God-realization.[7]

Vivekananda attempted to situate social service on the teachings of Advaita Vedanta, though for all intents and purposes, the philosophical base for his ideal of philanthropy and social work remained Pantheistic. This is because his arguments for the Vedantic perception of the unity of mankind appear more obfuscatory than expository. His idea of "humanity" does not designate the concrete individual but an abstraction like "soul"—something that does not die in a dying body—"*na hanyate hanyamāne śarīre*." This humanity has nothing to do with individual pain and suffering. Thus it would be difficult to support Dr. Bryson's effort to explain away the Swami's contradictions as his successful syncretism, because he "has drawn a network of logical, historical and rhetorical connections between Western humanism and traditional Hinduism sufficient to inspire belief and action. As a practical religious philosophy it works, that is, it sustains belief."[8] As Niranjan Dhar has demonstrated, "by trying to enlist himself in the Divine-regarding Vedantic camp, the Human-regarding Vivekananda has fallen victim to self-contradiction, and hence, fundamentally, his enterprise for creating Neo-Vedanta has been a failure."[9]

In the context of the above, let us examine some of the Swami's humanitarian ideas and prescriptions. First let us have a close look into his various pronouncements with respect to the downtrodden and exploited masses of India. He wrote an eminently rhetorical missive to his brother monk Ramakrishnananda in 1894:

> If you want any good to come, fling into the Ganges all those bells and other junk and worship every human being who is the embodiment of God, Naranarayana. . . . The living gods are dying without food and education. The merchants of Bombay are building hospitals for the treatment of bugs and have little qualms if human beings die. . . . Our country is sick, it's a madhouse everywhere. I salute those of you who have a little brains and I urge them to spread out like wildfire. Let them preach the worship of this universal God—something that has never happened before in our century.[10]

To Akhandananda he wrote: "You have read, 'Treat your mother and father as god!' I say, 'Treat the poor and the illiterate as gods.' Let the poor, the illiterate, the ignorant, and the oppressed be your gods. Know that service to them constitutes the supreme *dharma*. What more can I say?"[11] Wishing to inculcate self-reliance to the poor through education, he wrote to the editor of *Bharati:*

> Whenever I saw the level of comforts and education even of the poor in the cities of Europe during my travels, I used to shed tears remembering our poor people. Why this disparity? I found the answer—education. Their self-confidence is the outcome of their education and being self-confident their inner *Brahman* was aroused. On the other hand, ours is shrinking gradually.[12]

He wrote again to Akhandananda: "Who wants name? To hell with name. Even if I have to lose my name and identity while feeding the poor, [I shall deem it] my greatest fortune."[13] "I love the poor, the ignorant, the downtrodden, I feel for them—the Lord knows how much," he protested in a letter to the Dewan of Junagad State.[14]

He wrote to Haripada Mitra, praising the scope for social mobility and opportunities in the United States:

Everybody has hope, assurance, and opportunity in this country. He may be poor today but could be wealthy, educated, and famous tomorrow. [Here] everybody is keen on helping the needy. . . . But how many associations [*sabha*] are there in India for helping the poor, even though everybody laments over our dire poverty? . . . Oh God, are we human! . . . What are all those thousands of brahmin monks doing for the poor and the oppressed? They are simply shouting: "Don't touch me!"[15]

His altruistic exhortation in a letter to a member of the Vedanta class in London was typical: "The world is in need of those whose life is one burning love—selfless. The love will make every word tell like a thunderbolt. Awake, awake, great souls! The world is burning in misery. Can you sleep?"[16] He told Sudhir Chakravarti in 1897 that even though he had performed extremely severe austerity and *tapasyā* (meditation) in the past for the sake of liberation, he no longer wanted it until the entire human race had been liberated. Sudhir felt that Swamiji was truly an incarnation, and he was giving a hint to that effect.[17]

His most impassioned philanthropic outburst was expressed in his exhortation (to the Indians) "not to forget that the lowly, the illiterate, the poor, the ignorant, the cobbler, the scavenger" are "blood brothers."[18] He was splendidly rhetorical in his vision of new India:

Let her arise—out of the peasants' cottage, grasping the plough; out of the huts of the fishermen, the cobbler, and the sweeper. Let her spring from the grocer's shop, from beside the oven of the fritter-seller. Let her emanate from the factory, from marts, and from markets. . . . These common people . . . have suffered eternal misery, which has given them unflinching vitality. Living on a handful of grain, they can convulse the world. . . . And, besides, they have got the wonderful strength that comes of a pure and moral life, which is not to be found anywhere else in the world.[19]

He told his audience in California that unlike the American poor who are "lazy" and "indecent"—only fools and rogues are poor in the States—in India "the poor fellows work hard from morning to sunset, and somebody else takes the bread out of their hands and their children go hungry."[20] This statement, of course, flatly contradicts his observation that the poor in the Western countries are taken care of and provided with education, and thus their "inner Brahman" was on the ascendant.[21]

II

All this dithyramb for the downtrodden was in fact simply wishy-washy fashionable humanitarianism of a Bengali *bhadralok* (a member of the genteel society). His eloquent but somewhat condescending and patronizing speeches, generally misunderstood for his genuine sympathy for the poor, may be illustrated through a couple of episodes. Once during his wanderings in India, the Swami, a guest at a lawyer's home in Bombay, came running with his favorite hookah to meet his two fatigued and famished *gurubhāis*—Brahmananda and Turiyananda—who had located the absconding Swami after a tiring search. All the while he was chanting a Sanskrit verse deprecating the three vices of pride, glory, and fame. On hearing this Turiyananda at once felt that Swamiji had been freed from those vices. Then during the conversation Vivekananda remarked: "Brother, I don't know how religious I have been, but I am "feeling" too much (*kintu baḍḍa feel karchi*)—my heart is terribly depressed for all and is weeping profusely." Turiyananda's commented, "At that remark of Swamiji we were recalling the teachings of the Buddha."[22] Vivekananda persuaded a young initiate to pay one rupee for a snack worth a penny to the Muslim vendor in a railway station, because he felt that the poor seller had not earned enough that day and hence was waiting for the passengers of the upper-class compartments of the train. Recording this episode Manmathanath Gangopadhyay has observed:

> This was his specialty. Whenever and whatever he reflected upon, he used to think deep. We are concerned merely with the actual worth of things. . . . But Swamiji is feeling "Poor man, how great is his need, how many mouths he has to feed! Let them eat a square meal at least for one day."[23]

The Swami, however, let it be known that his feelings for the poor were not paternalistic. As he wrote to Saracchandra Chakravarti: "*ayameva viśeṣah—jīve jīvabuddhyā yā sevā samarpitā sā dayā, na prema. Yadātmavuddhyā jīvah sevyate, tat prema. . . . Tadāsmakam prema eva śaraṇam, na dayā.*"[24] ("Especially, service to beings by regarding them as beings is mere compassion, not love. And service to beings by regarding them as souls, is love proper. . . . Therefore, we must rely on love and not compassion.") Rhetorical statements such as this in Sanskrit have misled Swamiji's biographers into thinking that he never pitied the poor but was a genuine practitioner of *prema*. Yet actually speaking his magnanimity for the poor was not only condescending, befitting a middle-class *bhadralok,* but often somewhat eccentric. Once while walking toward home at night, he saw a beggar on the sidewalk and tossed him a coin from his pocket casually and walked away. When the befuddled panhandler discovered that the coin was in fact a gold coin, he ran to his benefactor to return the precious metal for fear being caught as a thief. The Swami now looked at the object and said: "I have given it to you, it's yours. I won't take it back. Just keep it hidden." Similarly he parted with his gold watch and chain when an admirer eyed it.[25] Reportedly he was extremely kind to the workers, laborers, and servants of the Belur Math. He often chatted with them and inquired about their welfare and creature comforts. He was so close to them that they were quite frank in their various depositions to him.[26]

An example of "the beautiful confidences he made out of the abundance of his heart"—to borrow Romain Rolland's felicitous phrase—can be culled from the diary of Sharacchandra Chakravarti, Vivekananda's disciple. Sometime in 1902 the Swami fed some Santal workers at Belur and said:

> "You truly are Narayan—today I have offered food to Narayan." He then told several disciples who were present on the occasion: "Could you mitigate some of their miseries? Otherwise, what's the use of donning the ochre robe? I feel like selling the *math* and stuff [*math-phat*], and distribute the money to the poor and the destitute. . . . When I see my countrymen unable to have a square meal a day, I feel like overthrowing all ritual worship [*śāṅkh bājāno ghaṇṭānādā*] and learning, and move in the villages collecting funds from the rich by persuading them with our character and *sādhanā* and thus spending life serving the poor."[27]

Exhortations like this—such as his lecture in New York on 10 June 1900—must have exercised an inspirational force upon the audience. Swami Abhedananda is reported to have told Turiyananda that he felt his *kundalinī* surging up while he was listening to Swamiji's New York lecture.[28] Swamiji literally forced Premananda to quit worshiping Ramakrishna and instead search out the poor and the indigent in the neighborhood. Premananda had to endure a lot of hardship and even humiliation in his efforts and had to satisfy his philanthropic *gurubhāi* by bringing a few poor children from some other localities into the monastery and bathing and feeding them. On being asked by Vivekananda—who had remained in his room on the second floor all the while—how he felt about his chore, the importuned and hapless Premananda had to admit that he felt he was serving the living God.[29]

III

Vivekananda's actual caste and class superiority were revealed, unwittingly, in his admonition to Indumati, the wife of his disciple

Haripada Mitra, against using the conventional suffix *dāsī* (literally, maid servant or female slave) with her name. As he wrote to her: "The Brahmins and the Kshatriyas ought to use *dev* or *devī* [literally, god or goddess]; the Vaisyas and the Shudras are to use *dās* or *dāsī*."[30] His class consciousness was unmistakable in his statement "Our mission is [to work for] the destitute, poor, illiterate rustics and peasants [*cāsābhūso*] first, and then, if there's time, for the upper classes [*bhadraloker janya*]."[31] One can easily notice this elite consciousness creeping behind the Swami's lumping together "the poor, the sinners, even the worms and the insects" as "His children" for whom "He is coming."[32] He had little faith in the capacity of the poor and the illiterates to obtain salvation. He told his friend Girish Ghosh that *Brahmajñāna* was realizable only through severe austerity and *sādhanā*. Merely seeing the Paramahamsa could not assure anyone of salvation. If it did, then even the servants of Dakshineshwar would have obtained their liberation.[33]

Vivekananda once told Sharat Chakravarti: "The mass of people in your country are like the sleeping Leviathan." Unfortunately most of them are not educated, and those who are, "dissipate their energy by getting married, procreating children, and making a family. . . . With the burden of a family would they find time to do anything great or think anything high!"[34] They are also lazy. While eating lunch with his friend "Siṅgī," the Swami elaborated on the need to consume "concentrated food," which included meat. When the friend reminded the monk of the difficulty for everybody to eat meat, the latter retorted:

> Why, they should simply eat less. Just quarter pound a day is enough. Know what, laziness is the root of poverty. If someone's boss reduced his salary out of anger, he would just reduce the quantity of milk for his son or eat only puffed rice as one of the daily meals. . . . Why can't they work harder in order to maintain proper food intake? They would while away their time in neighborhood socialization. How much could I say about how they waste their time![35]

He wanted "some renouncers ready to sacrifice their lives for others, instead of worrying about their families." These young *sannyāsīs* would be trained in a monastery that the Swami wished to found and "will go from door to door making people realize their pitiable condition . . . and instructing them in the ways and means of their welfare, and at the same time explaining to them in very simple and easy language the higher truths of religion."[36]

Needless to mention these ascetic warriors were to be recruited "from the highest classes, not the lowest." He could not yet trust the capacity of the masses, of whom he said: "I shall have to wait a little."[37] He recognized "inequality in nature" but insisted that "there must be equal chance for all . . . the weaker should be given more chance than the stronger. That is the Chandala needed more education than the Brahmin . . . because it is imperative to provide more help to those who are naturally backward" (*yāhāke prakṛti svābhābik prakhar karen nāi, tāhāke sāhāyya karite haibe*).[38] Attitudes such as these, together with his casual references to *muci* (cobbler), *methar* (sweeper), *jele* (fishermen), or *mudī* (grocer), were typical of the self-conscious Bengali *Bābu* (that is, *bhadralok*), who usually considered (still do) these people *chotalok* (lowly people). The multiple contradictions in the Swami's sermons and speeches were perhaps culture syntonic and thus spontaneous. Hence he remained impervious to the contradictions and lack of veracity in his claims and conclusions and could assert boldly: "Truth is my God" or "I do everything to be *sweet,* but when it comes to a horrible compromise with the truth, then I stop."[39] Dr. Rudra cites Lord Ronaldshay's report of how an Indian gentleman had told him "frankly that Hindus were not in the least troubled by contradictions where the teaching of the Vedanta was concerned." Thus Rudra observes that "although Swami Vivekananda was not consciously contradictory . . . his intention was subverted by his enthusiasm."[40]

It need also be noted here that the Swami's prescriptions for the poor were not original with him but inherited from his maternal uncle Kailaschandra Basu, who had been a social activist and who read a paper on the "Claims of the Poor" to the Uttarpara Hitakari Sabha (Uttarpara Benevolent Society), started by a local landlord to impart "education to the poor, to help the needy, to distribute garments to those who stood in need of them, to give medicine to the sick and to help poor widows and orphans." Kailas wrote in this paper that "lack of education was the sole cause behind the country's downfall and degradation and argued that by imparting education to the poor tenants the landlords themselves would come to be benefitted." In another lecture delivered at the Uttarpara Public Library he observed that "Bengal could never be prosperous unless the condition of the peasantry improved."[41] Educated Bengalis from the middle strata of society had viewed the upliftment of the poor as the foundation for their continued leadership in the professional and socioeconomic world. Swamiji was part and parcel of this enlightened middle class.

IV

The Swami, however, did not quite work out a concrete plan of action for his secular program of social regeneration. His ideas were rather vague and naive, albeit quite nice, as could be seen in his instructions to Alasinga Perumal of Madras:

> Try to get up a fund, buy some magic lanterns, maps, globes, etc., and some chemicals. Get every evening a crowd of the poor and the low, even the Pariahs, and lecture to them about religion first, and then teach them through the magic-lantern and other things, astronomy, geography, etc., in the dialect of the people. Train up a band of fiery young men. Put your fire in them and gradually increase the organisation, letting it widen and widen its circle.[42]

He also believed in teaching self-help to the poor. He complained to Shuddhananda that Akhandananda was wasting his energy by distributing rice to the poor villagers of Bhagalpur instead of spreading the Vedantic gospels and thereby teaching self-reliance. "Our job ought to be mainly teaching—spreading education for the cultivation of character and intellect," Vivekananda wrote.[43] At the same time, his letter to Akhandananda underscored the need for teaching self-help to the peasants:

> When they will realize their own situation and the need for their advancement, you will know then that your work is going on well. Moreover, one must not let the rich help the poor through kindness on a permanent basis. This will harm both [the rich and the poor] in the long run. The peasants are in a comatose state [*mritaprāy*]. The rich should merely help them regain their consciousness.[44]

Although the Swami's ideas for helping the poor to be self-reliant and not making them entirely dependent on the rich all the time were commendable, he did not follow them uniformly. Just the day before writing to Shuddhananda, he had written to Brahmananda instructing him to advise Ramakrishnananda to start a bureau for helping the poor. "The world can be bought by kindness and love. Lectures, books or philosophy—all these are secondary," he observed. He further instructed Brahmananda to cease offering foods to gods during worship and make do with water and *tulsi* leaf. The fund thus saved ought to be used for "the living god who resides in the body of the poor."[45] As early as 1894, he had advised Akhandananda to solicit the support of the social elites for his project. "Try to inculcate spirituality and philanthropy amongst the Thakurs (landlords) in the different parts of Rajputana. You have to act. . . . Go from door to door amongst the poor and lower class of the town of Khetri preaching religion."[46] As he wrote his disciples of Madras, his objective was "to bring to the door of the meanest, the poorest, the noble ideas that the human race has developed both in and out of India, and let

them think for themselves."[47] Dr. Chelishev rightly observes: "Vivekananda approached the solution of the problem of social inequality
from the position of Utopian Socialism, placing hopes on the good
will and magnanimity of the propertied classes."[48]

Obviously these armchair *dicta* and haphazard "plans" did not work
as desired. Marie Burke writes about Swamiji's "various and tentative
projects" and his writing "again and again . . . in this vein."[49] Within
less than a year, he was forced to concede defeat. "I have given up at
present my plan for the education of the masses," he wrote to Alasinga
on 12 January 1895.

> It will come by degrees. What I now want is a band of fiery missionaries.
> We must have a College in Madras to teach comparative religions, San-
> skrit, the different schools of Vedanta, and some European languages; we
> must have a press, and papers printed in English and in the vernaculars.
> When this is done, then I shall know that you have accomplished some-
> thing. Let the nation show that they are ready to *do*. If you cannot do
> anything of the kind in India, let me give it to people who appreciate it
> and who will work it out.[50]

He even volunteered to offer some financial help—"Very little now,
but I will continue it onward"—with the command: "So go on
working."[51]

It ought to be noted here that the Swami's sermons on the education and upliftment of the poor were not original with him. They
harked back to the ideas of his Brahmo mentor Keshab who had
established as early as 1856 an institution for the boys of the poor and
working classes, the Coolootollah Evening School, which was hailed as
"a novelty in India" by the *Hindu Patriot* (21 January 1858). It was
renovated in 1870 after Sen's return from England. Additionally he
started the Working Men's Institute through the Indian Reform Association founded on 7 November of that year. Keshab wrote in the
weekly magazine of the Association on 15 August 1871: "Those of
you, among our readers, who are farmers and artisans, do unite and
stand up. Exert yourselves, to the utmost to improve your condition. . . . Sleep no more. It is time, wake up. . . . Exert yourselves, put
forth effort, receive enlightenment."[52] In his letter to the Maharaja of
Mysore (23 June 1891) Swamiji revealed his Brahmo influence: "The
one thing that is at the root of all evils of India, is the condition of
the poor. . . . The only service to be done for our lower classes is to
give them education, *to develop their lost individuality*."[53]

Vivekananda did acquire a reputation for philanthropy among his
devotees and disciples, who were overwhelmed by his rhetoric for
the poor and the downtrodden. Following the opening day of the

Parliament of Religions in Chicago, the Swami, with his newfound celebrity status and as a guest at a prosperous home, "wept from the depths of his heart over the poverty and suffering of the Indian masses."[54] He proclaimed in a letter to Alice Hansbrough: "I may have to be born again because I have fallen in love with man."[55] He expressed *mahākaruṇā* (supreme compassion) eloquently in a letter to Mary Hale:

> . . . and may I be born again and again, and suffer thousands of miseries so that I may worship the only God that exists, the only God I believe in, the sum total of all souls; and above all, my God the wicked, my God the miserable, my God the poor of all races, of all species, is the special object of my worship.[56]

Echoing Ramakrishna's statement he told Sharat Chakravarti: "I am ready to be born a hundred thousand times for the sake of making a man out of single individual."[57] He proclaimed the primacy of philanthropic mission over the spiritual: "So long as even a single dog in my country is without food, my whole religion will be to feed it."[58] In the spring of 1897, Vivekananda told two boys in Darjeeling that he felt "greatly hurt" because he had "much pain" at the sight of a coolie woman "who met with an accident by getting dashed against a rock."[59] Sometime in 1898 he astounded Akhandananda as well as his physician in Darjeeling when they could not fathom the cause of his indisposition after having found him grave, silent, and morose, lying in bed with his head tucked in the pillow all day. At last they discovered that his condition was caused by the news of the Calcutta epidemic, resulting in the suffering of the people there.[60] He impressed Nagendranath Gupta by confessing that he was prepared to go to prison for helping his country. Gupta admiringly recalled the conversation and added: "He was not bidding for the martyr's crown, for any sort of pose was utterly foreign to his nature, but his thoughts were undoubtedly tending towards finding redemption for his country through suffering."[61]

One day when the Swami mildly admonished his intimate friend Girishchandra Ghosh for not studying the scriptures, the latter quipped that knowledge of the Vedas and the Vedanta would not help prevent social ills. To quote Sharat Chakravarti, who has recorded the incident, "as Girish began to depict the terrible state of society, Vivekananda sat speechless. Thinking of the pain and misery of the world, tears came into his eyes and as if to hide his feelings from us rose and went out of the room." Thereupon Girish, who was noted for his dramatic speech and flamboyance, said to Chakravarti: "Now did you see, dumbo [*bāṅgāl*], what a large heart! I don't respect your Swamiji as a Vedic *paṇḍit* only, but I respect him . . . for his compassion." Upon returning to the room, the Swami confessed: "Ah, Girishbabu, sometimes I feel that even if I have to undergo a thousand births to remove the misery of the world, even to remove the least pain from anyone, I am ready!"[62] A junior monk at Belur once heard Swamiji's loud wailing at midnight, and on inquiring the reasons for his cries was told that he was unable to sleep because his mind was disturbed and pained at the distress of his country.[63] Swami Brahmananda sincerely believed that "during his travel in the Western Ghats and the Mahratta province Swamiji used to shed tears at the poverty of the common people and the oppression of the rich."[64] Another monk, Swami Paramananda, wrote: "I have seen him weep. Having made sure that nobody was watching him, this great man wept piteously for the poor Indians inflicted with pain and suffering. His heart used to be heavy with the dire distress of the people."[65]

Vivekananda informed his admirer and patron Francis Leggett of his wondrous transformation from a misanthrope into an altruist. He wrote to Leggett:

> At twenty years of age I was the most unsympathetic, uncompromising fanatic; I would not walk on the footpath on the theatre side of streets in Calcutta. At thirty-three, I can live in the home with prostitutes and never would think of saying a word of reproach to them. Is it degenerate? Or is it that I am broadening out into the Universal Love which is the Lord Himself?[66]

These statements contradict the Swami's much touted natural sympathy for the low born since boyhood, his keeping bad company in early youth, and his singing devotional songs on the stage in 1889 (he was twenty-six then) in front of the actresses (usually prostitutes) employed by his friend Girish Ghosh.[67] He reportedly confessed to Swami Subodhananda that after his father's death he visited brothels and consumed alcoholic beverages in the company of his friends.[68] Swami Saradananda was frankly scandalized to see young Narendra—whom the Paramahamsa had regarded as divine—humming an erotic Hindi tune at the home of Dhirendranath Pal, a "moral derelict."[69]

In a letter to Nivedita, Swami Vivekananda declared dramatically: "What I mean is what I am, intensely personal in love, but having the power to pluck out my own heart with my own hand, if it becomes necessary 'for the good of many, for the welfare of many,' as Buddha said."[70] Swami Sadashivananda reports a dramatic encounter between the ailing Swamiji and Narasimha Chintaman Kelkar, editor of the *Keshari,* sometime in late January or early February 1902 during which, in the course of a conversation, Vivekananda became so emotional in his description of India's misery that his eyes revealed, simultaneously, sadness, grief, compassion, and love for every being. He then told Kelkar in angry despair: "What's the use of the Indians' lingering in such misery and degradation? They are suffering the torments of hell every moment, starving and feeling humiliation and hardship every day, surviving on mere subsistence, and burning in hellfire day and night. Death would have been far more desirable than this [life]!" Sadashivananda admitted that he had never before witnessed such an exuberance of patriotism and philanthropy.[71] A young correspondent from Maldah (West Bengal) wrote to Calcutta Radio (Akashvani) how in 1993 on the occasion of the centenary of Vivekananda's address to the World's Parliament of Religions at Chicago, he remembered Swamiji's slogan of *"jīve prem kare jei jan, sei jan seviche Īśvar"* ("one who loves a living being serves God"). While on the way to his uncle's home, the young man caught a fish, recalled Vivekananda's elebrated lyric of compassion, and so set the catch free.[72] He empathized with the sufferings of others because he said he was one with the universe: "I am in the sun, I am in the moon, I am in the stars, I am everywhere. . . . I am a voice without form."[73] And yet with all his cosmic compassion and his posthumous glorification by admirers and devotees, the Swami did virtually nothing for the permanent uplifting of the downtrodden. He neither had a firsthand experience of social work nor a theoretical understanding of the task he was preaching with so much passion and panache. Niranjan Dhar has pointed out that "Vivekananda never said anything about forming a national government by removing foreign control with a view to materializing his plan for eradicating poverty from India, even though this plan could conceivably work only through a structure such as a national government."[74] Even an admiring scholar has admitted: "Indeed I do not think that he intended to produce political or economic solutions of the problems."[75] He never exerted himself to tour the villages and teach religion to the masses. He preached mainly to the affluent and the affable in India and abroad. Sarala Ghosal was right when she told Sister Nivedita in plain terms: "Swami had good ideas—plenty—but he carried nothing out. . . . He only talked."[76]

V

Vivekananda scholars have made a mountain of socialism out of a molehill of the Swami's statement: "I am a socialist not because I

think it is a perfect system, but half a loaf is better than no bread."[77]
For him socialism was a kind of attitude opposed to individualism.
"The Indian people are intensely socialistic," he wrote. "But, beyond
that, there is a wealth of individualism."[78] On another occasion he
illustrated the socialistic attitude of the Hindus. The filial love between man and woman in Hindu society is an outcome of Hindu
socialistic attitude that forbids one to "load misery on hundreds of
others . . . for the sake of one man's or woman's exquisite pleasure."[79]
The same socialistic outlook prevents a Hindu from allowing the
widows to remarry because they had a chance in their life and must
accord the same to other unmarried maidens. Whatever these rather
bizarre explanations mean, it is certain that for Vivekananda socialism
did not constitute a rationally constructed ideology. It is extremely
doubtful that he had a firsthand knowledge of the socialist literature—
Utopian or Scientific. He, however, reportedly told Shuddhananda
that some British socialists, including Edward Carpenter, visited him,
and "finding in the religion of Vedanta a strong support for their
ideals, they felt much attracted towards its teachings"[80] (enshrined in
the dictum: "sameness for all.")[81] Quite expectedly Bhupendranath
Datta declared that his elder brother was the first Indian to preach
the ideals of socialism, though "his socialism was quite different from
modern socialism."[82] Even Dr. Arun Biswas, who has written an
entire book on Swamiji's socialism, has said virtually nothing on its
theory except that it was derived from the writings of his distinguished forbears and contemporaries, such as Rammohan, Keshabchandra, and Bankimchandra, and that the Hindu scriptures such
as the *Rgveda,* the *Śatapathabrāhmaṇa,* the Upanishads (especially
Vṛhadāraṇyaka and *Īśa*), and above all, the *Bhāgavadgītā* contained
the quintessential socialistic ideal of human equality and welfare. In
Biswas's terms Vivekananda preached the message of "spiritual socialism" (whatever that means).[83]

Nevertheless his socialism was at best and at most humanitarian
egalitarianism. Two Russian scholars have noted the "haziness and
abstract nature" of Vivekananda's "social ideals and world outlook as
a whole" as well as the unmistakable elitism of his social movement.[84]
He had almost no idea of a class struggle or the attainment of legitimate social goals through determined confrontation and compromise.
In fact he would have nothing to do with any conflict between the
rich and the poor.[85] He was also opposed to social reform. "Meddle
not with the so-called social reform," he wrote to Alasinga, "for there
cannot be any reform without spiritual reform first. Who told you
that I want social reform? Not I."[86] Later in his Madras lecture, he
would declare: "I do not mean to say that political or social improve-

ments are not necessary, but what I mean is this . . . that they are secondary here and that religion is primary."[87] Till the last day of his life, the Swami remained steadfast in his apolitical quiescence, without any understanding of the dynamics of social change. His final admonition was "India is immortal if she persists in her search for God. But if she goes in for politics and social conflict, she will die."[88]

Vivekananda once explained to Haripada Mitra his reasons for socializing with the Rajas of India:

> Just compare the results one can achieve by instructing thousands of poor people and inducing them to adopt a certain line of action on the one hand, and by converting a prince to that point of view on the other. . . . A prince has the power of doing good to his subjects already in his hands. Only he lacks the will to do it. If you can work up that will in him, then, along with it, the fortune of his subjects will take a turn for the better, and society will be immensely benefitted thereby.[89]

Supported by the Indian feudal chieftains in his work of spiritual regeneration, Vivekananda's Vedantism was instrumental in entrenching the traditional power structure with a powerful religious-moral rhetoric. In spite of his proclamation that he had seen the Indian masses during his peregrination and pilgrimage all over India, he almost never experienced their tribulation and torment. On the other hand, he had succeeded in eliciting the hospitality of influential patrons—the feudal princes or their influential ministers—who were amenable to the spread of Vedantism.[90] Yet he unhesitatingly proclaimed in a public speech:

> Ye, labouring classes of India, as a result of your silent, constant labour, Babylon, Persia, Alexandria, Greece, Rome, Venice, Genoa, Baghdad, Samarkand, Spain, Portugal, France, Denmark, Holland and England have successively attained supremacy and eminence. And you?—Well, who cares to think of you . . . but blessed indeed is he who manifests the same unselfishness and devotion to duty in the smallest of acts, unnoticed by all—and it is you who are actually doing this, ye ever-trampled labouring classes of India! I bow to you.[91]

His eloquent speeches like this have driven a scholar to conclude that "Vivekananda is great because he passionately loved his country, his poor fellow countrymen."[92] The Swami, however, knew better. His nonchalant attitude to what he said or how he said it was explicit in his admonition to his devotee Kiranchandra Datta: "Look here, we are like mammoths in the realm of ideas [*bhāvrājyer airāvat*]. We will stir up the ocean of ideas tumultuously. Let others provide the language. We haven't come for that."[93] He was disarmingly candid in his confession: "The Bengalis and the Irish in Europe, are races cast in the same mould—only talking and talking, and bandying words. These two nations are adepts [*sic*] only in making grandiloquent speeches."[94]

Christine Greenstidel (Sister Christine)

7

Secrets of Vivekananda's Popularity

I

FROM the various journalistic reports and the letters and reminiscences of some of Vivekananda's devotees and disciples, it is abundantly clear that his reputation in the West owed as much to how he looked and spoke as to what he said about himself and his spiritual message. His maiden speech at the Chicago conference, for which he has been justly famous, contained little original spiritual content but was an eloquent plea for toleration, global understanding, and universal love, as well as a bold assertion of his own religion, which he called "Mother of religions" and one "in whose sacred language, the Sanskrit, the word exclusion is untranslable." He also proudly declared that his nation had "sheltered the persecuted and the refugees of all religions and all nations of the earth."[1] These are the sorts of audacious claims made with feeling and style that elicited audience admiration. Even the opening phrase, "Sisters and Brothers of America," had so stirred the hearts of his hearers that, to quote the Swami himself, "a deafening applause of two minutes followed," and to cite a newspaper report of his speech on 19 September quoted by him, "Ladies, ladies, ladies packing every place—filling every corner, they patiently waited and waited, while the papers that separated them from Vivekananda were read."[2] Mrs. S. K. Blodgett, who was present at the Parliament and who later became Vivekananda's hostess in Los Angeles, "saw scores of women walking over the benches to get near him."[3]

Indeed it was the Swami's personality and rhetoric that created the greatest impression, as one can gather from the report of Rev. Mercer, a member of the General Commitee of the Chicago Parliament. The following quotation from this source perhaps demonstrates the spontaneous and sincere reaction of an eyewitness without any hidden agenda of his own. The Reverend reports on Vivekananda thus:

Swami Vivekananda of Bombay [*sic*], India, arose, *a magnificent figure of manly beauty, in his orange robe and turban, with striking, strong, and re-*

poseful countenance, and said: "Sisters and brothers of America," where-upon there arose a peal of applause in acknowledgment of the originality of the salutation, and *perhaps not less as testifying interest in the personality of the speaker.*[4]

One just needs to compare this report with that on the performance of the Brahmo representative Protap Mozoomdar: "When President Bonney presented P. C. Mozoomdar of India, author of the 'Oriental Christ,' . . . the audience greeted him with the wildest applause. Mo-zoomdar had been in this country ten years ago; *many had heard him then, and added to their welcome to India greeting to a friend.*"[5]

In his letter of 24 May 1894 to Professor John Wright, Viveka-nanda had claimed that his "place is in the Himalayas."[6] A Boston journal described his exotic background: "This monk has come from the mountains of India, where he wandered in solitude, occupied with spiritual meditations."[7] Most probably Vivekananda thoroughly convinced his enthusiastic admirer turned Hindu monk, Leon Lands-berg (Swami Kripananda), in December 1895, that he "would retire shortly to a Himalayan cave, never to return."[8] He similarly informed Sara Bull that years ago he had gone to the Himalayas "never to come back" but had to leave that abode of serenity because his "weak heart" could not bear the tragedy caused by the news of his sister's death by suicide.[9] In actuality, however, prior to coming to the United States, Vivekananda had been to Hrishikesh and Badrikashrama, the two famous places of Hindu pilgrimage in the Himalayas, twice, in 1888 and 1890. He was a traveling pilgrim in the Himalayas, and almost every account of his travels in northern India, especially by Akhanda-nanda, gives details not so much of his well-publicized *kathor tapasyā* (stern austerities and meditation) as of his eating, falling sick, or meeting various people. In fact he was terribly upset with Shivananda and Virajananda for having forced him to take the difficult mountain path from Mayavati to Kathgodam in the Himalayas, where he had to suffer severe cold due to a snowstorm.[10] He neither hailed from the hills nor graduated, as it were, to *sannyās* (ascetic life) from there.

The Swami's style—rather than the substance of his sermons—appealed to some people. When Josephine MacLeod recalled in her old age her first meeting with him on 29 January 1895 in New York, she remembered everything except what he was preaching. "He said something," Miss MacLeod wrote in the *Prabuddha Bharata* (Decem-ber 1949), "the particular words of which I do not remember, but instantly to me that was truth, and the second sentence he spoke was truth, and the third sentence was truth."[11] Naturally she was con-vinced that he was the famous medieval Vedantist Shankaracharya reborn. On 10 April 1944, Josephine wrote to her niece Alberta Sturges (Lady Sandwich): "You know, Swamiji said he was Shankara! He came back after 800 years."[12] Josephine really did not care much for what the Swami said. To her his physical appearance loomed larger than his spiritual and intellectual equipment. Recalling his lecture on the *Bhāgavadgītā* sometime in 1895, she wrote: "I saw with these very eyes (she pointed to her own eyes) Krishna himself standing there and preaching the Gita. That was my first wonderful vision. I stared and stared. . . . I saw only the figure and all else vanished."[13]

Vivekananda was also seen as Christ, while he hinted on a Buddha connection for himself. "I love the Swami talk," confessed an old English woman. "I can't understand much of the philosophy but his voice and gestures charm me. I seem to be seeing someone out of the Bible."[14] At an afternoon tête-à-tête in London with Mahendranath, Saradananda, and Henrietta Müller, Vivekananda declared solemnly: "This time I will give hundred years to my body. . . . This time I have to perform many difficult tasks. . . . This time I shall go on working till the last moment. . . . In this life [this time] I shall demonstrate my powers much more than I did in my past life [*pūrvavāre*]." Mahendranath wrote that though he could not distinctly remember his brother's exact language, he was able to recall that he hinted that he had been the Buddha in his previous life![15] The Swami, however, cautiously avoided comparing himself to, or calling himself an incarnation of, Christ. In fact he reacted angrily to an Indian's comparing him to Christ. "I learn from a letter from Sarada [Trigunatitananda] that N. Ghose had compared me with Christ and the like," he wrote to Ramakrishnananda. "Those might be o.k. for our country, but it might be embarrassing if that stuff is printed and sent here."[16] However he performed brilliantly in front of a bunch of Egyptian whores, weeping for their miserable, sinful life. The sight of a handsome monk in gorgeous robes shedding tears led the fallen women to exclaim in reverential wonder that they were beholding a veritable "*Hombre de Dios, hombre de Dios* ["Man of God"]!" The reporter of this scene, Madame Calvé, wrote: "He began to weep, as Jesus might have done before the woman taken to adultery."[17]

II

A significant factor behind the enormous popularity of Vivekananda's sermons among the educated, liberal middle-class folks of America and England was his rhetorical rendering of bold and bald statements with an excessively authoritative and nonchalant air. A typical example comes from a private conversation the Swami had with a Vaishnava visitor in 1897. "Babaji," he told the Vaishnava, "once in America I lectured to them on Shri Krishna. Captivated by that lecture, one exquisitely beautiful young lady, the mistress of a great many attainments and heiress to an immense fortune, renounced everything and retired to a solitary island and lost herself in the intoxication of meditation on the Lord."[18] Then most of his statements were combined shrewdly with some plausible ones punched with half-truths and even unqualified lies.[19] A typical example of Swamiji's persuasive preaching containing a strong and well-directed message is his statement in respect of his *guru* Ramakrishna's spiritual practices. "He never knew whether he was living or dying, or anything," the Swami informed his audience at a public lecture. "Sometimes, while talking, he would get so excited that if he sat on live charcoals, he did not know it. Live charcoals! Forgetting all about his body, all the time."[20] Ramakrishna does not seem to have made any claim in respect to his loss of body consciousness. What we have is a statement by Ram Datta in the *Jīvanvṛttānta* that the Master would often (*kathāy kathāy*) lose external consciousness like Mahāprabhu (that is, Chaitanya). Even once (*ekadā*) charcoal fire (*guler agni*) touched his body and penetrated his muscles. A scar mark on the left side of his stomach was formed in this way.[21] Vivekananda further told another story of Ramakrishna's love for the low-caste people and his desire to serve them.

> Now my Master would go to a Pariah and ask to be allowed to clean his home. . . . The Pariah would not permit it; so in the dead of night, when all were sleeping, Ramakrishna would enter the home. He had long hair, and with his hair he would wipe the place, saying "Oh, my Mother, make me the servant of the Pariah, make me feel that I am even lower than the Pariah."[22]

This is a colorful retelling of another episode described in the *Jīvanvṛttānta:* "[The Master] used to pray to the Mother: 'Mā, destroy my ego. . . . Let me be always aware that I am the lowest of the lowly and the poorest of the poor. Let me always feel that everybody, whether a Brahmin or a Kshatriya, or a Vaisya, or a Shudra, or such low caste people as sweepers or cobblers, beasts, birds, or insects, is higher than me.' . . . Sometimes he would sweep the latrine with a broom. Seeing this people used to make adverse remarks. Some thought that he was possessed by devil or that he had lost his head."[23]

"He is wonderfully clever and clear in putting his arguments and laying his train [of thought] to a conclusion," Mary Tappan Wright observed in her letter of 29 August 1893 to her mother. "You can't trip him up, nor get ahead of him."[24] Rev. Promotho Lall Sen of the Brahmo Samaj similarly observed: "Norendra Dutt ... was not known among his compeers for spiritual beauty (grace) or innocence. Cleverness and smartness characterised him."[25] When a *pandit* detected a grammatical slip in Vivekananda's conversation in Sanskrit with Chattambi Swami in Ernakulam sometime in December 1892, the Bengali *parivrājak* shut off the critic by declaring: "I need not follow grammar; grammar will follow me."[26] Most important, his talks were seldom dull. As one of his Indian admirers noted astutely, "whenever he had any occasion to deal with the same question he threw such new light on it and used such new similes and illustrations that it seemed altogether a fresh subject. . . . As a result, his talks never bored any one; rather the interest increased at every step and the people sat spellbound."[27] His bold assertions bearing his opinion on people and places were made with such force as to sweep his audience off their feet, as it were, even when his comments and conclusions made on two occasions were manifestly contradictory. A typical example in this regard comes from his observations on Western women. One day he told his visitors in London that the English women are very robust and masculine, and they move about in the streets like men. They do not marry before they are twenty-five or thirty, and they take especial care of their health. That is why the English children are so hale and hearty. At another time, in Calcutta, he praised the American women:

> How efficient are the women of America! They are more like men than women. They go to the market, buy stuff, keep accounts of their money and encash checks in the bank, and move here and there by bus or carriage. How marvelously brisk [is their movement]! They are scoring over men. There is not the least femininity in them—all are manly. Compared to them the English women seem pretty lethargic. They are too timid to accomplish anything by themselves or go out alone. They are not as energetic and clever [as the Americans]. The English lag almost half a century behind the American.[28]

Questioned by Chakravarti as to the inconsistencies in his statements, the Swami so overwhelmed his disciple with his explanation that the latter confessed: "Nobody could help accepting Swamiji's arguments because they were charged with an uncanny force, sweeping all counter argument and reasoning."[29]

Vivekananda had little qualms in contradicting himself for winning an argument. At the Congregational Church in Evanston, Illinois, he declared: "Because the Hindu is kind to dumb animals many believe that we believe in the incarnation of souls in lower orders. They are not able to conceive of kindness to dumb animals being other than the result of superstition."[30] But he responded to a question from a devotee whether humans could be born again as an animal of lower order by insisting that such a rebirth was quite possible because rebirth is predicated on karma (work). "If people behave like an animal," he added, "then they would be attracted toward an animal self [paśuyoni]." When the inquirer protested that the law of evolution precludes the possibility for a human being's regressing into a lower animal, the Swami argued that the evolution for animal to human could be reversed because there is only one existence, and everything basically belongs to a single whole.[31]

Tom Allan's wife Edith recorded a most dramatic incident. On being asked by someone in the audience to speak on philosophy, Vivekananda thundered: "So you want philosophy. Then you must be prepared for cannon balls." Mrs. Allan added her personal impression of the Swami's peroration: "We got them." Frank Rhodehamel wrote on the same incident. "There to his word Swamiji bombarded the audience. His stress on monism . . . reached . . . a climax of explicit and impassioned expression; cannon balls flew to right and left," writes Marie Burke, paraphrasing the reports on these lectures made by Ida Ansell. According to Rhodehamel "audiences were jolted out of hereditary ruts, and New Thought [a materialistic religious movement akin to Christian Science] students, so-called, were subjected to scathing, though constructive criticism without mercy."[32] Another report from Rhodehamel's diary has the Swami declaring like Lord Krishna of the Bhāgavadgītā:

> "Be brave! Be strong! Be fearless! . . . Even though you know you are going to be killed, fight till you are *killed*. Don't die of fright. *Die fighting*. Don't go down till you are knocked down." The diary continues: "Then with his right arm extended he thundered, 'Die game! Die game! Die game!' That one sentence rang through those last lectures 'Die game! Die game!'".[33]

No doubt this forcefully suggestive but grammatically dubious phrase "die game" worked wonders in the ears and minds of his devotees. In this connection one needs to note Vivekananda's thundering admonition to his disciple Chakravarti: "Be a hero, utter *abhīh*, *abhīh*" [fearless]. Tell everybody, '*mābhaih*, *mābhaih*—fear is death, it's hell, it's blasphemy, it's perversion.'" Saracchandra writes: "Speaking thus the corners of Swamiji's blue lotus-like eyes seemed be tinged with the rays of the sun. As if *abhīh* itself has been personified and sitting before the disciple as his master." The completely flabbergasted Chakravarti thus had little hesitation in regarding his guru as a blue-eyed (*nīlotpalanayan*) messiah.[34] Alice Hansbrough recalled part of one such conversation in which the Swami declared majestically and mysteriously: "You heard that Christ said, 'My words are spirit and they are life.' So are my words spirit and life; they will burn their way into your brain and you will never get away from them."[35] Indeed as a New York newspaper has it, the Swami was "an orator by Divine right."[36] He truly was what an Indian scholar has said admiringly "*vāk pati*" (lord of language).[37] "His conversation was like Ganga at the flood. There was really no interrupting him," Reeves Calkins had observed with uncanny perspicacity.[38]

Statements such as those cited above were made with flair and panache. Mahendranath often has observed the transformation of his brother's personality on the podium. He would enter the lecture hall with a smile and then gaze at his audience. Next he would walk up the stage and stand still, before parading up and down the stage, his arms akimbo, like a lion. When he began his lecture, his smiling visage would be slowly replaced by that of a very powerful personality full of *ojas:* his eyes wide open but calm, his voice different—altogether a different individual. He would begin his talk in slow pace and low pitch and then raise his voice until its cadence would be confident and commanding. Often he would be so carried away by his own talk that both his hands would move to and fro and he would point his fingers to the audience. As Datta has written: "This expressive movement of his limbs was particularly noteworthy. It was very pleasant and yet authoritative. Barring an experienced and skilled actor, ordinary folks would be hard put to communicate deep feelings and thoughts through the movement of the hand."[39] That Viveka-nanda was a consummate actor who could effectively alter his visage to express his mood is attested to by Mahendranath who saw various expressions on his brother's face—that of a wise old man, a vigorous young man, and a frivolous pleasure-seeking adolescent—in a number of photographs taken at the same time.[40] Datta also reports the Swami's claim that he often channeled his own awakened power into his audience with a view to drawing their sole attention to his sermons.[41]

From Datta's graphic description of Swamiji's sermon and its impact on the audience, one can get an almost firsthand idea of his style. To quote Datta:

One night there was a lecture on Rajayoga in London. The lecture came to a conclusion. About one hundred fifty to two hundred well-dressed

men and women from distinguished families sat on cushioned chairs
placed on the carpeted floor of the room and listened to the lecture in
English. Swamiji was lecturing in his usual manner and his facial expression was normal. All of a sudden, his countenance assumed an inscrutable
calm expression. Even his gaze underwent a change. He lifted his both
hands as if to shower benediction. It seemed a new individual had materialized from his body. After a few moments of silence, a rhythmic tone
emanated from him. He began to recite a benediction in Sanskrit. . . . He
uttered one word at a time and directed his gaze at something above
silently . . . before uttering another word. In this way the recitation took
a while to finish. Swamiji's entire nervous system [*snayupuṅja*] changed,
as it were. He became a new man, as if he was the world's greatest man.
As he recited, the listeners became so overwhelmed that they pushed back
their chair and knelt down, bending their head, with folded hands. All
were silent and it seemed there was nobody in the room except the
Swami. . . . No one understood the meaning of the benediction but the
voice [of Swamiji] was so powerful that it seemed to command the audience: "It is not the time to sit on a high chair, kneel down and keep your
head bent."[42]

The Swami's principal listeners and benefactors, especially at The
Chicago Parliament of Religions and subsequently elsewhere in the
United States and in the United Kingdom, were mostly women of
the upper middle and higher classes. As Rajagopal Chattopadhyaya
explains:

It should be realized that the Parliament went on for 17 days in 1893,
and many of those days were on working days. Naturally, other than
highly motivated men who were interested in attending the Parliament,
visitors from other areas, and religious professionals, most of the audience
was composed of ladies. That was so because women did not go to work
in good numbers yet in the USA and did not have to take a vacation in
order to attend the Parliament.[43]

Vivekananda, however, provided his very personal analysis in this
regard. As he wrote to Ramakrishnananda: "Men of this country
begin to earn from their early youth but the women go to the university to educate themselves. That is why you will notice that women
constitute ninety percent of the audience in any meeting. The boys
are no match for them [*"choṅārā tāder kāche kalke pāy nā"*]."[44] A total
stranger to the world of extroverted, educated, and affluent women,
he was charmed by their generosity, kindness, and frankly unqualified
admiration for and obsession with a handsome, young, witty, and
somewhat enchantingly naive virgin male from a distant land. The
charming and charismatic ascetic was also capable of violent mood

swings, which invested his personality with a powerful mystique. Indeed his temperament made him an awesome personality, which elicited people's respectful fear and fascination for the man. It is doubtful if all his female admirers fell for the "sublime philosophy of the Vedanta." On the other hand, it is quite likely that they were attracted by the personality of the young man wearing "a turban of white silk which set off to advantage the swarthy complexion of his cleanly shaven face." "His pleasing address, his Bengali fluency as a speaker, his command of English, his judicious silence on some points, his claiming some important Christian doctrines as Hindu," no doubt also contributed to his popularity. "The main cause, however," according to the anonymous author of *Vivekananda and His Guru,* "was curiosity, of which the Americans have such an abundant supply. Any great novelty attracts attention. . . . The Swami was the first Indian who visited America in the supposed dress of a sannyasi."[45] The *Amrita Bazar Patrika* of Calcutta shrewdly observed on 14 November 1893: "The Americans wanted to see . . . a genuine Hindu, not Christianized, humanized or Europeanized. They fancied they had found one such in Vivekananda. His figure, deportment and tenets attracted the greatest attention."[46]

There is, of course, another explanation for the Swami's popularity, especially among the social elites, who included, inter alia, the prominent Chicagoans George and Belle Hale; the Detroit businessman Thomas Palmer; Walter and Frances Goodyear of Goodyear Rubber Company; Sara Bull, divorced wife of the famous Norwegian violinist Ole Bull; the well-known soprano Emma Thursby; the fashionable and impetuous socialite Josephine MacLeod; and Francis Leggett, a wealthy New York businessman. As Dr. Jackson has observed, these were "people with excess time and too much money, who have been jaded by more conventional religion and who are forever searching for an alternative." To quote Jackson once more, "it is that members in the upper levels of society are better educated and more cosmopolitan in their tastes than the working class, circumstances that create greater openness to foreign conceptions."[47]

There were some specific reasons why Vivekananda's Vedanta initially impacted a small number of well-to-do predominantly female audiences in America. Indian culture and philosophy had already exerted an exotic attraction for the liberal and cosmopolitan elite of the United States. Sister Devamata explained in her diary: "As students in the past have gone to Paris to study art and to Germany to study music, so they will in time turn to India to acquire . . . the most efficient method of developing the religious consciousness."[48] Then the wealthy and educated American men "were too deeply absorbed in the tasks of earning a living to pay the heed [as did their spouses] to exciting new doctrines." Next America at the end of the century was witnessing a resurgence of moral drive and "the emphasis in Vedanta upon purity may thus have offered a deeply reassuring anchorage to certain women whom their own culture had previously given a great anxiety in just this respect." Beyond all this, however, there was the irresistible romantic figure of the guru that "supplied a concrete object for adoration entirely within the context of such a purity." A veteran Vedanta nun told Dr. Veysey that "in her opinion all truly 'advanced souls' were physically beautiful."[49]

An important factor for the easy comprehension of Swamiji's sermons and lectures by his audience, as well as their acceptance of much of what he preached, is that he interpreted the Vedanta by situating its principles on the Western value system. The West values science, and so he said:

> To my mind, if modern science is proving anything again and again, it is this, that we are one—mentally, spiritually, and physically. . . . We are absolutely one. . . . That is exactly the teaching of the Advaita. . . . The Self is the essence of this universe, the essence of all souls; He is the essence of your own life, nay, "Thou art That." . . . Thus we see that the religion of the Vedanta can satisfy the demands of the scientific world.[50]

Again as Western idealism accepts democracy and attacks discrimination, so he declared: "The work of the Advaita . . . is to break down all privileges. . . . Once a gigantic attempt was made to preach Vedantic ethics. . . . I mean the Buddhistic attempt to break down privilege."[51] Finally the West follows Christianity. Thus Vivekananda attempted to show that as an oriental religion, Christianity is only a form of Hinduism. He declared in a sermon in San Francisco: "This mass of Vedas eternally exists and all the world is the manifestation of this mass of words. . . . If there is something here that is not in the Vedas, that is your delusion. It does not exist."[52]

Lastly one must recognize Vivekananda's flair for impassioned lecturing—a skill he could very well have picked up from the Protestant missionaries or from the literature on their style of preaching. Alexandre Vinet had written as early as 1870 on homiletics as a "combat" for the preacher ("orator"), whose sermons to his audience ("bench of corrupt judges") assumes an aggressive tone as an admonition from the agent of the Divine. Hence he can take recourse to "invention" and eloquence grounded in the commonplace. Though in all probability the Swami never read Vinet's book, he nevertheless instanced its principles. He was a master of invention and simplification and possessed "an exceptional repertoire of rhetorical and performative gestures," and thus his speeches and sermons displayed a remarkable "intellectual and physical intensity." Once he struck a table with great force to make a point and caused a watch lying on top of it leap into the air—an act that "created a visible sensation."[53] Manomohan Ganguly observed that Vivekananda's style "smells of gun-powder."[54] On another occasion he confessed to Goodwin after a lecture: "Goodwin, I am a nut, nothing is right with me. I find something appears in the air in front of me. I stare at that and keep on rambling without making any sense of what I speak. I hope the people hadn't found me a crazy guy yet."[55]

The Swami's occasional confession that he had lost sense of the substance of his sermons had a curiously ironical truth about it. He indeed was capable of the most specious and puerile argument to prove a point or score a victory over his critics. For example with a view to highlighting the values of spiritual-religious goal in life and critiquing the English utilitarian philosopher Jeremy Bentham's (1748–1832) ideas, he declared in London: "The Utilitarian wants us to give up the struggle after the Infinite . . . and, in the same breath, asks us to take up ethics and do good to society. Why should we do good? . . . Why should I do good to other men, and not injure them? If happiness is the goal of mankind, why should I not make myself happy and others unhappy? What prevents us?"[56] He had little idea or appreciation of Bentham's *felicific calculus* (greatest good for the greatest number) and its raison d'être, nor did he have much understanding of the idea of human freedom assured by making it universal, thereby submitting it to the rule of law. However this sermon was one of the earliest of the Swami's talks that made him popular in the English metropolis.[57]

There is also the eyewitness account of Vivekananda's humiliating a skeptical member of the audience in his lecture in London—a retired Anglo-Indian civil servant—who questioned the integrity of the Indian *sādhus*. To quote Mahendranath: "Swamiji then transformed his serene visage into a terrible form and, turning to the right toward his critic, who sat near the fire-place, spat fire for thirty-five minutes. He recounted the history of the cruelty and barbarity of the English in the countries around the globe since the days of Hengist and Horsa [the fabled Saxon chiefs who had been invited by the British king Vortigern in the fifth century]." He then stopped and, regaining his previous calm, resumed his sermon from where he had left due to the interruption.[58] Reportedly Vivekananda's audience stood up at the end of his sermon and told him: "Swami, you have taught us a grand lesson of forbearance. . . . You are a saint, you are a real great man."[59] Mahendranath considers his brother's peroration to be one of the few celebrated "impeachments" in the history of the world and marvels at his wondrous knowledge of history.[60] Dr. Srikumar Banerjee observed cautiously on Vivekananda's sermons and speeches: "Amidst a series of calm equable sentences . . . we suddenly come across an utterance that is ablaze with passion. . . . The unseen aspiring fixes of revelation cast a halo, a tinge of glory upon the sobre pedestrianism of reason."[61] In the final analysis, it was his forceful style, colorful language—and not necessarily the contents of his sermons—together with his charisma and sheer personal charm that endeared Vivekananda to his audience in India and abroad. Wendell Thomas got it right when he observed that "the first swami to visit America was a bold, well-meaning, lovable impressionist."[62]

8

Vivekananda's Ramakrishna

I

ON his return to Calcutta after his first visit to the West (1893–96), Vivekananda told his interviewer, Narendranath Sen, editor of the *Indian Mirror,* that his intention had been "to elicit, as a spiritual master, the respect and sympathy of the mighty Western world by preaching the deep secrets of Vedantic religion there and make them our mentors in mundane matters."[1] During his second visit to the United States, the Swami declared that his messages were "an attempt to echo . . . [Ramakrishna's] ideas."[2] In two lectures in New York and London, he underscored his conviction in Ramakrishna's message that "religion can be given and taken more tangibly, more really than anything else in the world." He further insinuated his own credentials by declaring that his late Master had said that "only those who have attained spirituality can communicate it to others, can be great teachers of mankind. They alone are the powers of light."[3] He preached what he proudly called "Practical Vedanta" to his Western audience. For them it meant that "the Vedanta recognises no sin, it only recognises error. And the greatest error . . . is to say that you are weak, that you are a sinner, a miserable creature."[4] To the Indians, however, the Vedanta lion roared: "I do not believe in God that cannot give bread."[5] He interpreted the principles of the Vedanta to suit the requirements of his age, his watchword being "dynamic religion and united India."[6]

He is said to have especially espoused the cause of the poor, the downtrodden, and women. His mission was to galvanize the Indian people into a program of self-help and self-improvement—to bring to a successful fruition the work of their British masters who had "aroused the sleeping Leviathan."[7] This awakening was to be predicated on a comprehensive program of education of the masses, whose upliftment was to be accomplished by preaching the gospel of equality. He wanted to assimilate the message of practical Islam, that is,

103

the message of equality with the message of personal salvation of the Hindus. That is what he meant in a letter to his Muslim friend in Nainital: "For our own motherland a junction of the two great systems, Hinduism and Islam—Vedanta brain and Islam body—is the only hope."[8]

All this was a far cry from the Paramahamsa's constant emphasis on "realization of God first" and his advice for total quiescence and passive surrender to *Jagajjananī* ("Mother of the Universe"—an appellation of Goddess Kali)—"mew mew" like a kitten profusely and piteously.[9] He had admonished his devotees: "You people talk of doing good for the world. Is the world a small place? Who the hell are you to do good to the world? Meet Him by means of spiritual discipline. Realize Him if He gives you the strength, then you can do good to everybody, otherwise not."[10] But the Swami had little patience with the spiritual qua spiritual. He considered a quest for the Divine to the neglect of "humanitarian works" as imbecile behavior.[11] He was also quite contemptuous of ecstatic enthusiasm. Toward the end of his guru's life, at the Shyampukur residence, Narendranath openly inveighed against the Paramahamsa style of dances and trances indulged in by several eager young devotees of the Master. He boldly declared that shedding tears, experiencing horripilation or "even a temporary withdrawal of normal consciousness" was "the result of nervous weakness."[12] He in fact disdained mysticism because "these mysticisms, in spite of some grains of truth in them are generally weakening." He claimed that he had come to this conclusion on the basis of his lifelong experiences with it.[13] Thus he had little qualms in mimicking and making fun of Ramakrishna's *samādhi* shortly after his death.[14] As a matter of fact, both the Master and his disciple projected a fundamentally different image to their followers. The Paramahamsa had been popular as the *pāgal thākur* (mad master)—childlike, naive, and unsophisticated. The Swami, on the other hand, appeared to his admirers as a veritable princely ascetic, indeed a *mahāyogī*—regal, heroic, humanitarian, and intellectual.[15]

II

However, Vivekananda's new image of Sri Ramakrishna was built by reconciling the latter's asocial devotionalism to the former's social activism. The Paramahamsa of the Swami's ideal was a unique prophet of modern India. Hence Vivekananda dramatized his experience of altered state of consciousness by his Master's touch, interpreted Ramakrishna's erotic devotionalism as the purest form of Hindu spirituality, and depicted his caste conscious, androgynous, but frankly misogynist, mentor as "the Saviour of women, Saviour of the masses, Saviour of all, high and low" as well as declared that he was the greatest of all *avatāras*.[16] He was convinced that "India can only rise by sitting at the feet of Shri Ramakrishna" and hence "his life and his teachings are to be spread far and wide, are to be made to penetrate every pore of Hindu society."[17] His absolute necessity for a redeemer figure like his Master explains his efforts to discover a new meaning in the Ramakrishna phenomenon. He told Nivedita that Ramakrishna "lived that great life," and he "read the meaning."[18] He discovered that the Paramahamsa had "spoken of the Vedanta as an all-comprehensive and synthetic religion," which he was preaching.[19]

And that was not all. Vivekananda now claimed: "Buddha and Chaitanya are boring but Ramakrishna Paramahamsa is the latest and the most perfect—full of knowledge, love, renunciation, liberality, and the desire to save mankind."[20] The new Ramakrishna was not to be the conventional godman—or even a godlike man, as he had once regarded the Master over a decade ago[21]—but was to project the image of a saintly superman. This delicate balancing of the traditional *avatāra* image with the modern prophet motif informed Vivekananda's interpretation and propagation of his guru's message in the world. Though he recognized the political value of an *avatāra* for a religious movement, he publicly announced his disapproval of such "orthodoxy" as belief in an incarnation.[22] He in fact clearly told Prasannakumar Shastri in 1899 that he did not "preach that the Master was an *avatāra*."[23] His ideal godman and prophet was a militant mystic—an amalgam of a yogi (saint) and a Kshatriya (warrior). He indeed was influenced, inter alia, by Thomas Carlyle's "Great Man" idea.[24] The Swami's ideas in this regard are articulated in his letter to Dewan Haridas Desai: "It is a character, a life, a centre, a God-man that must lead the way. . . . That centre, that God-man to lead . . . was the great Ramakrishna Paramahamsa."[25]

III

The Swami's quest for a special image of his Master led him to critique the existing biographies of Ramakrishna. His reaction to those published in the 1890s was far from favorable. He was particularly vehement in his denunciation of his cousin Ram Datta's *Śrīśrīramakrishna Paramahaṁsadever Jīvanvṛttānta* (1890). As he complained to Alasinga Perumal, his most important disciple in Madras:

What nonsense about the miracle of Ramakrishna! . . . Had Ramakrishna
nothing to do but turning wine into the Gupta's medicine [alluding to
the popular herbal concoction patented in Calcutta by D. Gupta & Co.]?
Lord save me from such people! What materials to work with! If they
can write a real life of Shri Ramakrishna with the idea of showing what
he came to do and teach, let them do it, otherwise let them not distort
his life and sayings. . . . I read a Bengali life sent over. . . . I am simply
ashamed of the Bengali book . . . . *Bosh and rot.*[26]

He was, however, quite appreciative of Akshaykumar Sen's biography of Ramakrishna in verse, the *Puńthi.*[27] As he wrote to Ramakrishnananda from the United States: "The book on the Master sent
by *śāṅkcunnī* [Akshay's nickname, literally meaning, goblin, for his
homely appearance] is very beautiful. . . . I just read [it]. Give him a
hundred thousand hugs from me."[28] The *Puńthi*'s primary appeal for
him lay most probably in its delightful *payār* (rhyme) so dear to
the Bengalis. Moreover such a work, meant primarily for a Bengali
audience, educated as well as uneducated, was unlikely to be translated into any other language—Indian or foreign—and hence was
likely to be confined to an enthusiastic readership. Nevertheless he
wished not to take chances with any published biography of the Master. As he observed: "But its chief fault is that it lacks a description
of the *śakti* at the outset. Ask him to emend this in the second edition.
Always remember that we now stand facing the world. Do everything
bearing in mind that people are listening to our every word and
watching our every move."[29] He in fact warned Ramakrishnananda
against using the Paramahamsa's expressions *verbatim* in any communication to foreigners. Thus he advised his *gurubhāi* to translate the
Master's phrase *kāminī-kāñcana* (woman and wealth) as *kāma-
kāñcana.* "You must convert *kāminī-kāñcana* into *kāma-kāñcana*—lust
and gold etc.—in other words, you must express the universal import
of his sermons."[30] He believed, as he would write a couple of years
later, that the Westerners were rich and strong because "the Dharma
of the Westerners is worship of Shakti—the Creative Power regarded
as the Female Principle."[31] He now proffered a few suggestions for
improvement of Sen's text:

Tell *śāṅkcunnī* to write these things in the third chapter titled "Propagation": Whatever has been accomplished by the Vedas, the Vedanta, and
the incarnations, he [Ramakrishna] has demonstrated in life by himself.
He was the explanation and thus nobody can comprehend the incarnations, the Vedas, and the Vedanta without first understanding him. The
satyayug has started the day he was born. Now all discrimination is over
and everybody including the Chandal will be treated with equanimity. He

has wiped out all distinction between man and woman, rich and poor, scholar and *jñānī*, and the Brahmin and the Chandal. He is also the terminator of all feuds and thus all [animosities] between the Hindus and the Muslims or the Hindus and the Christians are gone. All those squabbling due to differences belonged to the other age. In this *satyayug* the tidal wave of his love has united all. Tell him to expand these thoughts in his own language.[32]

Like Akshay, even ŚrīM could not help being nicked by the horn of the charging bull of a critic. It must be noted that Vivekananda had enthusiastically applauded M's enterprise a few years before his travel to the West. In a letter from Antpur, he had written: "Thanks! 100000 Master! You have hit Ramkristo in the right point. Few alas, few understand him!"[33] But when he read M's own translation of his diary as *The Gospel of Sri Ramakrishna* in 1896, probably in manuscript form before its printing in 1897, he did not like the stuff Mahendranath had written. He wrote to Trigunatitananda: "Ramakrishna Paramahamsa is God—could that sort of thing work in this country? M—has a tendency to put that stuff down everybody's throat, but that will make our movement a little sect."[34] However, the Swami executed a volte-face next year. In October 1897 he wrote to Mahendranath from Rawalpindi: "Dear M. *C'est bon ami*—Now you are doing just the thing. Come out man. No sleeping all life. Time is flying. Bravo that is the way. Many many thanks for your publication."[35] Again in November of that year, he wrote ŚrīM to applaud his second part of *The Gospel:*

> My dear "M." Many thanks for your second leaflet (leaves from the *Gospel*). It is indeed wonderful. The move is quite original and never was the life of a great Teacher brought before the public untarnished by the writer's mind, as you are presenting this one. The language also is beyond all praise, so fresh, so pointed, and withal so plain and easy. I cannot express in adequate terms how I have enjoyed the leaflets. I am really in a transport when I read them! Strange, isn't it? Our Teacher and Lord was so original, and each one of us have to be original or nothing. I now understand why none of us attempted his life before. It has been reserved for you, this great work.
>
> In a postscript the ebullient correspondent added another comment on the work: "The Socratic dialogues are Plato all over; you are entirely hidden. Moreover, the dramatic part is infinitely beautiful. Everybody likes it here in the West."[36]

Even when the Swami found a work on the life and *logia* of his Master quite acceptable in all essentials, he still noticed something in it to cavil at, as was the case with Sureshchandra Datta's collection of

Ramakrishna's sayings in Bengali, *Śrīramakrsnadever Upadeś* (1886), which contained a short but comprehensive biography of the Master titled *Śrīśrīramakrishnalīlā*. Commenting on this work, Vivekananda wrote to Brahmananda: "I just read the *Śrīramakrishna-Jīvanī* [referring obviously to *Ramakrishnalīlā*] by Suresh Datta. Good. But why did he print those examples . . . ? Shame on him! What great sin!"[37] To Ramakrishnananda he wrote: "Suresh Dutta means well and writes well. Let this work circulate—it might be of some use. But how darn much do they understand him?" He in fact ordered Ramakrishnananda: "You must not identify yourself with any Life of Him written by anybody, nor give your sanction to any."[38] The Bengalis thus generally disappointed the Swami, as none of them could write an "original" piece (he had gone as far as he could to concede that in M's *Gospel,* "the move is quite original"), that is, one that would depict Ramakrishna as a dignified and enlightened reformer acceptable and respectable throughout the world.

He considered the Madras disciples as "at least far superior to the Bengalis, who are simply fools and have no souls, no stamina at all,"[39] though he did not hesitate to lambast Alasinga and "this pack of Madras babies," who "cannot even keep a counsel in their blessed noodles! Talk nonsense all day, and when it comes to the least business, they are nowhere!"[40] However the mercurial monk changed his mind again a few months later and confided to Alasinga in a letter of 30 November 1894: "I have all hope in Madras." He now suggested to him that Kidi (nickname of Singaravelu Mudaliar, another disciple) write a biography of the Master:

> The life of Shri Ramakrishna was an extraordinary searchlight under whose illumination one is able to really understand the whole scope of Hindu religion. He was the object-lesson of all the theoretical knowledge given in the Shastras (scriptures). He showed by his life what the Rishis and Avataras really wanted to teach. . . . The Vedas can only be explained and the Shastras reconciled by his theory of Avastha or stages—that we must not only tolerate others, but positively embrace them, and that truth is the basis of all religions.

He especially cautioned Alasinga to "avoid all irregular indecent expressions about sex etc. . . . , because other nations think it the height of indecency to mention such things, and his life in English is going to be read by the whole world."[41] A few months earlier, Vivekananda had approached Kidi with the same proposal: "Take thought, get materials, write a sketch of Ramakrishna, *studiously avoiding all miracles*. The Life should be written as an illustration of the doctrines he preached."[42]

But he showed his disenchantment with his south Indian hopefuls in his letter to his Bengali *gurubhāis:*

Of course I never had any confidence in the Bengalis, but the Madrasis couldn't do anything either . . . not one independent thought crosses anyone's brains, all squabbling over the same old, torn wrapper—that Ramakrishna Paramahamsa was like this and that and those fantastic tales—stories having no end. . . . Today you have your bell, tomorrow you add a horn, a fan the day after; or you introduce a bedstand today, and tomorrow you have its legs silver-mounted, and people help themselves to a hotchpotch concoction, and you spin out two thousand cock-and-bull stories. . . . This is called imbecility in English.

In the postscript the writer observed: "It won't do by just calling him an incarnation. You must manifest power."[43]

Vivekananda's double disappointment with regard to a model biography of his master could be partly explained. Most probably he found the Bengali works full of *verbatim* reproduction of Ramakrishna's talks in patois, often full of crude and obscene expressions, as well as indecent and uncritical reports, including eyewitness accounts, of the master's *ati bhayānak* (very scary) and *atīva bhayaṅkar* (extremely horrible) *sādhanās* with the *bhairavī brāhmaṇī* as well as his intimate encounters with Mathurmohan.[44] Certainly he felt uncomfortable with any reference to the Master's obsession with Naren. He admonished his brother monks at Alambazar for having published the late Paramahamsa's loving remarks on him. "Why did you tell the *Indian Mirror* that Paramahamsa Maśāy used to call Naren this and that? All that junk and stuff!" wrote the angry and exasperated Swami.[45] His dislike for the works by the south Indians stemmed probably from the fact that they depicted Ramakrishna in the conventional motif of the Indian hagiographical tradition. The Bengali works were embarrassing whereas the Madrasi ones were dull; both were eminently *unoriginal!*

IV

It is quite possible that Saradananda's *Līlāprasaṅga* was influenced by Vivekananda's ideas and suggestions. Indeed the Preface ["Grantha-Paricay"] to the part titled "Gurubhāv—Pūrvārdha" clearly states that the author, "following the footsteps of Swami Vivekananda, attempted to tell the reader that great life . . . the realization of a little of which has made Swami Vivekananda and others, including ourselves, dedicate their lives at the lotus feet of the Master."[46] It is also quite likely that ŚrīM dared not publish his *Kathāmṛta* until toward the end of Vivekananda's life.[47] Nikhilananda's concern for projecting the right image of the Paramahamsa was most certainly inspired by the ideas of the Swami whom he greatly admired.[48] Most probably the real reason for Vivekananda's praise for the second part of M's own translation of his *Kathāmṛta* as the *Gospel* was the fact that it partly reflected (in M's commentaries) the Swami's ideas of a godman.

As Freda Matchett has demonstrated, Vivekananda distorted the mystico-spiritual experiences and teachings of his master with a view to aligning them to the classical Vedanta of Shankara, which the Swami "regarded as the basis of his own universalized form of Hinduism."[49] Although the Master himself admitted that his personal experience fell within the ambit of the Shakta, Vaishnava, and Vedanta traditions, he undoubtedly was influenced more by the Vaishnava teachings, for example, his preference for the *Bhāgavadgītā*, the *Bhāgavata Purāṇa*, and, above all, the *Ādhyātma Rāmāyaṇa*, which represented a synthesis of Vedantic nondualism (*advaita*) and Vaishnava devotionalism (*bhakti*), as well as some tantric element (Sita being identified with Prakṛti). Ramakrishna saw in the *Ādhyātma Rāmāyaṇa* the harmony of *jñāna* (knowledge) and *bhakti*. It is thus clear, as Dr. Matchett concludes, that Ramakrishna's spiritual experience and teaching cannot be identified with any one Hindu tradition, because they were derived from and "shaped by a tradition where much synthesis had already taken place."[50] Edward Dimock has observed that "there is an eternal borrowing and reborrowing of ideas and doctrines . . . among religious sects in India, until the lines of derivation become very blurred indeed."[51]

Vivekananda not only made a Vedantin out of Ramakrishna but even attributed to the latter the teaching that "all of religion is contained in . . . the three stages of the Vedanta philosophy, the Dvaita, Vishishstadvaita, and Advaita."[52] Moreover he made a prophet out of his guru, who could never have recognized himself as a savior-figure born to enlighten the world. Though he believed himself to be an *avatāra*, Ramakrishna never did see himself in the role of a messiah, nor did he ever undertake any spiritual exercise for the sake of others. His reported experiments with various *sādhanās* were not an exercise in any systematic practice of various faiths or paths. He undertook them because "they were all there in Bengal to observe and cultivate."[53] The Master's dictum of *yata mat tata path* should not be taken as a solemn pronouncement about the validity of the religions of the world. Rather it should be treated, as he himself would have preferred, as a commonsensical observation that "states of consciousness in which one feels assured of one's own union or identity with Reality may be reached by various means and from starting points which are grounded in very different assumptions as to the nature of that Reality."[54] Ramakrishna ought to be seen in his own terms detached from Vivekananda's Vedantin messiah. "When Ramakrishna is separated from Vivekananda, it becomes clear that the latter's presentation of his master has been in fact a misrepresentation."[55]

Sometime in late 1896, Saradananda asked Vivekananda why the latter had not written Ramakrishna's biography for Professor Max Müller. The Swami replied in his characteristic dithyramb:

> I have such deep feeling for the Master that it is impossible for me to write about him for the public. If I had written the article Max Müller wanted, then I would have proved, quoting from philosophies, the scriptures and even the holy books of the Christians, that Ramakrishna was the greatest of all prophets born in the world.[56]

He had in fact contemplated writing an interpretive biography of his Master. As early as 1895, he had informed Brahmananda: "I am sending you a very short biography of Ramakrishna in English. Get it printed and translated into Bengali and sell it at the great festival [Ramakrishna Festival]—people do not read books that are distributed free. Put a nominal price. Celebrate the festival with great éclat."[57]

Most probably he read this biography as a public lecture in New York on 23 February 1896. Though this biography is short, it is shot through with the author's very personalized interpretation of Ramakrishna's preachings and teachings and his claims on behalf of the Ramakrishna phenomenon.[58] In many respects this short biography is original in its interpretation of Ramakrishna's contributions. It is not Saradananda's Great Master [title of the English translation of the Lilāprasaṅga] but Vivekananda's "My Master" that is familiar throughout the world, and "My Master" is Vivekananda all over. It is important to remember in this context that Max Müller had warned Vivekananda against coloring his guru's life with "the irresponsible miraculising tendencies of devoted disciples," thus confirming the Swami's own attitude on the subject.[59]

Ramakrishna's new image was further refined in the Swami's lecture "The Sages of India" delivered in Madras on 11 February 1897. As he declared the Paramahamsa combined the

brilliant intellect of Shankara and the wonderfully expansive, infinite heart
of Chaitanya; one who would see God in every being, one whose heart
would weep for the poor, for the weak, for the outcast, for the downtrodden, for every one in this world, inside India or outside India; and at the
same time whose grand brilliant intellect would conceive of such noble
thoughts as would harmonise all conflicting sects, not only in India but
outside of India, and bring a marvellous harmony, the universal religion
of head and heart into existence. . . . [T]his great intellect never learnt
even to write his own name, but the most brilliant graduates of our
university found in him an intellectual giant. He was a strange man, this
Shri Ramakrishna Paramahamsa.[60]

Vivekananda's inspired hyperbole with respect to his Master was at
its highest and best in his claim made in 1901: "It is my opinion that
Shri Ramakrishna was born to vivify all branches of art and culture
in this country."[61] The Swami used to say: "Each one of the Master's
children is 'original.' Whosoever is not so, cannot be his child."[62]
This boast describes Vivekananda quite aptly.

V

Since Vivekananda's days the life and *logia* of the Paramahamsa
have been written and interpreted by a variety of researchers both in
India and abroad. Almost all the biographies of Ramakrishna have
relied on the interpretation of the Master's life provided by the Ramakrishna Order founded by Vivekananda. One of the Swami's Brahmo
contemporaries, Krishnakumar Mitra, astutely observed: "It is true
that Narendranath became the disciple of Ramakrishna, but this disciple made his guru 'unsectarian.'"[63] The much publicized Paramahamsa is not only the greatest incarnation who ever descended on
earth but also the patron saint of renascent India. The projection of
Ramakrishna as the universal redeemer was made in total disregard
of the Master's pronounced casteism and misogyny.[64]

On the other hand, Ṭhākur Ramakrishna of the householder disciples such as Mahendranath Gupta or Ramchandra Datta, while
trapped in the ivory tower of divinity, still has a human face—an
unsophisticated bucolic brahmin and a semiliterate ecstatic possessed
of charming simplicity and naïveté.[65] The authentic godmad Gadadhar—neither a social reformer nor a Vedantin nor even a *tāntrik*
in any meaningful sense but an enthusiastic freewheeling *bhakta*—
was transformed into a modern messiah.[66] If Ramakrishna appeared
as a mere *bhagavān* (god) to most of his devotees and disciples, he
had become something even more—*bhagavāner bābā* (God's father),

greater than God—at the hand of the "cyclonic" Swami.[67] Vivekananda once confessed: "I say, I am a slave of Ramakrishna—I am even ready to steal and rob for the sake of establishing his name in his land of birth and *sādhanā* as well as helping, however minimally, the *sādhanā* of his disciples."[68] He certainly did not commit these crimes, but with a view to making a scholar out of his semiliterate Master, he resorted to his wonted colorful exaggeration bordering on the ridiculous when he, reportedly, told Max Müller "the story of Ramakrishna's learning Sanskrit under the professorship of a fairy."[69] In fact he threw up a challenge to his *gurubhais:* "Without me, who would have made your Master known to the world!"[70] Nobody dared to suggest any name then, nobody can, even to this day!

Josephine MacLeod

9

Vivekananda and Women

I

THOUGH nurtured in a male-dominated and frankly misogynic culture, Swami Vivekananda nevertheless succeeded in endearing himself to scores of women devotees and admirers in England and America, especially those in America. Most of them never had any inkling of or real interest in the religious message he was preaching in their land. They, however, provided the young monk with shelter, companionship, and security, chaperoning him to his various public meetings all over the United States. The Swami admitted candidly in a letter to Ramakrishnananda: "They treat me like a kid and escort me to markets and malls. They do everything; I could not do even a quarter of a quarter of their work" [*sikir sikio karte pārini*].[1] He had paid an eloquent tribute to the American women in an earlier communication to his brother monk by claiming that "there are no women in the whole world comparable" to the American. "How pure, free, self-reliant, and kind they are! . . . Good God! When I see them, bang! I am at wit's end!" [*ākkel gudum*] confessed the enchanted young monk.[2] The American maidens appeared to the ascetic even more than just the embodiment of purity itself. In his inspired lexicon, they were "pure as the icicle on Diana's temple and withal with much culture, education, and spirituality in the highest sense."[3] They were also compared with two Hindu goddesses—the beautiful Lakshmi and the intellectual Saraswati in his letters to his *gurubhāi* and a college friend.[4] And they appreciated the Swami's worth and showed him respect precisely because they were "great scholars in science and philosophy."[5] He declared that "the average American woman is far more cultivated than the average American man. The men slave all their life for money, and the women snatch every opportunity to improve themselves."[6] He in fact went to the length of asserting that "in this country, women are the life of every movement and represent all the cultures of the nation."[7] In short as Swamiji would have it, "they are the grandest women in the world."[8]

115

Deep down in his heart, the Swami indeed had been aware of the magnitude of love, kindness, respect, and material and moral support provided by the American women. He was quite forthright in his acknowledgment in this regard in his letter to Raja Ajit Singh:

American women! A hundred lives would not be sufficient to pay my deep debt of gratitude to you! I have not words enough to express the depth of Oriental gratitude—"If the Indian Ocean were an inkstand, the highest mountain of the Himalayas, the pen, the earth, the scroll and time itself, the writer, still it will not express my gratitude to you!"[9]

Actually he discovered his latent strength as a public speaker and a public figure, thanks to the encouragements and reinforcements he received from his female admirers, who, in a way, acted as his public relations agents. In fact he was fashioned as a prophet and a spiritual leader of titanic proportions by such American women as Christina Greenstidel, Edith Allan, Josephine MacLeod, Sara Bull, Ida Ansell, and a few others. Swami Nikhilananda was quite right in his observation that "Swami Vivekananda is America's best gift to India."[10]

Nevertheless Vivekananda's attitude to American women remained basically schizophrenic: grateful and grudging. Though pampered by them generally, he must have resented having to play a Hindu mystery man at the home of his Boston hostess, Kate Sanborn, whose notice he had attracted when he journeyed by train from Chicago to Massachusetts in 1893. Most probably during his initial months in the United States, he had not yet internalized his newly formed image of a princely ascetic from the Orient. He thus may have been embarrassed, even enraged, by Mrs. Sanborn's driving him through the streets of Boston in a horse-drawn carriage furnished with a liveryman. He might have been upset even more after having read the report of his city tour in the newspaper.[11] He probably had this ride or any such pompous show in mind when he observed in his letter to Alasinga: "Just now I am living as the guest of an old lady in a village near Boston. . . . I have an advantage in living with her . . . and she has the advantage of inviting her friends over here and showing them a curio from India!"[12] The Swami's gratitude to American women was the outcome of his deep indebtedness to their generosity, and in spite of it or precisely because of it, he hated them for their naive enthusiasm for a stranger in their midst.

He, however, criticized American women as glibly as he had complimented them. In a fiery sermon, he challenged his audience to show him "a dozen spiritual women in America." "Nice dress, wealth, brilliant society, operas, novels," he quipped. "There should also be spirituality, but that side is *entirely absent* from Christian countries. They live in India."[13] In an earlier public lecture, he had claimed that "the Hindu women are very spiritual and very religious, perhaps *more so than any other* women in the world."[14] Later he observed that the American women, though intellectual, were "not steady, serious and sincere."[15] And in Boston, in particular, his verdict was that "there the women are all faddists, all fickle, merely bent on following something new and strange."[16] He told Sharat Chakravarti that he found Western women driving vehicles, working in offices, attending schools or working as professors quite masculine. It was only the Indian women who were truly feminine with their characteristic humility and bashfulness.[17] He even told Chakravarti that the American sluts and studs (*māgī minsegulo*) used to be sexually aroused after hearing his lectures.[18] A lady who had listened to him say in a lecture in Pasadena that Indian women were more moral than the lustful Western women, exclaimed at his secretary, Mrs. Hansbrough, trying to escort him out of the lecture room: "You little fool! Don't you know he hates you?"[19]

II

Even though he was careful about giving public vent to his real attitude to femininity in the United States and preached "We should not think that we are men and women, but only that we are human beings,"[20] he was quite vocal in his antifeminine invectives in his letters to his Bengali cohorts. Thus he wrote to Akhandananda from Almora: "I am a fighter [*vīra*] and we will die in the battlefield. It does not behoove me to sit idle like a woman here."[21] He took his south Indian disciple to task for not rising against the Christian missionaries: "I know, my son, I shall have to come and manufacture *men* out of you. I know that India is only inhabited by *women* and *eunuchs*."[22] His androcentrism was so pronounced that he once told Nivedita: "Yes, the older I grow, the more everything seems to me to lie in manliness. This is my new gospel. Do even evil like a man!"[23]

He attacked the Vaishnavas of Orissa and Bengal viciously. "Look at this nation," observed the Swami in a conversation with Surendranath Sen. "Through the preaching of that love broadcast, the nation has become effeminate—a race of women! The whole of Orissa has been turned into a land of cowards, and Bengal, running after the Radha-prema, these past four hundred years, has almost lost all sense of manliness!"[24] He advised a visitor at Almora in June 1897 to "use the whip left and right" on those who were indulging in the erotic

Radha-Krishna songs.[25] He interpreted the poems of the aesthete Rabindranath Tagore (who had taught the young Narendra a number of songs composed by himself to be sung at the Brahmo Samaj)[26] as effeminate and warned Nivedita about the Tagores: "Remember that that family has poured a lot of erotic venom over Bengal."[27] He ridiculed Premananda and Yogananda who, as devotees of the late Paramahamsa, followed the path of devotion, as effeminate in that theirs was an attitude of a helpless and hapless woman (*dīnāhīnā bhāv*). He admonished them to get rid of such a mentality by reflecting: "I am the Soul, how could I be sick? '*Dīnāhīnā*' for what?"[28] He similarly ridiculed Christianity as effeminate devotionalism [*meyelī bhaktir dharma*] in a conversation with his friend Priyanath Singha.[29]

Even while praising publicly a Hindu woman for her gallantry, he unwittingly revealed his gender bias. Thus he told his audience in Boston that one of the mutineers (of 1857) led by the Rani of Jhansi regarded the queen as "a goddess" and reportedly confessed to the Swami that "when overcome, she fell on her sword and died like a *man*."[30] From Turiyananda's reminiscences we come to know how Swamiji found inspiration for his life as a renouncer after having read an admonition in a Hindi couplet etched on the walls of a saint's cottage in Vrindavan. The couplet ran like this:

> O desire, you are the lowliest of
> the lowly, like a woman of the caste
> of sweepers or tanners. Had you not
> come inside me, I would have remained
> a Brahman.[31]

This kind of antagonistic attitude toward women as an impediment to an ascetic career found its expression in their being regarded as whores. At the Baranagore Math, Vivekananda and his nude monastic cohorts would cry out on seeing women visitors enter the monastery, "The *māgīs* are coming" to alert the young ascetics to cover themselves. They later substituted the word *māgī* for *mogī* or Burmese (they are called *mog* in Bengali) lest any of the women overheard them.[32] Women are not only the living manifestation of lust or desire, they are also, unlike the detached and remote Shivalike renouncers, meddlesome. "I am always dragging other's pain into me . . . just as women," Vivekananda once confessed to Marie Halboister, and asked her: "Do you think this has any spirituality in it? Nonsense, it is all *nervous bondage*."[33] He did not consider women capable of mature behavior. He declared in Madras, rather nonchalantly, that "through centuries of slavery, we have become like a nation of women." He explained the predicament:

> You scarcely can get three women together for five minutes in this country or any other country, but they quarrel. Women make big societies in European countries and make tremendous declarations of women's power and so on; then they quarrel, and some man comes and rules them all.[34]

III

Vivekananda always projected the image of himself as a "Man of Fire and Flame, a regal, majestic figure, forceful, dominant," in the admiring prose of Mary Funke of Detroit.[35] He was not just a seeker of God; he was also a protector of the meek and the helpless. Even as a six-year old child, he, reportedly, rescued his companion from imminent death from being crushed under a horse-drawn carriage by courageously pulling him to safety.[36] He told Sister Nivedita how he rescued a helpless English woman deserted by her cowardly male escort from a charging mad bull by simply taking up "his stand." "The animal suddenly stopped, a few paces off, and then raising his head, retreated sullenly."[37] He told her another story of his youthful gallantry in the streets of Calcutta, where he rescued another damsel in distress in a carriage dragged by a runaway horse by boldly restraining the wild beast.[38] There is also the story of his Tarzanlike empathy with ferocious beasts. At a hunting expedition organized by his patron, the Raja of Khetri, the Swami confronted a tiger but refused to shoot the animal, saying: "Sadhus need no guns to protect them. Even a tiger could not harm them. . . . Let no creature of God have any fear from me."[39] He, however, did not hesitate to shoot a deer for sheer fun—a Kshatriya feat that earned the great Vedantist monk the admiration of a devotee: "The Swamiji was a dead shot."[40]

The Swami often provided such instances of his gallantry and prowess to his Bengali admirers and devotees. He narrated his encounter with a high-ranking police officer in Calcutta, responding to the latter's attempt to persuade the young monk to renege on his *gurubhāis* of Baranagar Math, who were suspected of treason against the government, by flexing his "exercised powerful frame" and "thereby cowing the puny officer down."[41] Once as a co-passenger to some Englishmen in a first-class train compartment, he subdued the "racist" imperialist white men trying to kick him out of the car by simply showing them his muscles. "You may shove me," declared the proud and powerful Bengali, "but before that all of you get ready to be thrown out of the running train. Just examine my biceps and triceps before you get up to shove me out."[42] Another episode, with its perfect jokebook character, involved his subduing two British army officers in a first-class train compartment. When on seeing a monk entering the car, one of them remarked contemptuously "Here comes a log" and the other "No, here comes an ass," the indignant Swami sat in between them and said with perfect equipoise and nonchalance: "And I am sitting between the two." The two British bullies were overpowered by the monk's personality and command of the English language.[43]

The Swami's concept of manliness—standing for both the Bengali words, *manusyatva* (humanity or humaneness) and *purusatva* (masculinity or manliness)—often emphasized the latter. In a letter to Mary Hale, he clearly defined his idea in this regard. With a view to inspiring her, he wrote: "'The gods themselves have no clue as to women's moods and man's fate, what to speak of human beings?' My instincts may be very feminine, but what I am exercised with just this moment is, that you get a little bit of manliness about you." He pointed out that this manliness would inculcate "individuality" and "backbone," which she, her "brain, health, beauty . . . haughtiness, spirit, etc." notwithstanding, did not possess.[44] His most sincere prayer to the gods (conceived as the primal father and mother) was: "Oh Thou Lord of Gauri, O Thou Mother of the Universe! Vouchsafe manliness unto me! O Thou Mother of Strength! take away my weakness, take away my unmanliness, and—*Make me a Man!*"[45] He declared in Madras: "Men, men, these are wanted . . . strong, vigorous, believing young men, sincere to the backbone, are wanted. . . . It is man-making theories that we want. It is man-making education all round that we want."[46] The Swami's gendered emphasis on manliness contrasted sharply with the conception of *manusyatva* (meaning "the completely developed state of all the qualities of humanity") of the Bengal renaissance as enunciated by Bankimchandra Chattopadhyay, who had "taught the necessity of cultivating all the human faculties, mental as well as physical, to attain *manusyatva,* one of the primary goals of *dharma.*"[47]

In spite of his powerful, vital, and masculine image, his own penchant for manliness, and his insistence on training a band of men with "muscles of iron and nerves of steel,"[48] Vivekananda "did not possess what might be called an athletic physique [*pāloanī cehārā*]," to quote his friend and devotee Manmathanath Gangopadhyay. "On the other hand, his arms [*bāju*] and fingers were smooth and tapered."[49] This description of the Swami agrees with the one given by Dr. Edgar C. Beall in *The Phrenological Journal:* "One of the most striking peculiarities of this man is the femininity indicated in nearly every contour of the figure, face, head and hands. He has probably as perfect a conic hand as could be imagined."[50] He in fact never did any physical exercise since his college days nor was he inclined to it. Even after having been advised by his physicians to do regular physical exercise during his voyage to the West, he preferred to chat with Nivedita on board the *S.S. Golconda*.[51] During his Indian peregrination in 1890, he had come in contact with the famous mystique and yogi Pavhari Baba at Ghazipur and wished to learn from him the science of *hathayoga*. He, however, soon found out the sheer difficulty of practicing it, for the techniques and postures of *hathayoga* called for regular physical exercise and conditioning as well as a strict dietary regimen. He gave up the idea, declaring that he had been importuned by the Baba's insistence on learning Vedanta from him and thus had to leave to save the mystique from embarrassment.[52]

IV

Vivekananda's contempt for Indian women was hardly distinguishable from his condescending attitude to them. The latter has been interpreted by his devotee biographers as his real respectful outlook on femininity.[53] For example he wrote: "we call women lowly, wretched, despicable, and impure. Consequently, we have become beastly, slavish, unenterprising, and poor." He also wrote: "Could you uplift your women? Only then there is hope, otherwise there will be no salvation from this animal life."[54] His impassioned plea for women's education was based on his claim expressed in his characteristic style: "With five hundred men, the conquest of India might take fifty years: with as many women, not more than a few weeks."[55] Even his remark in a lecture on Hindu women's chastity and spirituality in Chicago, "The idea of perfect womanhood is perfect independence," which was an obvious non sequitur, because it neither followed from the preceding statement nor led to the one immediately after, has been interpreted by an admiring analyst as "the strongest argument for women's liberation."[56] The Swami would even unabashedly flatter women to realize his objective. With a view to recruiting a worker for propaganda against Pandita Ramabai Saraswati, an Indian Christian woman in the United States trying to raise funds to help child widows of India, he asked Miss Sarala Ghosal, editor of the *Bharati,* to volunteer to preach Vedanta in the West. He wrote to her:

If anyone like you go, England will be stirred, what to speak of America!
If an Indian woman in Indian dress preach the religion which fell from
the lips of the Rishis of India—I see a prophetic vision—there will rise a
great wave which will inundate the whole Western world. Will there be
no woman, in the land of Maitreyi, Khana, Lilavati, Savitri, and Ubhay-
abharati, who will venture to do this?[57]

Only a few months later, he was to write a letter persuading Margaret
Noble to come to India for social work: "India cannot yet produce
great women, she must borrow them from other nations. Your education, sincerity, purity, immense love, determination, and above all,
the Celtic blood make you the woman wanted."[58]

V

Vivekananda inherited his gender consciousness from his culture,
which extolled the ideal of a de-erotized woman as a mother figure
and condemned the sexual female as an ogre and an exteriorizing and
fettering element—an impediment to the realization of the divine. As
Robert Goldman has argued,

in many texts women are idealized as pure, spiritual, and nurturant when
they are de-erotized and placed in clearly defined and sexually tabooed
blood relationships such as those of mother, sister, or daughter. In other
words, when emphasis is placed on their sexuality, they are often vilified
for this aspect of their nature and condemned as temptress, seductress,
or whore.[59]

The *Rgveda* had highlighted the Hindu woman's ontological inferior-
ity by labeling her "fickle-minded and uncontrollable."[60] Even the
quintessentially feminine figure, Pancacūḍā the nymph, is made to
confess to Narada in one of the lores of the *Mahābhārata* that

God created women with all kinds of vices and they were the worst possible sinners. They were so deadly that death, hell, snakes, etc. all combined
stood on one side and women on the other. They were falsehood incar-
nate, without the knowledge of the *sastra*-s or control of their senses, and
were obsessed with ornaments, dresses, food and drink, etc.[61]

The *Śatapathabrāhmaṇa* (III. 2.4.6) has it that women are unfaithful
by nature and "always went in for handsome men and those who
could sing and dance well."[62] Also Vivekananda's upbringing in an
androcratic culture precluded any meaningful contact with females

other than his own direct relations. As was the case with a middle-class Bengali family of the nineteenth century, young Narendra's association with women was limited either to siblings or cousins or aunts and the elderly. With both groups he could be free, frivolous, even wanton. The tragic death by suicide of his dear sister Yogendrabala at the tender age of twenty-two could possibly have distressed him and sensitized him to the predicament of Indian women as well as to the need for their upliftment through education.[63]

Nevertheless his upbringing squared very well with his later ascetic life, which was based on Ramakrishna's misogynist dictum against *kāminī-kāñcana,* especially the phobia of a sexual female. At the same time, an attitude of obsequious passive surrender to woman as mother became concomitant to this unmistakably misogynist consciousness. The only women he and his ascetic cohorts came in contact with were the elderly female devotees of the late Paramahamsa, including his relatively young widow, Saradamani, who was venerated by the young monks not just as the wife of their beloved guru but as a veritable goddess à la Ramakrishna's insistence on her divinity. Thus the young Sarada became the Holy Mother, Śrīmā, for Ramakrishna's boys. This ambivalence on the part of the Bengali *bhadralok,* reared in a culture of *machismo,* could be seen in their labeling woman Shakti, the primal force and the ultimate source of power while at the same time taking her for granted. The Swami was a product of this culture that lavished verbal glorification on the female while subjecting her to every kind of hardship and domination in real life in the name of chastity, purity, and spirituality.

For Vivekananda, as for all the monks of the Ramakrishna Order, renunciation, meaning repression of natural sexual urges, constituted the highest ascetic ideal. He literally indoctrinated the beautiful Hale sisters, especially the most attractive of them, Mary, into remaining a virgin. He wrote to her:

This hideous world is Maya. Renounce and be happy. Give up the idea of sex and possessions. There is no other bond. Marriage and sex and money are the only living devils. All earthly love proceeds from the body. No sex, no possessions; as these fall off, the eyes open to spiritual vision. The soul regains its own infinite power.[64]

He also wrote her a letter quoting from Tulsidas's devotional poems full of erotic phraseology and imagery. He disparaged the philosopher's attempt to know God rationally and wrote: "We are here dying for a kiss of His lips." He then, rather suggestively, and within quotes, wrote (apparently citing from Tulsidas): "Take your nonsense back to your own home and send a kiss of my Love—can you?" He concluded his letter with a bit of self-conscious embarrassment: "Excuse my mad scribbling, excuse my foolery in trying to express the inexpressible."[65] Later he would attack the Vaishnavas of Bengal and Orissa severely and even label Rabindranath's poems as "erotic venom."

On the other hand, the mercurial monk was violently vocal in his insistence on chastity. When someone told him that some American physicians had advised sex to a young man from India suffering from a disorder due to sexual repression, Vivekananda exploded: "You doctors in this country who hold that chastity is against the law of nature, don't know what you are talking about. You don't know the meaning of the word purity. You are beasts! beasts! I say, with the morals of a tomcat if that is the best you have to say on the subject."[66] He was oblivious of the fact that Ramakrishna's so-called "madness" had been diagnosed by the Master's family members and employers as an outcome of his self-inflicted continence, and they hastened to get him married.[67] Vivekananda expatiated on chastity as a means of strengthening the mind. From Frank Rhodehamel's report on the Swami's sermon to a packed gathering in San Francisco, we learn that "as a practice to develop purity, he expounded the theory of looking upon every woman as one's mother."[68] "The Hindu nation is not given to marriage," he is reported to have declared in Boston on 16 May 1893, "not because we are woman haters, but because our religion teaches us to see in every woman his mother, and no man wants to marry his mother. . . . We consider marriage a low, vulgar state, and if a man does marry it is because he needs a helpmate for religion."[69]

Vivekananda's twin ideals for the woman were those of a loving mother and a chaste wife on the one hand or that of an all-renouncing nun on the other. She must either dedicate herself to her son and husband or to humanity at large. "O India! Forget not that the ideal of thy womanhood is Sita, Savitri, Damayanti," the patriot-prophet of modern India reminded his readers.[70] "The ideal of womanhood in India is motherhood—that marvellous, unselfish, all suffering, ever-forgiving mother," he announced in California. He further declared that the mother "deserved worship" because she "was a saint in bringing . . . [her] child into the world . . . by keeping her body pure, her mind pure, her food pure, her clothes pure, her imagination pure, for years in expectation of becoming a mother."[71] Indeed the Swami's sermon had the canonical imprimatur of his culture. The *Mahābhārata* extolled the character of Parvati, a woman who practiced *dharma* as well as *sahadharma* (with her husband, Lord Shiva), and declared that there was no other god for a woman but her husband, by attending on whom she attained heaven. The great Kaurava warrior and lifelong bachelor Bhisma, on deathbed in the battleground, un-hesitatingly advised the eldest of the Pandava brother, Yudhisthira, that women should always be loyal, forgiving, naive, truthful, pious, as well as attractive to their spouses. Yudhisthira heard an anecdote from the sage Markandeya of a housewife who neglected a brahmin alms-seeker (a grave offense) to attend on her husband and, on being reprimanded by the angry ascetic, "gave him a good harangue as to the duties and ideals of a married woman, the theme of which was that a married woman should worship her husband before all others."[72] We thus see that the Hindu texts identified an ideal woman with an ideal wife. "In other words," concludes Dr. Mukherjee, "it was rather an ideal wifehood, and not an ideal womanhood, that all these authorities were describing at great length."[73]

While citing the examples from the Hindu epics and Puranas of women who were all chaste wives loyal to their spouses without de-mur, the Swami did not bother to talk about independent-minded women such as Draupadi of the *Mahābhārata*.[74] On the other hand, his inflated mother-consciousness was so acute that he found even the Western countries, whose women he had lambasted earlier, worship mother with equal fervor and devotion. He thus gave a fantastic description of Roman Catholic practices and wrote:

> In the religion, Jehovah, Jesus, and the Trinity are secondary; there, the worship is for the Mother—She, the Mother, with the Child Jesus in her arms. The emperor cries "Mother," the field-marshal cries "Mother," the soldier with the flag in his hand cries "Mother," the seaman at the helm cries "Mother," the fisherman in his rags cries "Mother," the beggar in the street cries "Mother"! A million voices in million ways, from a million places—from the palace, from the cottage, from the church, cry "Mother," "Mother," "Mother"! Everywhere is the cry "Ave Maria," day and night, "Ave Maria," "Ave Maria"![75]

VI

Vivekananda inherited the ideal of giving up *kāminī-kāñcana* from Hindu culture, as well as an obsession with fair skin (something his mentor, Ramakrishna, had exhibited often) from Bengali culture. He showed himself a typical Bengali and disarmingly vulnerable in his candid confession in a letter to a friend (having cautioned him to treat his letter as strictly confidential) that "the American women are very beautiful" and by contrast "even the prettiest woman of our country will look like a black owl there."[76] In a letter to his monastic brother, he observed that the American women belonged to "the race of the titans" (*virocaner jāt*) and that they are extremely body-conscious and thus "always keep their body clean and made up."[77] He noticed that "in the West, men of forty years and women of fifty years are still young," and "the secret is that they do not marry at an early age." However, he also noticed that the upper-class women "suffer the torment of death to make themselves shapely in appear-ance" "by squeezing the waist, making the spine crooked, and thus displacing the liver and spleen and disfiguring the form!" He even observed that "as a matter of fact, the dress of the English and the German women is not good" because "they do not generally follow the Paris fashions." He noticed, too, the Western women dancing with exposed face, shoulders, and upper part of the body to view.[78] It seems that he did not find this exposure particularly offensive, for we have his preference for female curves, which he made explicit to Nivedita by confessing that "fat plump spinsters were good—but thin never."[79]

He could not also remain fundamentally detached from feminine influence. On his own admission, he was somewhat spoiled by one sister Jeany, who could "jump and run and play and swear like a devil and talk slang at the rate of 500 a minute" and who did not "much care for religion." Another admirer, one Miss Phillips, got the Swami quite excited about starting a monastery at her mountain resort.[80] Then in spite of his braggadocio and equating heroism with absti-nence and activism with masculinity, he remained mysteriously am-bivalent with respect to a proper male identity. His especial fondness for and his alleged identity with Shiva since childhood is particularly significant.[81] As a god Shiva represents the quintessential erotic as-cetic—capable of supreme renunciation but possessing "a highly con-trolled but potentially uncontrollable sexual dynamism."[82] He is the great ethyphallic deity who exercises total control of his virility. The Swami's career as a self-asserted monk and a renouncer of the world shows his Shivalike self-willed control, which made him a *sannyāsī* of great spiritual potency. But he seems to have succeeded in transmut-ing his natural maleness into a supranormal spiritual masculinity only in a limited sense. So long as he remained free from closeness to a young adoring female, there was little problem, though there were some rumors about his indiscretion with respect to associating with some women during his stay at Mrs. John Bagley's residence in De-troit.[83] However, the advent of Nivedita in his life at the apex of his worldwide reputation as a spiritual leader coincided with his declining health and disturbed the *ataraxia* of the Vedantic monk who had once seemed "inly-pleased" to his admirers.[84]

Margaret Noble (Sister Nivedita)

10

Vivekananda and Nivedita

I

VIVEKANANDA came in social contact with adult women for the first time in the United States. His early patron, Mrs. George Hale, was a maternal figure, and her daughters and nieces—the two Marys and the two Harriets, the so-called Hale sisters—were like his own sisters with whom he was friendly and open—"elder brother, sage, and child combined," in Marie Burke's elegant prose.[1] A comparatively young woman, though a few years older than Vivekananda, Josephine Mac-Leod was strangely but strongly fascinated by him. Her feelings toward him at first sight had more to do with how he looked—"the fiery missionary whose physique was like a wrestler's and whose eyes were deep black"[2]—than what he said ("He said something, the particular words of which I do not remember."[3]) She also admired Vivekananda's "long, thick black hair" and even once "crept behind him with a pair of scissors and cut off a lock of it" to the utter befuddlement of the embarrassed young monk.[4] Tantine (Josephine's nickname) so identified herself with Vivekananda that she appropriated his sense of mischievous humor and even practiced it on Swami Brahmananda at the Ramakrishna Math in Bangalore. She surprised the reclusive but unsuspecting Rakhal Maharaj who avoided meeting her daily by suddenly leaping in front of him exclaiming: "Naughty boy, now how will you escape?"[5]

In one sense Vivekananda's relations with his women devotees and admirers could be characterized, à la Ramakrishna, as *madhur bhāv*—a kind of divine love having all the qualities of the erotic except the carnal.[6] This sanitized sex or divine love seemed to act as a surrogate for normal heterosexual relationships. The Great Master had sustained the interest of his male admirers in his erotic community of Dakshineshwar by performing frenzied *kīrtan,* dance, nudity, and *samādhi*. Vivekananda's attraction consisted in his sharp intellect, fluent speech, colorful sermons, and above all, his sheer personal charm.

Ramakrishna had been the cynosure of the male eye; the Swami became the apple of the female eye. Although the Paramahamsa was Kali the Divine Mother or Shakti to his male admirers, his great disciple became the Buddha, Jesus, Arjuna, Othello, prince, raja, or prophet, and above all, Shiva, to his female (and also to a number of male) devotees.

II

The Swami's problems began when he encountered a very intelligent and persistent devotee who was also a mature adult in the person of Margaret Noble. From the very beginning, his attitude and behavior toward her was markedly different. In many respects she was Vivekananda's alter ego: flamboyant, rhetorical, energetic, and possessed of immense personal charm and charisma. He projected to her an image of himself as *manly*—physically and morally unassailable—and *godly*, the Shiva manifest. From Sister Nivedita's writings and speeches, we come across some details of the Swami's early life which, though not corroborated by any other source, throw interesting light on his idealized image. He once told her, for example, that "when he was eight years old, sitting at play, he developed the power of entering in *Samadhi*."[7] He also gave a brilliant account of what might be regarded as a mystical soccer with a blazing ball. The Sister writes that he used to see a light at sleeping time. "In later life, he would often . . . describe the light he saw. Sometimes it would come as a ball, which a boy was kicking towards him. It would draw near. He would be one with it, and all would be forgotten. Sometimes it was a blaze into which he would enter."[8]

Initially Margaret was attracted by the young monk's good looks and his carefully cultivated image of a virgin male of immense intellectual and spiritual potency. She first met him sometime during the last week of October 1895 at the fashionable residence of the London socialite Lady Isabel Margesson, where the Swami delivered his second address at the Balloon Society. She describes her first enchanting encounter with her future guru "seated, facing a half-circle of listeners, with the fire on the hearth behind him . . . in his crimson robe and girdle, as one bringing . . . news from a far land, with a curious habit of saying now and again 'Shiva! Shiva!' and wearing that look of mingled gentleness and loftiness, that one sees on the faces of those who live much in meditation, that look, perhaps, that Raphael has painted . . . on the brow of the Sistine Child." We are told by the awestruck Margaret that the Swami chanted Sanskrit verses for his audience, thrilling them with "those wonderful Eastern tones," which they found "at once so reminiscent of, and yet so different from, the Gregorian music of our own churches."[9]

Since her early youth, Margaret "manifested a fondness for the society of intellectual men," according to the testimony of her brother Richmond.[10] Her first reaction at hearing the Swami's sermons was that he "had said nothing new." But on cogitating on his emphasis on self and renunciation, she changed her mind. As she wrote later, "it dawned on me slowly that it is not only ungenerous, it was also unjust, to discuss in such fashion the message of a new mind and a strange culture."[11] However, Margaret the intellectual was also an incorrigible romantic at heart. Richmond even mildly accused her "of being too romantic."[12] A woman with a penchant for dreams and fantasies, Noble had her personal dreams shattered by the time she met the handsome Indian. Her two previous love affairs had ended in tragedy. Her first lover and fiancé succumbed to tuberculosis just before their marriage. She was jilted by her second lover, who abandoned her for another woman of his choice.[13] To her, then, the Swami appeared not only as an exotic romantic figure but also as a true intellectual—someone who could fill the void in her life of unrequited romance.

He, too, on his part, projected and continued to maintain an image of a hero—the great renouncer and sacrificer who was also a manly man possessed of infinite courage and compassion. He even hinted in a conversation with her that he was an incarnation of the Buddha and the Christ. He first said: "I have a superstition . . . that the same soul who came once as Buddha came afterwards as Christ." Then to quote Margaret's report, "his voice had sunk lower, as he talked, till the tones had become dream-like. But finally, almost in soliloquy, he shook off the mood that had stolen upon him, saying with a long breath, 'Yes, yes! these things have been, and they will again be.'"[14] Noble was charmed by the young man's nostalgia, and this drove her to recapitulate his longings:

How homesick he had been for the sound of July rains, as he had known them in his childhood in Bengal! How wonderful was the sound of water and rain, or waterfall, or sea! The most beautiful sight he could remember was a mother whom he had seen, passing from stepping stone to stepping stone across a mountain brook and turning as she went, to play with and caress the baby on the back. The ideal death would be to lie on a ledge of rock in the midst of Himalayan forests and hear the torrent beneath, as one passed out of the body, chanting eternally, "Hara!! Hara! The Free! The Free!"[15]

This is hardly spiritual stuff. It's a classic example of superb story-telling, tickling romantic sensibility. "His conversation was like Ganga at the flood. There was really no interrupting him," Reeves Calkins observed with uncanny perspicacity.[16]

It was the Swami who, according to Nivedita's account, solicited her service for India. "I have plans for the women of my country," he told her, "in which you, I think, could be of great help to me." He also added, by way of conveying his earnestness to her: "Thousands of Indian women are waiting, and will lift their heads when a woman from the West comes to fight with them, live with them, and show them the way."[17] The effect of this appeal was a foregone conclusion. Nivedita remembered the occasion vividly: "I knew that I heard a call which would change my life."[18] She was perhaps beguiled by the monk's equivocation and intentional innuendos. And she was an attractive woman whose charm was hard to ignore. According to her friend Eric Hammond, Margaret was "a young but distinctive woman with luminous grey eyes, with hair of light golden brown, with a complexion radiant in its clearness, with a smile ingratiating and alluring. Of medium height; alert in every muscle and movement, eager, enterprising, dauntless."[19] Vivekananda wept one day in her school, feeling sorry for the uneducated children back home, and said with his characteristic innuendo: "The problem seems hopeless but I am searching for a solution. If the mountain will not come to Mohammed, Mohammed must go to the mountain. If the poor cannot come to school, the school must go to them, to the plough, to the factory, everywhere." Moved by this dramatic and energetic appeal and utterly overwhelmed by the force of its misunderstood message, she offered herself completely to the orange robed patriot. This was her offer of service and love to the superman of her fancy. Sadly she suffered another blow in this third and final episode of the heart, when her overtures were overturned by the man who recoiled into the safe haven of asceticism and declared: "I am a monk."[20]

III

Vivekananda never wished to sever the relationship with his female admirer even when she seemed potentially troublesome. It is reasonable to speculate that he really desired her to come to India. In November 1896 when she agreed to come, he wrote to her assuring her of his help and telling her indirectly that he was an incarnation himself. "For my own part, I will be incarnated two hundred times, if that is necessary to do this work among my people that I have undertaken." He also told her: "Yes, in India . . . that is where you belong."[21] When she responded by expressing her resolve to go, he fired one of his most dithyrambic salvos: "Let me tell you frankly that I am now convinced that you have a great future in the work for India. What was wanted was not a man, but a woman—a real lioness—to work for the Indians, women specially." He promised: "on my part I will stand by you unto death. . . . 'The tusks of the elephant come out, but never go back'; so are the words of a man never retracted."[22] He, of course, had not figured out how he would utilize her services about which she, too, had but a naively vague idea. He also needed to alert her against any further show of her true feelings for him while in India. He therefore admonished her against making any personal (that is sexual) overtures while continuing to shower colorful encomiums on her to sustain her resolve for India. From India (he had returned home in August 1897), he continued his correspondence with Noble, warning her not to involve him personally in her work nor to become personally entangled with him in any way.[23] Yet though he did not have any concrete plan for her, he certainly had no desire to avoid her company. Hence his ambivalence and innuendo in all his letters to Nivedita.

Since her arrival in Calcutta on 28 January 1898, Margaret had remained virtually idle, passing her days listening to the Swami's perorations on renunciation, philanthropy, and Vedanta. When she asked for work, he pointed to the bank of the Hooghly River and said: "Live in the sun. Look at what is going on around you. Everything is so beautiful! Don't make any plan. That is not your job."[24] After having tarried for several months at Belur, Noble began to regret her decision to quit her job in England and come to a strange land thousands of miles away. She complained to Josephine, who had come to visit India along with Sara Bull: "What am I doing for so long? Why doesn't the Swami speak to me about work?"[25] Because Vivekananda had not planned or prepared any tangible and viable social-spiritual project for Margaret and because he probably wished her to continue to stay in Calcutta, he subjected her ostensibly to a training in asceticism. He wanted her to become Indian in spirit and as such would not put up with her expression of love and loyalty for England. In fact he told her that her patriotism and her love for her race was a sin. She had come to India for the sake of, and depending on, the Swami, and she had hoped to find him a congenial and compassionate mentor. She thus found it terribly oppressing to put up with his somewhat hostile indifference.[26]

What caused this sudden and sullen hostility? We get a clue in this regard in Margaret's observation. On arrival in Calcutta, she had noticed her master's tormented life and wrote about it later: "It was the personality of my Master himself, in *all the fruitless torture and struggle of a lion caught in a net*."[27] Another female disciple of the Swami, who had been impressed with his "forceful virile figure," had seen him pace up and down like "the lion in the cage," howling "Azad, Azad, the Free."[28] Vivekananda had sermonized on renunciation and chastity on the part of a monk and claimed that "spiritual giants are produced only where the vow of chastity is observed."[29] At the same time, he had lectured in London encouraging his female audience to think of God or a personal deity (*iṣṭa*) as husband.[30] On another occasion, he related to them the story of a young handsome *sādhu* being propositioned by an unsuspecting pretty princess to be her husband and his heroic rejection of this overture by proclaiming his status as a world renouncer.[31] He also "knew that Nivedita's feelings towards him, besides being known to himself, were known to others and that . . . misconceptions and gossips might arise which, in the interests of public morality, must be prevented."[32] Earlier he had, in another context, admitted that even a renouncer and monk could be "seen to shiver in fear of public opinion."[33]

Yet he could not quite overcome the temptations of a normal life, which he had discarded so easily in his early youth. His so-called renunciation amounted to no more than giving up the hassles of a householder's life and taking refuge in a monk's career. Now with a buxom woman at his beck and call, he was torn between male instincts and monkish injunctions. He once confessed to Nivedita: "These shadows of home and marriage cross even *my* mind now and then."[34] He further confessed to her, albeit conceitedly: "I would undo the past if I could—I would marry—were I 10 years younger—just to make my mother happy—not for any other reason."[35] But then he told her at another time that "marriage was horrible, it was the door to birth and so on" and that "he would go out into the world and preach *smashing* truths . . . give up, give up, give up." Although she adored the Swami's mood when these words were spoken, she was struck by "the violence and utter unreasonableness of much that he said."[36] The fetters of an austere life embraced without much inner soteriological anxiety often proved too much for the monk torn between the two worlds he found unacceptable. He openly confessed his dilemma to one of his European disciples in the Sister's presence: "How I wish a law could be broken. If we were really able to break a law we should be free. What you call breaking the law, is really only another way of keeping it."[37] During a conversation with Chandicharan Bardhan, sometime in 1897, Vivekananda confessed to his own feelings of lust: "Once in me rose the feeling of lust. I got so disgusted with myself that I sat on a pot of burning tinders, and it took a long time for the wound to heal."[38] He, of course, had ready recourse to an almost Epicurean justification for an ascetic life. "He who is alone is happy," he wrote in a letter to Miss Halboister of Wimbledon. "Do good to all, like everyone, but *do not love* anyone. It is a bondage, and bondage brings only misery. . . . To have nobody to care for and never minding who cares for one is the way to be free."[39] He reminded Nivedita: "Never forget to tell to yourself and to teach your children as the difference between the firefly and the blazing sun, between the infinite ocean and a little pond, between a mustard-seed and the mountain of Meru, such is the difference between the householder and the sannyasin."[40]

IV

Vivekananda's ambivalence with regard to natural male urges reached its tragic finale in his sojourn to Amarnath (Kashmir) in the company of his female devotees, including Nivedita. Apparently the Swami had received an offer from the Maharaja of Kashmir to open a center for Sanskrit studies in Kashmir and had decided to impress the prince with a few Western disciples—trophies, as it were, he had won in his recent exploits overseas. Probably he wished to spend the hot and sultry summer months in the coolness of the hills along with his female disciples, recent arrivals from temperate zones, who needed to be adjusted to the tropical climate of India slowly. It is also quite reasonable to suppose that he needed Nivedita's company in a secluded environment away from his cohorts and his other disciples. He had been trying to respond to her overtures but needed an appropriate environment to teach her the ultimate spiritual lesson, his own divinity. In the guarded language of Miss Reymond, "he wished . . . to devote a considerable amount of time to Nivedita. He knew her very well: her devotion to himself, her dependence upon him, and at the same time, her inherent capacity for self-abnegation. This journey to the mountain heights would be symbolically helpful to her."[41]

Vivekananda's party of pilgrims, consisting of four Western women, Nivedita, Josephine, Sara, and Mrs. Patterson, wife of the American Consul-General of Calcutta (who had been the Swami's hostess in America), and four monks, Turiyananda, Niranjanananda, Sadananda, and Swarupananda, set out for Naini Tal on 11 May 1898. From there they traveled to Almora, where the Swami's two English devotees (Captain John H. and Charlotte Sevier) had been staying, and finally they proceeded to Amarnath. In actuality this was no ascetic or austere pilgrimage but, from Naini Tal onward, a gala sight-seeing with a slow-moving caravan of coolies, supplies, ponies, tents and so forth. This was the Swami's way of inducting, or better still, indoctrinating, his Western devotees into the ways of the Indians. The entire pilgrimage also afforded him the opportunity to observe these women, especially Nivedita, at close quarters. During this journey (sometime in June 1898) Vivekananda the *kāminīkāñcanvirahī* ("deprived of/indifferent to woman and wealth") was converted to the efficacy of love. The monk who had earlier enjoined his audience to regard every woman as a mother, now conceded that "though the love of a mother is in some ways greater, yet the whole world takes the love of man and woman as the type. *No other has such tremendous idealising power.* The beloved actually becomes what he is imagined to be: This love transforms its object."[42] He not only talked approvingly and adoringly of marriage but even "broke out into [a] fierce invective against asceticism as savagery.'"[43]

During an open air meal at the Mogul Gardens, Achabal, Vivekananda announced his intention to take "his daughter" alone to a mountain cave in Kashmir—the temple of Amarnath, the phallus (*lingam*) representation of Shiva, the Lord of Immortality (*amarnāth*).[44] Before setting out for his destination, he told Nivedita that he had planned to impart some secret teachings to her there, but her account, which is the only firsthand source for the episode, suggests nothing by way of Swamiji's special training for his spiritual daughter. Reportedly on his way to the shrine, he talked only of Shiva, the supreme renouncer, told his beads regularly, kept his fasts, and interestingly enough, bathed often in the ice-cold water, in spite of his extremely fragile health, apparently in Nivedita's presence.[45] The Sister also provides a vivid and often imaginative description of the ailing monk's behavior inside the temple of Amarnath—his efforts to demonstrate his identity with Shiva by touching the base of the *lingam* in seminude condition despite the cold. On entering the sacred grotto, Nivedita writes on the basis of Vivekananda's personal deposition,

> to him, the heavens had opened. He had touched the feet of Shiva. He had to hold himself tight . . . lest he should swoon away. But so great was his physical exhaustion, that a doctor said afterwards that his heart ought to have stopped beating, and had undergone permanent enlargement instead.

The Swami explained to her that this near-death condition confirmed the "fact" that he was Lord Shiva Himself. "How strangely near fulfillment had been those words of his Master [Ramakrishna], 'when he [Vivekananda] realizes who and what he is he will give up this body.'"[46] Vivekananda also told her that "in these brief moments he had received from Shiva the gift of *Amar*—not to die, until he himself had willed it."[47]

Nivedita, however, never shared this spiritual experience of her guru. She was to be ritually dedicated to the ice *lingam* by the Swami. She had felt a "wild joy" in anticipation of this moment. She saw him prostrate before the deity, but then, he simply disappeared from the sanctum. "Lost, abandoned, she was choked by a cry of revolt."[48] "It is such a terrible pain," she was to write to her friend Nell Hammond a few days later, "to come face to face with something which is all *inwardness* to someone you worship, and for yourself to be able to get little farther than the external."[49] The Swami, who really had no definite design with respect to the alleged secret lessons for her, confessed in tearful eyes, albeit with his wonted equivocation: "Margot, I have not the power to give you what you want. You do not now understand. . . . You will understand better afterward."[50]

The actual contents of the Sister's diary, especially her conversation with Swamiji at Amarnath, are deleted from the authorized version of her *Notes of Some Wanderings with the Swami Vivekananda*, edited by Saradananda. The original unexpurgated manuscript of her diary contains the following conversation between the master and his disciple. "Oh Swami—it hurts me to speak to you like this," Nivedita told him apologetically but unequivocally. "I want to have a real understanding. Are we Guru & disciple, or are we just a man & woman? Because, if we are Guru & disciple, you ought to help me. But you never do. You speak to me as if [I] were not a woman, but you don't carry out the other side." She then continued: "Then we are not just an ordinary man & woman. You must remember that." "I can't do it, Margot. I'm not a Ramakrishna Paramahamsa" was his disarming confession.[51] Most probably she was simultaneously aware of the tantric ritual of *ṣoḍaśīpūjā* or virgin worship and of Ramakrishna's ritual dedication of his wife to the Great Mother. She had hoped to be dedicated similarly to Lord Shiva.[52] He was, after all, her *iṣṭa*, and didn't he encourage his women devotees to regard their *iṣṭa* as a *vallabha* (beloved) or a husband?[53] Her heightened excitement, which she records as her anticipation of "wild joy," resembling, uncannily, a moment of erotic arousal, was definitely caused by her belief that she was to be dedicated to her guru, who was the incarnation of the great God Himself. Hence her disappointment and rage reveal an utter sense of frustration. Vivekananda's confession could be interpreted as an admission of his inability to achieve the Paramahamsa's total indifference to women and thus his personal anxiety about his vulnerability.

All that talk about God's granting the monk the boon of *icchāmṛtyu* (voluntary death) was another way of protecting his incarnational identity even though his body was degenerating fast. More important he quickly transferred his loyalty from Shiva to Kali. His encounter with the divine phallus had left his body broken and soul bleeding. "He complained bitterly of the malady of thought which would consume a man, leaving him no time for sleep or rest, and would often become as insistent as a human voice." He now became a devotee of Kali, the Universal Mother. Nivedita found him "always singing the songs of Ramprasad, as if he would saturate his own mind with the conception of himself as a child."[54] It is important to bear in mind that Vivekananda had grown up on Ramakrishna's admonition that the safest recourse for a man in the company of a woman was to behave like a little child. Long ago the Master had told Naren: "The state of the son [*santānbhāv*] is the purest state."[55] Indeed he had slunk off to the shrine of the Goddess Kṣīr Bhavānī on 13 September and returned holding a bunch of marigold flowers. "I offered them to Mother," he told Nivedita and others. Then he said with a sigh and a smile: "No more 'Hari Om'! It is all 'Mother,' now! All my patriotism is gone. Everything is gone. Now it's only 'Mother, Mother!'" "I am only a little child," he added further.[56] At the same time, he befuddled his disciples with his enigmatic statements: "I may not tell you more now. . . . But spiritually, *spiritually*, I was not bound down." He said further that "there could be bliss in torture." He wrote in his poem on Kali: "Who dares misery love, dance in Destruction's dance, and hug the form of death."[57]

V

To make any sense of Vivekananda's puzzling behavior and enigmatic statements in conversations with his disciples in Kashmir, we need to recognize the inner struggle of the ailing young monk, his physical pain and suffering, and his mental anguish. Nivedita refers to his sense of utter disequilibrium when she writes that "he spoke of this time once, as 'a crisis in his life.'"[58] It seems that his crisis really was the outcome of his realization of the fragility and artificiality of his public image of a vital and militant monk. As has been noted earlier, he did not take to cowl out of any inner compulsion and that is why his cravings for a good life persisted throughout. Even after he had met his spiritual mentor Sri Ramakrishna accidentally at a party in a neighbor's home, young Narendranath remained, albeit passively, a potential candidate for marriage, in spite of the Parama-hamsa's vehement disapproval. That his marriage proposal initiated by the women of his family failed to materialize was not due to any unwillingness on his part but because of a breakdown in the negotiations between the families of the intended bride and groom.[59]

He was known to be an avid advocate of good health. On his return to Belur from the West, he advised all his cohorts to boil and filter their drinking water and showed them the postures of Del-sarte—a system of calisthenics for developing bodily grace and poise.[60] He told his disciple Chakravarti that "the physically weak are unfit for the realisation of the Self" and quoted his Master's admonition that "one with even a little physical defect is incapable of obtaining divine grace" to become a *siddha* [one who realized Brahman].[61] The Swami told Nivedita about his athletic exercises of childhood and of his sheer physical prowess in the face of imminent danger. He advised Brahmananda to pay special attention to health first and everything else next.[62] He offered Ramakrishnananda some advice on health and hygiene.[63] Even the modern admiring scholars sincerely believe that "literally, throughout his life, he [Vivekananda] regularly did physical exercise."[64] The Swami also earned a reputation for cleanliness. Achalananda reported how Swamiji kept a strong watch over cleanliness in the Math. He would see that every bed had been made and the sheets dusted and kept in the sun everyday, and he would become very upset with anyone with dirty fingernails or trying to wipe wet hands on the cloth he was wearing. Reportedly his instructions on cleanliness were derived from his Master's teachings.[65] He made his devotee Mrs. Hansbrough scrub the bathtub at his Turk Street residence in San Francisco over and over again and yet complained that it was not clean enough for him.[66] He also made fun of the Westerners who, according to him, "do not wash their mouth after meals" because, supposedly, "to rinse . . . mouth before others is disgraceful," and consequently their "teeth gradually decay." Further he described their habit of blowing nose in a pocket handkerchief sarcastically.[67]

Yet this hygienically sensitive *pahalwan* (athletic) Swami or Her-cules was a young man of fragile health with a markedly unhealthy lifestyle.[68] He had been a diabetic since his late teens—most probably a case of genetic complication.[69] He often suffered from dyspepsia or diarrhea,[70] from fever due to liver troubles, and from gallstone.[71] Sometimes he had to be prescribed opium as an antidote to stomach ailments.[72] He also suffered from lumbago, most probably due to insufficiently exercised muscles.[73] His personal lifestyle did not betray any concern for cleanliness or hygiene. For example he once startled his *gurubhāi* by drinking dirty river water by way of purifying himself before meeting his guru's widow, Saradamani.[74] Then he himself harbored a few filthy habits from his childhood days. As a boy of ten, he became addicted to snuff powder which he pushed through his nostrils by means of a pencil. Consequently he often expectorated nasal and oral phlegm everywhere. Even while asleep under a mosquito net, he would spit out or blow his nose on the net itself.[75] As an adult he continued his incorrigible spitting habit. He would have little hesitation in spitting on the freshly painted walls of Balaram Basu's living room. Ultimately Balaram had to provide his careless guest with a spitula and beg him to expectorate therein. In London as a guest of Henrietta Müller, the Swami regularly spat into the fireplace to the utter disgust of the old cleaning maid, who, however, put up with this filthy habit of "a great loving man," of whom she was quite fond.[76] While staying at the residence of of Lady Margesson, he needed a special pot in the toilet to spit into it while sitting on the commode.[77] Reportedly Vivekananda inherited the dirty habit from his family. In fact his great grandfather Rammohan was nicknamed "the spitting Datta." His father and also his brother suffered from the same habit.[78] Priyanath Singha described young Naren's study at his maternal grandfather's home as an unkempt small chamber with books strewn everywhere, broken bottles of medicine and a hookah and a clay tobacco bowl, ashes on the floor, and a stringed instrument (*tāmburā*), together with a drum underneath the dirty canvas bed. Singha concluded that Naren was "oblivious of the need to please himself."[79]

Vivekananda had his own diagnosis of his multiple illnesses. He had suggested that his diabetic condition was caused by his monastic lifestyle. At another time he wrote that his diabetes was caused by indigestion due to "excessive brain work" and that it was not a worrisome disease. "Do not give yourself up as lost because some symptoms of diabetes are noticeable in you," he wrote in an article in *Udbodhan*. "Those are nothing in our country and should not be taken seriously into account." He would even advice against consulting physicians. He wrote, "Most of them will harm you more than do any good; and so far as possible, never take medicines, which in most cases kill the patient sooner than the illness itself."[80] He complained against the medical practitioners:

Those wretched doctors have been my bane. They claim to be omniscient and able to do anything by their medicines. They promptly prescribe a pill for a mere upset stomach. The damn doctor does never say, "To hell with medicine, just walk a few miles."[81]

All these "insights" did not do the Swami any good. He was progressively ill and disabled because of his aggravated condition. His diabetes worsened during the summer of 1897.[82] He deplored his ill health in a letter to the wife of his disciple: "Due to my illness my life has become unreliable."[83] Contrary to his own counsel against taking medicines, he was once so overwhelmed by shoulder pain that he had to request Premananda to send him some medical drug.[84] His condition did not improve the next year, for he complained in 1898 of several attacks of fever and insomnia.[85] At Amarnath his deliberate demonstration of mystical experience, following an arduous trek to the shrine of Lord Shiva, cost him an enlargement of the heart. During the fall of 1898, he suffered from bouts of asthma. On 27 October he had his chest examined by a specialist, who advised him to take care of himself. The monks of Belur made every effort to prevent him from meditating, fearing that "the Great and Final Meditation might come upon him at any time, and that he might throw off the body like a worn-out garment."[86] He refused to be daunted by his disease. His letter to Mary Hale shows his fighting spirit: "You need not be alarmed with me as the disease will take two or three years at worst to carry me off. At best it may remain a harmless companion. I am content. . . . Death I have conquered long ago when I gave up life."[87] Even in the midst of growing complications, he wrote to Brahmananda from New York: "I don't have any sickness. I am again off on my peregrinations. I don't care. Don't fear . . . Hail, Mā the Warrior ["*Jai Mā, Jai Mā, Raṇaraṅginī*"]. . . . *Wa guru ki fateh* [Victory to Master]."[88] But he was becoming aware of the increasing infirmity of his body and his diminishing willpower. "My health and spirit are totally exhausted," the dying patient wrote to Ramakrishnananda around 1900. "I find it impossible even to hold conversations with people. . . . I am telling you again—I am almost dead and absolutely unwilling to meet anyone."[89] In the end his diabetes degenerated into dropsy. M. Rolland writes that "his feet swelled and certain parts of his body became keenly hypersensitive. He hardly slept at all."[90] He died on 4 July 1902, probably of a cerebral hemorrhage. Rolland has observed shrewdly: "This Hercules had death always sitting by his side."[91]

VI

Vivekananda's poor health was partly a genetic endowment and partly, no doubt, the result of his personal habits and lifestyle. He probably had a heart attack in England sometime in 1896 in the presence of John Pierce Fox and his younger brother Mahendranath. He reportedly told Fox that he felt his heart was "failing," adding, "My father died of this ailment . . . it is a family disease."[92] He alluded to his diabetic attack in Madras in a letter to Mary Hale: "Well, it was in Southern India . . . that an old hereditary disease made its appearance. The tendency was always there, and excess of mental work made it 'express' itself."[93] Fond of good food from the early childhood, he ate meat and milk products, especially ice cream, excessively, and was a chain smoker. His personal unhealthy lifestyle, coupled with his overbearing attitude, led to the disaffection of a few of his erstwhile admirers such as Ashton Jonson, Edward Sturdy, and Henrietta Müller. Miss Jonson, who had once been enthusiastic over Vivekananda's sermons, was shocked to see a yogi and a saint suffering from severe physical ailment, and when she inquired of him how he had contracted his diseases, her curiosity was readily interpreted by him and his friends as condemnation of human illness by a Christian Scientist. Jonson wrote to Mrs. Bull:

> I no more condemn or criticise him than I do a child who falls down and hurts itself. If am asked to recognise that Swami is manifesting the highest Divine consciousness in this disease . . . I do not feel that the highest consciousness can ever demand a diseased body in which to manifest. Of course I do not pretend to worship Swami's feet as Miss Noble does.[94]

Sturdy, who had admired Vivekananda and in fact brought him to England, was disillusioned with him after he had seen "very little of Sannyasa" and much "humbug and sham" on the Swami's part and on that of the monks of the Ramakrishna Order visiting England. In particular Sturdy was appalled by Vivekananda's addiction to tobacco and refused to recognize him as "a God walking the earth."[95] Similarly Miss Müller, a genuine patron of the Ramakrishna Order and the Swami's hostess in London, "completely severed her connection with Swami Vivekananda's movement to spread Hinduism and. . .returned to her Christian faith" after having followed him to India and contributed financially to his work.[96] She had noticed Swamiji's involvement in his family affairs, found the Hindu phallic worship abominable, and above all did not quite like the idea of a spiritual personality taking ill, and detested his intimacy with Nivedita.[97] Vivekananda, on his part, remained absolutely impervious to any criticism of his habits. As has been noted in chapter 4, he regarded his critics as fanatics.[98]

VII

Vivekananda's personal crisis, caused by his failing health and diminishing credibility, was further compounded by his sudden awareness of his feelings toward his closest female disciple. The outcome of this psychosomatic problem was his initial attempt to project himself as a troubled titan or a suffering hero, using the Jesus motif, and then his descent into oblivion. As he wrote to Nivedita: "Suffering is the lot of the world's best and bravest. . . . In my sane moments I rejoice for my sufferings. Someone must suffer here—I am glad it is I, amongst others of nature's sacrifices."[99] Projecting the image of a suffering Prometheus, he wrote to her again: "We are all sacrifices. . . . The worship is going on. . . . Those that are willing, escape a lot of pain. . . . I am determined to be a willing one."[100] He wrote to her at another time: "the clouds may gather over me, but I am the same infinite blue. . . . These tin-pot bodies and foolish dreams of happiness and misery—what are they? My dreams are breaking."[101] A third letter to the Sister has his dreams as its subject: "Dreams, oh dreams! Dream on! Dream, the magic of dream, is the cause of this life, it is also the remedy. Dream, dream, only dream! Kill dream by dream!"[102] In yet another missive from the Swami, this tragic hero theme with suggestive but deliberately equivocal allusions to "sacrifices," "willing one," "foolish dreams of happiness and misery," and "dreams . . . breaking" continued with an explosive denial of his physical and emotional predicament:

> Black and thick are the folds of sinister fate. But I am the master. I raise my hand, and lo, they vanish! All this is nonsense and fear. I am the Fear of fear, the Terror of terror. I am the fearless, secondless One, I am the Ruler of destiny, the Wiper-out of fact.[103]

Vivekananda had already made it clear to others that he was a fighter. "I have always behaved like a hero," he wrote to Brahmananda. "I want action as fast as electricity and as firm as lightning."[104] He told Nivedita how the late Paramahamsa once put his hands round his shoulders and said: "This is a *hero*."[105] He related to Turiyananda the fascinating account of how he lectured to a band of wild American cowboys who were shooting indiscriminately at and around him. He ultimately forced them to acknowledge: "Here is our hero."[106]

Vivekananda's projection of the image of an ailing warrior was a sublimated form of the Vedantic lion courting the Celtic lioness. His undeniable fascination for her made him so possessive of the woman that he did not take kindly to her admiration for and association with the Scottish intellectual Patrick Geddes. By 1899 she had become quite skeptical about her Indian mission. She had not been helped by her guru, who really had no concrete plans for her except that he wished to keep her near about him for some reason. He told her: "Do not work yourself out. It is no use; always remember. . . . Duty . . . is necessary for a time as a discipline; beyond that, it is a morbid dream."[107] He even advised her to go back to England because "there was no money here—and no hope of any" for her desperate but feeble attempt to run her school for girls.[108] Even though she persisted in her project for some more time, she eventually conceded defeat and told her guru: "I knew my school was a waste of time."[109] In spite of his vague encouragement, "Things shall look up for us, never mind,"[110] things had not been looking up for Nivedita. She even questioned her decision to affiliate with Indian work and wrote to Miss MacLeod: "My own life,—where was it? Lost—thrown away like a cast-off garment that I may kneel at the feet of this man. Would it prove a mistake; an illusion; or was it a triumph of choice."[111]

Vivekananda advised Nivedita to abandon her original project of a girls' school and instead accompany him to Europe, apparently to raise funds for a home for widows and girls. Since December 1898 he had been thinking of returning to the West for the treatment of his deteriorating health. On 11 April 1899, he wrote to Christine Greenstidel about his condition and intention:

> My complaint, I do not know what. Some say asthma, others nervous weakness of the heart brought on by overstrain. Anyhow, last two months the terrible fits of suffocation, which used to remain for days, have not come. Yet unlike other asthmatic people I feel a little weakness in the heart always. Whatever it be, dyspepsia certainly has a great deal to do with it, I am sure. . . . A sea voyage will be good indeed. . . . Anyhow, this summer I am sure to be in England.[112]

In spite of the Swami's good time with his disciple during the entire "heavenly voyage,"[113] this was a period of frustration for the latter, causing a sense of utter void in her. Thus when she met the famous sociologist Patrick Geddes in March 1900 at the home of Francis Leggett in New York, she found him "a light—beautiful and lovable" and "like one starving, she sat down with avidity to the intellectual feast Professor Geddes spread before her."[114] She even followed Geddes to Paris where she was to act as his research assistant and secretary—a job she soon found too difficult to perform.[115] Meanwhile her drifting away to Geddes had been reciprocated by Vivekananda's hinting about his "really understanding what non-attachment means" and his hope "very soon to be perfectly non-attached,"[116] followed by his coolness toward her and his visible interest in other women of Paris, where he had been invited to represent Hinduism and Vedanta in the Paris Exposition Universelle. Turiyananda reports how Swamiji, while looking admiringly at a beautiful woman, saw the face of a "grimacing monkey."[117] He also met the attractive but eccentric Emma Calvé and went out of his way to cultivate her friendship, somewhat flirtatiously, to the utter chagrin of Nivedita. He watched Emma perform Carmen at the Opèra Comique and after the performance met her backstage to tell her that Carmen was a true woman who did not lie but was "of the superb race of women" who wished "to die of . . . desire." He also made her sing the French national anthem, the *Marseillaise,* the next day when she visited the Leggett residence. Needless to mention "the Swami's whole attitude upset Nivedita completely."[118]

In his letter to Nivedita, the Swami tacitly acknowledged his feelings while protesting: "I never had any jealousy about what friends you made. You are free, have your own choice, your own work."[119] She of course knew that she had irritated her master and wrote to Josephine: "I was not worthy or ready to accept the personal in Him. . . . Swami has cut me off by a well-deserved stroke."[120] She blamed herself for having upset him by her letter in which she "complained, she blamed, and she sought for guidance and solicitude."[121] "I wish I had not *struck* back at Swami in writing my last letter to him," she confessed. However as she continues, her letter was written to find an answer to her agonizing question: "But why did you do it *that way,* Swami?"[122] His response to her anguish and anger caused by his indifference and by her disappointment with Geddes had already been made and it was cruel and clear. He had told her that he was "free—BORN free"[123] and advised her in Brittany (where he had gone in September 1900 at Sara Bull's retreat) to live in solitude because she dared to differentiate evil from good. Later Nivedita would refer to her experience as "that anguish in Brittany."[124] When she finally took leave of her guru and departed for England, he gave her his generous benediction which really sounds much like a release from his spiritual care: "Go forth into the world, and there, if I made you, be destroyed! If Mother made you, live!"[125] One of Vivekananda's devotees has claimed that "it was only in order to impress upon Nivedita the significance of her new and deeper life that Swami Vivekananda engaged himself into a conflict with Nivedita. That goal was directed towards protecting Nivedita from herself, from the blindness of her half-views, and from the partiality of her conception of life."[126]

Vivekananda similarly reacted against Nivedita's apparent infatu-

ation with the Japanese aesthete and art critic Tenshin Okakura (Kakuzō) (1862–1913), who came to Calcutta in January 1902. The
Swami at first hailed the oriental as his long lost brother and the latter
reciprocated with characteristic courtesy by claiming Vivekananda for
the East.[127] Reportedly Okakura came from Japan to invite Swamiji—
about whom he had been told by Josephine in Japan sometime in
spring 1901—to his country, though the invitation could not be hon-
ored because of Vivekananda's declining health. However, Nivedita's
romantic adventurous spirit was rekindled by Okakura's advent in
her life since their first meeting in early March 1902, and she began
spearheading a "revolutionary" group (somewhat reminiscent of the
romantic Young Italy of Giuseppe Mazzini) with the Japanese. She
grew quite fond of the artist whom she often referred to by various
adoring nicknames such as "Nigu," "Chieftain" (cf. "King" for Vivekananda), "Banner Chief," or "Genghis," in her letters to Josephine.
She shocked MacLeod by writing to her how she had entered Okakura's bedroom in the middle of the night to nurse the ailing Nigu.
Josephine even warned her about her "physical awakening."[128]

Okakura had had a failed romance back home before leaving for
India and, reportedly, he propositioned Nivedita, though to no success.[129] She informed Josephine how one day lying ill at her residence
Okakura had felt her company and conversation had "opened out
whole fields of love" to him which he had not hitherto known. Although she wrote that she had "not the faintest idea of what he
meant," she "recognised the hunger out of which such words were
spoken."[130] She was aware that she "had been a temptation" to the
man.[131] She must have had some occasional confrontation with her
admirer. "Nigu and I had a sad misunderstanding," she had written
to Josephine on 28 July 1902, "and I fear we may not even meet
again. The worst of it is I do not know how to be angry in his case,
and can only feel the great blank made by the loss of his friendship—
and oh so sorry if there is any pain for him!"[132]

Nivedita's temporary diversion must have been occasioned by her
need for one. Increasing awareness of the impending death of her
beloved guru who had caught her fancy, and also somewhat tired of
the constant temper tantrums and mood swings of the terminally ill
monk, she might have sought relief in the company of a man, an
intellectual, who was paying her adoring attention. The Swami had
noticed his "daughter's" interest in the Japanese visitor and, as she
recalled after his death, he had told her: "Well, Margot, I see. . . .
You have had your Brahmo conviction, and your Tagore conviction,
and now you have these convictions [meaning Okakura and revolutionary organizations]. And they will pass, as others did."[133] By Ta-

gore conviction, he obviously alluded to her enthusiasm for the Brahmos, including Devendranath Tagore, in 1899. He also did not quite appreciate her intimacy with Dr. Jagadish Chandra Bose, even though she played mother to the brilliant young scientist. The Swami was so upset with the Sister's fondness for Bose that while discussing about him "he broke out in one of his strong moods" and exploded into a rage against marriage, householder's life and the like and reportedly chanted the merits of renunciation—"give up, give up, give up."[134]

Vivekananda's undeniable fascination for Nivedita, conflicting as it did with his image of a world renouncer, resulted first in his identification with Shiva and then with Kali. The hapless hero turned into a helpless child. The helpless child was none other than the helpless monk whose ascetic vows seemed to have emasculated the male within. The process of this transformation was facilitated and hastened by his growing physical infirmity during the advanced stage of his illness. No doubt he once declared: "No rest for me! I shall die in harness! I love action! Life is a battle, and one must always be in action."[135] One notices flashes of put-on self-control and self-confidence even amidst his multiple miseries. Thus his letter to Sara Bull showed the militant and activist monk at his rhetorical best: "If the Lord has made me His hack to work and die on the streets, let Him have it. Yes, let the world come, the hell come, the gods come, let Mother come, I fight and do not give in."[136] But ever since his return from Amarnath, he had become quiescent. His disciple Chakravarti "found him sitting cross-legged, facing the East, apparently in total abstraction" and was told by his guru that Shiva had entered his brain since his *darśan* of Amarnath. Brahmananda remarked that "since returning from Kashmir, Swamiji does not speak to anybody; he sits in one spot rapt in thought." The Swami was acutely aware of his approaching end. "He spoke of the divine Voice that he heard at the temple of Ksir-Bhavani."[137] The fighter was getting weaker and increasingly exhausted. He wrote to Brahmananda: "No more lectures and stuff [*lecture-phecture*]. Peace!"[138] He wrote to Mary Hale: "As for me, I am tired . . . of eternal tramping; that is why I want to go back home and be quiet. I do not want to work any more."[139]

VIII

Both the Swami and the Sister were tormented by the repressed emotions that had erupted spontaneously between them, which they could neither overcome nor transcend despite the vehemence of their

monastic vows. Hence Vivekananda's various innuendos and metaphors give vent to his inner feelings. At the same time, his lack of
adult male experience with women rendered his efforts clumsy and
naive. Nevertheless he came close to confessing to his inner turmoil
one day at the Ridgely Manor in the fall of 1899. In a conversation
with Nivedita at the Manor, the ailing and disturbed monk romanti-
cized his terminal illness and insinuated at his apostasy by declaring:
"This body is going anyway. I shall go with hard tapasya—I will say
10,000 OMs a day—and with fasting. Alone, alone by the Ganges—
in the Himalayas—saying Hara Hara, the Freed One, the Freed One
. . . I shall take the initiation of sannyasa once again . . . and I will
never come back to anyone again." He then confessed with "that lost
look" that he could no longer achieve concentration ("he had lost his
power of meditation") and finally said with "a smile—and a sigh": "I
have lost all—lost all for you Mlechhas!"[140]

True to her feelings, Nivedita had already expressed her sentiments
toward the Swami frankly and sincerely, and, as noted above, had in
fact proposed to him—an overture he, apparently unhappily, declined
by declaring his celibate status as a monk. However even though she
became quickly disenchanted with her Indian mission and somewhat
angered at the Swami's antics at Amarnath, her love for him remained
steadfast, as can be noted in one of her letters:

> I came to India with little or no dependence on the personal side of the
> Swami. In that awful time at Almora, when I thought he had put me out
> of his life contemptuously, it still made no difference to the essentials.
> Now he is the whole thing, for good or for evil; instead of growing less,
> I have grown infinitely more personal in my love. I am not sure but his
> least whim is worth the whole, and now when one turns to him in thought
> the heart grows free. Blessed be God for making it possible to love like
> this![141]

Margaret was an impulsive woman who had committed herself to the
cause of her guru, and she determined to stick to her decision even
after her "illusion" had been "broken into fragments" on the cold
hard rocks of Amarnath.[142]

Yet at the same time it ought to be recognized that Nivedita never
really intended to be a nun and a celibate.[143] It seems that she "took
the vows of lifelong celibacy, obedience, and poverty" under duress
when she was initiated by the Swami as a *naiṣṭhika brahmacāriṇī* on
25 March 1899. This very Christian sounding triple vows of chastity,
celibacy, and poverty was an ad hoc ritual, most probably contrived
by Vivekananda for a Catholic initiate. She was not made a nun or a
sannyāsinī—something that bothered her, not because she loved being

a nun but because, most probably, she took her status of *brahmacārinī* for one meant for a second-class disciple of the Swami.[144] She would have loved to lead a normal life of a householder with a husband of her choice. She was quite vocal about her conception of womanhood, wifehood, marriage, and love in a letter to Josephine written a couple of years after Vivekananda's death:

> We have rated nunhood so high that wifehood has seemed low beside it. But more and more I have come to feel that this untrue. In the one vow as in the other, there is daily faithfulness of word, thought and deed required of us—and the fulfillment cannot be too austere. . . . I feel that . . . Swamiji was a *man,* could see women only from the outside. All that He taught us was true, of course, but it was not the whole truth. I almost venture to say that He lived in many things more truly than He spoke. . . . He lived as if women were minds, *not* bodies. . . . And my conclusion is that . . . marriage is a *puja*—a ritual—a temple—a worship . . . that widowhood is nunhood . . . And I am *sure* that the nun is the true wife. . . . I am sure too that there is no special thing called wife or a wife's love. Love is one, undifferentiated, when it is true.[145]

She also told Josephine in no uncertain terms: "The union of the sexes is not impure. . . . We don't *want* the union etc.—not because it is impure—but because it is a new load to carry."[146] It is on record that she formally and finally severed her connection with the Ramakrishna Order when she chose to participate in the Indian nationalist movement—something that clashed with the stated policy of the Ramakrishna Mission.[147]

Perhaps the tormented monk failed in the end to cope with his frustration and anger resulting from the repression of his human emotion on the one hand and with the guilt caused by his violated monkish conscience on the other. The male within, who had long remained suppressed, was awakened, unfortunately, at a time when the body was decaying hopelessly. The carefully cultivated and widely publicized *lokattara tyāgī* (ultramundane renouncer) and *vīra sannyāsī* ("heroic ascetic") had been able neither to celebrate the spontaneous outburst of eros nor to transcend it. He remained checkmated, like an ensnared lion! The Swami's private inner universe and his outer world were in disarray. Broken in body and spirit, he thus sank into spiritual infantilism—state of a *puer aeternas*—just like his mentor Ramakrishna and into nihilism, so violently expressed in some of his letters to Nivedita. The Sister was acutely aware of her guru's destructive disposition that resulted from an anticipation of the untimely end of a powerful life of multiple possibilities. She confessed to Josephine just a couple of months before Vivekananda's death: "He is so ill that *my* attitude towards Him must be that of soothing by any concession at any time, without troubling about sincerity or consistency . . ."148

She also was being gradually aware of her failing femininity—something like a psychic castration. Since her sojourn to Amarnath, and especially during her visit to the West (1899–1901), Nivedita had undergone a transformative experience. She had decided on her future course of action in India. "I believe now that I have something to do for grown-up India and for Indian men," she had written to Josephine from Norway.149 More important, she had come to a definite understanding of her relationship—emotional and spiritual—with the Swami. She not only came to acknowledge openly and unequivocally that she was "his daughter," she also appeared to have modified her earlier feminine desires and disposition.150 She wrote to Josephine admitting her "womanism" as the "protest of . . . [her] individuality against becoming impersonal"151—something she now resolved to overcome. One cannot fail to notice the transformation of the caring, compassionate, sentimental, and quintessentially feminine Margaret into a hardened, detached, and impersonal, almost masculine, *sann-yāsinī* and social and political activist in her confession to Josephine a few years later. As she wrote to her dear friend Yum Yum: "Do you know I am growing more and more sure that I am a man in disguise. I don't seem to be a woman at all! What do you think?"152 Vivekananda, too, desperately searched for an explanation that would give due recognition to—if not resolve the conflict between—two emotions, two personalities, as it were. Indeed a realization of a multiplicity of selves within a single personality would not only be honest but would be the supreme testimony to the realization of the Vedantic *Weltganze*. One cannot fail to notice his admission in this regard concealed under his usual enigmatic rhetoric in a letter to Mary Hale: "I was Jesus and I was Judas Iscariot; both my play, my fun. . . . Did you ever enjoy evil! . . . I enjoy the good and I enjoy the evil. . . . Now I am going to be truly Vivekananda."153

11

Vivekananda's Conquest of the West

I

WHEN Vivekananda arrived in Chicago, he had little idea of what his objectives were in the United States other than participating in the World's Parliament of Religions, even though he had told his brother monks and disciples back home that he was going to seek financial and technical help from the Americans for his developmental work in India. In fact as he wrote to his patron Ajit Singh, from Japan en route to the States, if he had the cash sent by the Raja through bank transfer with him he "would have bought some Japanese artwork and returned home." "I would have given up my plan on visiting the States," he admitted.[1] However he quickly discovered his potential. Following the Parliament (sometime in the early winter of 1893), he enlisted himself with the Slayton Lyceum Bureau of Chicago with a view to earning money from his public lectures for his patriotic projects.[2] This enterprise prompted him to make himself provocative, and he did so with a panache—by directing his animus against the missionaries, calling them murderers, doctors of drunkenness, and harbingers of disease, until his enthusiasm ran into troubled waters in Detroit during the winter of 1894.[3]

Bishop Ninde of Detroit was greatly shocked and angered by the Swami's speech on 14 February 1894, which scandalized his audience with an unqualified assertion of the greatness of the Hindus and the meanness of the Christians. According to the *Detroit Journal* (16 February 1894),

the bishop had ceased to take any stock in the Hindoo, because of his propensity for attacking the Christian religion, as well as for what he considered his untruthfulness as displayed in his lecture on Wednesday evening. The bishop had traveled in India extensively himself, and in an interview with the Journal after the lecture said the monk had evidently been talking for the purpose of creating an impression.[4]

The Swami's behavior surprised even his devotee and biographer, Marie Burke, who writes: "The question sometimes arises how Swamiji, who saw divinity everywhere and continuously, could at the same time see the evil and anguish of the world and give himself fully to its removal." She cites the authority of a monk of the Ramakrishna Order, the late Swami Ashokananda, whose conceited explanation of Vivekananda's profession of universal love and divinity in humanity and his meanness is worth quoting here:

> There is a logical contradiction here. . . . But what a blessed contradiction! . . . You see, when man transcends his relative being and yet still lives in his body on this plane, there comes an extraordinary state. That is the state in which one can cast one's mind into any mood one likes. And it will be a total mood or total mode. . . . You find such contradictions in all great lives.[5]

Vivekananda comes through his writings and preachings as a highly complex individual who was capable of demonstrating at once intellectual strength, stubbornness, superstition, naiveté, and nativist chauvinism. He could be very selfish, even mean, to his best well wishers and friends for sheer personal reasons and at the same time extraordinarily compassionate for the unknown and unseen poor humanity of the world. His spiritual mentor, Ramakrishna, who had loved young Naren dearly and declared that he was one of the seven magis (*saptarṣi*) brought down from the high heavens by the Paramahamsa himself in the guise of a divine child,[6] once remarked shrewdly: "People will never understand him fully."[7]

II

Vivekananda alienated his well-wisher and guide in Vedic studies, Pramadadas Mitra of Benares, because the latter considered the Swami's belief in Ramakrishna's *avatārahood* a "perversion," and Vivekananda found Mitra's intimacy with the "white-skinned missionaries of the Hindu religion . . . repelling."[8] Even Protap Mozoomdar, whose kindness and initiative as a member of the selection committee for Asian speakers at the World's Parliament of Religions led to the acceptance of Vivekananda's unsponsored late personal application for participation, shockingly experienced Swamiji's wrath and was forced to comment: "Of course, we must not grudge this man a little temporary fame, but his lies will find him out."[9]

The Swami's admirer and sponsor in England, Edward Sturdy,

once respected the young "exponent of Vedanta" and believed that
his teachings, "if persevered with and continued, will very largely
modify the thought of the Western world, and help to turn its mind
from the tremendous love of luxury and wealth, in which it has forgotten itself."[10] As we have noted above, even he and two other
erstwhile Vivekananda admirers, Henrietta Müller and Ashton Jonson, were disillusioned with the Swami. Even though the latter
thought of Miss Müller as a woman of "violent temper," "overbearing
conduct," and "awfully vacillating mind,"[11] and Dr. Lewis Janes pronounced her to be "mentally unbalanced,"[12] some of Henrietta's accu-
sations appear to be justifiable, though one must not ignore her
especial ire over Nivedita's closeness to the Swami. Likewise Jonson's
concern, debunked as a Christian Scientist's superstition, was genuine enough.

Even Vivekananda's favorite "sister" Mary Hale once expressed her
shock and disgust at his letter containing his scathing remarks at his
critics. Mary wrote back in February 1895:

> I confess dear Brother, to a feeling of terrible disappointment—a year
> ago such a letter from your pen would have been an utter impossibil-
> ity. . . . Where is the great & glorious soul that came to the Parliament
> of Religions, so full of love of God, that his face shone with Divine light,
> whose words were fire, whose very presence created an atmosphere of
> harmony & purity, thereby drawing all souls to himself? It is our turn to
> cry "My!!!"

She later submitted to the Swami's angry rhetorical rejoinder and
begged "forgiveness o'er and o'er."[13]

Vivekananda also succeeded in alienating his great benefactor, the
New York artist Elizabeth Dutcher, who had graciously invited him
to stay and preach at her retreat in Thousand Island Park and even
added a three-storied new wing to her cottage for his accommoda-
tion. A sincere Methodist, Dutcher "often felt distressed by the
Swami's revolutionary ideas. All her ideas, her values of life, her con-
cepts of religion, were it seemed to her, being destroyed. Sometimes
she did not appear for two or three days." The ungrateful and unfeel-
ing guest, however, gave his own brand of explanation for his hostess'
behavior. "Don't you see?" Vivekananda told his devotees at Thousand Island, "this is not an ordinary illusion. It is the reaction of the
body against the chaos that is going on in her mind. She cannot
bear it."[14]

The flamboyant young French poet Jules Bois, who had admired
"the messenger of the old Barattha [Bharat], with his dark nimbus of
hair, his imposing carriage" sitting "like a Buddha of the Himalayas

transported to a suburb on the Seine," later shed much of his romantic notion of Vivekananda and Vedanta. "To Vivekananda I owe much in human enlightenment," Bois noted in 1927 with an unmistakable touch of Gallic irony. "To him I am indebted . . . for a deeper adoration of the Christian faith."[15]

In spite of his best efforts, Vivekananda failed to raise the requisite funds for his Indian developmental project. Deeply conscious of his failure in this regard and blaming the Indians for not telling the Americans that the Swami was "a real Sannyasin and no cheat,"[16] he took a vacation in the summer of 1894 and thought of a new strategy. He did some creative thinking, which began to take concrete shape from the fall of 1894. Even so as late as 21 September 1894, he felt quite discouraged about his prospects in the United States. "I hope to return soon to India," he wrote to Alasinga on that day. "I have had enough of this country."[17] From June 1895 through 1896, he thought of writing a book on Vedanta. In his letter of 6 May 1896, he informed Alasinga of his "discovery":

> All of religion is contained in the Vedanta, that is, in the three stages of the Vedanta philosophy, the Dvaita [Dualism], Vishishtadvaita [Qualified Monism], and Advaita [Nondualism] . . . the three stages of spiritual growth in man. . . . The first stage, i.e., Dvaita, applied to the ideas of the ethnic groups of Europe, is Christianity; as applied to the Semitic groups, Mohammedanism. The Advaita, as applied in its Yoga-perception form, is Buddhism etc. . . . I wish to write a book on this subject.[18]

In an earlier letter to his Madrasi disciple, the Swami had counseled: "Do not for a moment think the 'Yankees' are practical in religion. In that the Hindu is practical."[19]

III

The result of the Swami's intellectual endeavor was his change of mind in respect to returning home immediately and the beginning of a new mission in the West. According to Burke, Vivekananda "was acting in accordance with the divine will."[20] As early as 30 December 1894, he had declared in an interview at the Brooklyn Ethical Society: "I have a message to the West as Buddha had a message to the East."[21] A few days later, he wrote to Sir Subrahmanya Iyer: "at present I find that I have a mission in this country also."[22] He articulated the nature of his message a year later:

The dry, abstract Advaita must become living—poetic—in everyday life; out of hopelessly intricate mythology must come concrete moral forms; and out of bewildering Yogi–ism must come the most scientific and practical psychology—and all this must be put in a form so that a child may grasp it. That is my life's work.[23]

His fully formulated message was delivered first in London in four lectures on Practical Vedanta during 10–18 November 1896.[24] He was convinced that he had realized his world mission and declared in Madras after his triumphal return from the West: "That I went to America and England was simply for propagating these ideas. I did not care at all for the Parliament of Religions or anything else; it was simply an opportunity; for it was really those ideas of mine that took me all over the world."[25] This explanation of his reasons for visiting the West ran counter to an earlier one he had proffered to his monastic brethren. Swami Brahmananda recalled Vivekananda's refusal to preach religion until he had succeeded "in removing the poverty and misery of the country" and his decision "to go to the land of Croesus [meaning, the rich Western countries], to . . . find some way out."[26]

Vivekananda's grand vision of Hindu evangelism in the world was predicated on the premise that "the principles of the Vedanta not only should be preached everywhere in India, but also outside." As he wrote further, "our thought must enter into the make-up of the minds of every nation, not through writings, but through persons."[27] This global Vedantization required him "to preach unto mankind their divinity, and how to make it manifest in every movement of life."[28] And in various sermons delivered in the United States and England, he harped on the latent divinity in humanity. He declared that though he was teaching the eternal verities of the Hindu religion, he indeed was the pioneer teacher in the world: "I was born for this, and it was left for me to do!" roared the Vedanta lion of India.[29] It was an audacious challenge from a colonial native to the metropolitan West—a powerful response to the West's *mission civilisatrice* for the non-European world—a dramatic reversal of the concept of "white man's burden" into that of a "brown man's burden." The scientifically progressive and materially prosperous West had yet to learn the secrets of authentic spirituality from the colonized Orient.[30]

It is a fact that Vivekananda said nothing new. Over a generation before Narendranath's birth, Henry Thomas Colebrook, professor of Sanskrit at Fort William College, had argued that "the Vedas or rather the Vedanta, constituted the authentic tradition of India." Later Brahmananda Keshabchandra Sen suggested that India should learn practical knowledge from Europe and in exchange should teach the world religious wisdom. Keshab wrote in his "Religion of Love" (1860) that the religion of the Brahmo Samaj "is not the religion of any particular community, epoch or country: it is *universal religion;* it is a Human Catholic Religion.'"[31] It is Sen's concept of universal religion that the Swami had imbibed in his early youth as a regular visitor to the Brahmo Samaj and now appropriated and preached in Chicago.

In an interview with the representative of the *Prabuddha Bharata* in September 1898, Vivekananda described his movement of uniting the orthodox and the reforming sects of the Hindus of India in a common love for the Vedas.[32] This emphasis on the Vedas was not original with him. Almost a generation ago, Rajnarain Basu had extolled the *Śruti* with such eloquence and clarity that the Sanatana Dharmaraksani Sabha (Association for the Preservation of Traditional Religion) of Calcutta bestowed on him the honorific title *Hindukula-śiromaṇi* (Chief of the Tribe of Hindus). Even the *London Times* published Basu's lecture *Hindudharmer Śreṣṭhattva* ("Superiority of the Hindu Religion") with favorable comments.[33] However the editorial of the *Indian Mirror* had observed, as early as 21 May 1894 (when the Swami was preaching and lecturing in the States), that "if Hinduism is a mere doctrine and if that doctrine is to be found only in the Vedas or that section of it known as the Upanisads, what is there to distinguish it from Brahmoism?"[34] Vivekananda drew on all these ideas of his forbears, which he now claimed as his own.[35] Even his scathing self-criticism that the Bengalis "are the most worthless and superstitious and the most cowardly and lustful of all Hindus,"[36] which has received respectful accolade from conscientious Bengalis as an epitome of objective assessment of his racial character by a true son of the soil, echoed the language and tone of such English critics as Richard Orme (1770s), Bishop Reginald Heber (1820s), and, above all, Thomas Babington Macaulay (1830s).[37]

IV

The Swami's originality as a preacher lay in his Vedantic exegesis and messages.[38] Unfortunately his success as a Vedantist in the West was owed to his distortion of the traditional Advaita system as expounded by Shankaracharya. Ironically, however, he was universally regarded as an upholder of this traditional Advaita, indeed an incarnation of the great Shankara himself, though, in fact, he effected a radical departure from the former's tradition by underscoring the efficacy of personal experience (*anubhava*) and denying the validity of the scripture (*Śruti,* that is, the Vedas) as the source of *Brah-*

majñāna or *Brahmavidyā* (knowledge of Brahman).[39] For Shankara, *Brahmavidyā* as the *parā-vidyā* or transcendental knowledge cannot be attained without the aid of the Vedic revelation which, though a lower knowledge or the *aparā-vidyā,* yet remains the sole *śavda-pramāna* (valid knowledge composed of *śavda* or words) for Brahman.

The Swami seems to share Shankara's view that the primary limitation of inferential reasoning is its reliance on perception, that dry reason or *śuska-tarka* is not adequate to the discovery of spiritual reality, which is known through direct experience or *anubhava.* However as Professor Pande has argued, "Shankara's Vedanta . . . was critical of *shuska-tarka* but favoured *shrutyanugrihita-tarka*" (reasoning founded on the *Śruti* or the Vedas).[40] Even though he places *Śruti* within nesceicne or *avidyā,* it still is the prime means to attain *parā-vidyā.* It is the Vedic revelations that provide access to the true nature of the self—*Ātman-Brahman*—which is identified with *moksa* or liberation.[41] Vivekananda, on the other hand, appears to debunk reason altogether and equate *moksa* with the superconscious state of mind (*samādhi*) or, as he explains, with direct perception or concentration or meditation (*pratyaksa*). For him religion or spirituality proper belongs to the realm of the superconscious.

Vivekananda's emphasis on the superconscious state, that is, *nirvikalpa samādhi,* had no *imprimatur* from the Upanishads, the primary source of the Vedanta. In the *Chāndogya* and *Vrhadāranyaka* Upanishads, the word *samāhita* occurs, but it connotes a "collected" state of the mind. *Samādhi,* as Dr. Comans has demonstrated, forms "a part of yogic practice which has entered into the later Upanisadic literature."[42] Even Shankara, who makes a "very sparing use of the word *samādhi,* . . . does not consider the attainment of *samādhi* to be a sufficient cause to eradicate false knowledge [*mithyājñāna*], and . . . cannot therefore be the cause of liberation."[43] Agehananda Bharati regarded Vivekananda as an exemplar of "inane eclecticism."[44] Mircea Eliade "did not feel attracted to the suave, moralizing writings of Vivekananda . . . [and] considered his works of propaganda and 'popularization' to be hybrid and non-Indian."[45]

Vivekananda's distortion of Shankara can be explained. He wanted to make a Vedantist out of his guru, Sri Ramakrishna, who was neither well versed in the Vedas[46] nor converted by his mentor Totapuri into a Vedantist. The Master had claimed that the pinnacle of his Vedantic training was reached with his *nirvikalpa samādhi* which even astounded the *nyaṅgtā* Vedantist from the Punjab.[47] Also Ramakrishna believed in direct experience of the Divine through *bhakti.*[48] The Swami, once skeptical and contemptuous of *samādhi,* realized the need to explain it as a vehicle for *Brahmajñāna* (knowledge of

Brahman), if Ramakrishna was to be proclaimed the world's greatest
Vedantist. "Brother," Vivekananda wrote to Shivananda soon after
he had earned a celebrity status in the United States, "the contents
of the Vedas, the Vedanta, the *Purāṇas,* or the *Bhāgavadgītā* won't
be comprehensible without studying Ramakrishna Paramahamsa."[49]
He thus reformulated Advaita. In his work of reconstruction, he was
influenced by the Brahmo Samaj which had devalued the *Śruti* as well
by the scientific methods (which put reliance on the *āptas,* that is, the
discoverers of spiritual laws), on the one hand, and by his insistence
on making Ramakrishna a Vedantist, on the other. The Swami's de-
emphasis of the *Śruti,* that is, his debunking of intellectual method,
chimed very well with his Master's anti–intellectual stance.[50] Yet he
sought to posit a process of attaining *Brahmajñāna* that he felt had
satisfied the demands of science, the leading intellectual force of his
day. In the final analysis, however, Vivekananda's Vedanta seeks to
propound a philosophy that is founded on the despair of reason. It
seeks to achieve *Brahmajñāna* not through reason but through spiritual intoxication. Moreover as Dr. Rambachan has demonstrated, the
Swami's analysis of *anubhava* and *pratyakṣa* as superior to intellection
is "unconvincing and unsatisfactory."[51] Whether or not he deliberately
manipulated the canonical sources for easy comprehension by lay
communities, it is a fact that "Vivekananda was primarily a preacher,
not a scholastic or pundit,"[52] and he simply could not apply the necessary intellectual rigor in his study of the Hindu tradition. On the
other hand, he almost secularized, even vulgarized, Vedanta by making it practical, that is, an instrument for economic survival, as is
evident in his calling a failed banker of Paris turned coachman (for
the sake of earning a living independently) "Practical Vedantist."[53]
Professor Veysey astutely observes that the "Americans never made
contact with 'pure' Hinduism when they became interested in this
Asian movement."[54]

V

Having announced that "India must conquer the world,"[55] Swami
Vivekananda described his progress in the West with much aplomb
and fanfare: Ramakrishna "to-day is worshipped literally by thousands in Europe and America, and to-morrow will be worshipped by
thousands more."[56] He also boasted in a letter to Ramakrishnananda
of his popularity: "I cause tumult wherever I go. They call me 'Cyclonic Hindu.' . . . *I am a voice without a form.*"[57] He further boasted
that he had "helped on the tide of Vedanta which is flooding the

world" and predicted that "before ten years elapse a vast majority of the English people will be Vedantic."[58] He even hinted at his use of supernatural power (*mahākarana śakti*) in this regard and declared: "I have conquered America before I visited the country."[59] He was so gratified with his Vedanta classes in London that he thought that India should conquer and occupy England by spiritual force.[60]

In his *World's Parliament of Religions,* Dr. Chattopadhyaya has analyzed the various newspaper reports on the Chicago Parliament and demonstrated that "Swami Vivekananda's performance was neither extraordinary among the Indian participants [there were twenty Indian participants of whom six had their papers read *in absentia*] nor did he exceed all fellow delegates from India in over-all influence and recognition, not to speak of important delegates from America and Europe who represented Christianity and Judaism."[61] Vivekananda's boast about "a defeaning applause" to his address[62] cannot be found in Barrows's two-volume history of the Parliament of Religions as well as in the reports in the *Chicago Tribune.* The *Boston Evening Transcript* reports of 30 September 1893 "that painted an intimate picture of him . . . does not look like a dispassionate report, as "the interviewer relied on what Swamiji told him about himself."[63]

With a view to convincing his Indian disciples about his fame, Vivekananda deliberately denigrated the performance of his fellow Indians. He wrote to Alasinga that the latter's uncle S. Parthasarathi Aiyangar's paper "was like the tradesman's catalogue and it was not thought fit to be read in the Parliament." He further commented on another fellow Indian Manilal Dvivedi's paper which "had to be cut short." As he wrote: "I had a good long time given to me over the ordinary half hour."[64] He then observed in a letter to his *gurubhāis* in Calcutta that the Brahmo representative Protap Mozoomdar (who had actually been instrumental, as a member of the Selection Committee of the Parliament, of accommodating Vivekananda as a representative of the Hindu monastic order) "was very cordial at first but when all the men and women of Chicago began to flock round [Vivekananda] in overwhelming number, then brother Mozoomdar [*Majumdarbhāyā*] had a heartburn."[65] His most unjust and unkind invective was hurled at the most popular and acclaimed speaker at the Parliament, the Buddhist Hewivitarane Anagarika Dharmapala: "unfortunately he was not a good speaker."[66] To Ramakrishnananda the Swami wrote about Dharmapala: "Dharmapala is a fine boy. He has not much of learning but is very gentle."[67] Vivekananda bragged before his brother in London: "That bloke Dharmapala made himself a representative [of Buddhist religion], but with his little learning he arranged a lecture. I found him an ignoramus and thus I worked hard to lecture about the Buddha to people—after all the Buddha is also one of our *avatāras*."[68] However as Chattopadhyaya cites from the report of the *Chicago Tribune* of 27 September 1893: "Particularly interesting was the address of H. Dharmapala, who made clear the similarities of the doctrines taught by Christ and by the great prophet of India and the East." Chattopadhyaya has found that "the *Chicago Tribune* coverage (258 lines) of a single speech by Dharmapala exceeded the sum-total of all the coverage (206 lines) that Swami Vivekananda actually received."[69] Gyan Banerji had shrewdly observed long ago:

> On going through [Vivekananda's] . . . Epistles one is at once convinced that whatever temporary success he achieved in America was due solely to propaganda. . . . In these letters he has run down the Brahmos, the Christian Missionaries, the orthodox Hindus, the present Hinduism, the Brahmins, and whom not. . . . No man who aspires to be a religious teacher can ever write such letters.[70]

As could be expected, he was accorded a hero's welcome when he returned home via Ceylon (Sri Lanka). During his journey from Colombo in Ceylon to Almora in the Himalayan hills, Vivekananda was generally addressed variously as "Revered Sir," "Your Holiness," and the like. At a Hindu temple at Colombo, he was received with shouts of "Jai Jai Mahadev—All hail highest Deva."[71] In Madras the Swami was presented with offerings of fruits and coconuts, like God in a Hindu shrine. Influenced by his glowing reports, the editorial of the *Indian Mirror* of Calcutta observed on 21 January 1897: "It is impossible to over-estimate the value of his services in America to the cause of Hinduism. Hundreds of men and women have enlisted themselves under the standard, which he unfolded in America and some of them have even taken to the bowl and yellow-robes. . . . The tide of conversion seemed to have rolled back from the East to the West—the tables were completely turned—and the Hindu mission in the West was crowned with a greater and more glorious success than what has ever been vouchsafed to Christian mission in the East.[72] Quite expectedly in Calcutta, the horses of his carriage were taken out and it was pulled by devotees and students.[73] His stature had grown so enormous after his return from the West that his new disciple from eastern Bengal, Sharacchandra Chakravarti, actually worshipped him as God Shiva with *dhuturā* flowers (*datura*) typically used in Shiva worship.[74]

At Pamban he was greeted by a band playing "See the conquering hero comes,"[75] while the Raja of Ramnad "prostrated himself at the

Swami's feet weeping for pure joy and afterwards helping to drag the Swami's carriage in place of horse."[76] Indeed the Swami had, in his gait, speeches, and letters, deliberately projected the image of an almost Napoleon-like *vīra* (hero). Since his early youth, he had admired two flamboyant Europeans—the Nicean Giuseppe Garibaldi and the Corsican turned naturalized Frenchman, Napoleon Bonaparte. He particularly admired the latter because he "raised himself to the pinnacle of glory through self-reliance and strong character." According to an eyewitness report, while

speaking of Napoleon, he himself had become like Napoleon. It was as if he himself were directing the fight of Jena and Austerlitz. "There goes the enemy—far away—they are flying—stop them—forward the eastern brigade—do not let a soul leave the field alive. . . . We have won the battle—we have conquered," he cried in joy and sometimes with one hand and sometimes with both hands raised he expressed his joy at the imaginary conquest and sang the French battle songs of victory.[77]

Some of Vivekananda's letters to his *gurubhāis* and followers contain military rhetoric that reveals his fascination with Napoleon-like exhortations and commands in the battlefield. For example he urged Alasinga: "Have fire and spread all over. Work, work. . . . Have infinite patience, and success is yours. . . . Onward, my brave boys. . . . Onward and forward to the breach, you are irresistible.[78] He admitted in a letter to Brahmananda: "I have always behaved like a hero. My work must have the speed of electricity and be as steady [*atal*] as thunder."[79] Two years later he wrote again to Brahmananda from New York with delirious fervor:

Don't worry, do not fear. Everything before you will be swept away. . . . Hail to *Mā* who delights in battle! . . . Truly speaking, there's no greater vice than cowardice. . . . Take one blow and deliver ten—that is manliness. . . . Have no fear. She is coming and you will conquer all, you will conquer the whole world with great power. . . . Again, onward, forward![80]

Reportedly the Swami learned the technique of defying danger from a holy man of Benares, who commanded him, then fleeing from a band of attacking monkeys, to halt and confront his chasers with courage. His encounter with the monkeys taught him the lesson that one must tackle problems heroically.[81]

His famous photograph taken at the Parliament of Religions shows the visage of a young hero attired in magnificent robe and headgear—a pose he must have perfected at the behest of his royal devotee, Raja

Ajit Singh. Another photograph of the Swami taken at the Parliament shows him like a Napoleon with his right hand tucked inside the lapels of his robe. M. Rolland suggests an interesting parallel between the psychology of Vivekananda and Napoleon. As he writes, "he suffered from the excess of power which insists on domination and within him there was a Napoleon."[82] The distinguished gun manufacturer and inventor, Sir Hiram Maxim, who is said to have seen Vivekananda at the World's Parliament of Religions in Chicago, considered him as a Napoleon.[83] Swamiji's brother Mahendranath commented on his posture and gait: "A commanding, defiant, and nonchalant attitude indifferent to the world's problems and concerns. He waves hands and points fingers to rule the world, as it were—Napoleon-like movements and postures, as if everybody will be quiet at his orders."[84] Vivekananda's majestic announcement in 1897 that "it is my ambition to conquer the world by Hindu thought—to see Hindus from the North Pole to the South Pole" made an awestruck visitor admit that he saw in the Swami "the very Napoleon of religion."[85] Watching the kaupīna-clad Swamiji parade on the roof of Alambazar Math, young Kalikrishna (later Virajananda) felt Vivekananda was like a Napoleon of the spiritual realm under whose feet the earth was trembling and giving away.[86]

Here is a clue to the real attraction for Vivekananda: it certainly did not lie in what he spoke. In general this would be the pattern for his popularity, and as discussed earlier his personality and performance towered over the substance of his peroration. It ought to be remembered that Vivekananda had been a consummate actor since his childhood; he had, according to Sister Nivedita, organized a theater club and staged a number of plays in which he always acted the part of a king. When at college Narendranath "used to attend divine services held in the Brahmo churches, and was one of the actors on the stage which was erected at the house of the late Babu Keshub Chunder Sen to represent a religious drama."[87] Admittedly the Sister herself was greatly influenced by his princely personality, for she always referred to him as "raja" or "king" in most of her letters to Josephine MacLeod. An admiring scholar has unhesitatingly declared in his characteristically colorful Bengali that this great "Kshatriya" had "shot out of the times of Homer or the Mahābhārata" and, as an illustration of the monk's Kshatriya qualities, proudly quoted the remark of an eyewitness to the Swami's hunting a deer for fun: "The Swamiji was a dead shot."[88]

VI

There is indeed some justification for Vivekananda's boast before the Holy Mother: "Mā, by your grace, I have made the white man my horse" [*Mā, sāheber cheleke ghoḍā karechi, tomār kṛpāy*], meaning he had brought a number of Westerners under his control.[89] He did create a following in the United States and England, comprised of a number of liberal and progressive minded middle- and upper middle-class folks. Yet in spite of his Napoleonic style and his much vaunted claim for world conquest, he simply failed to make a dent in the religious life of mainstream America. According to an eyewitness account,

> in the beginning, crowds of people flocked to his lectures. But they were not of the kind that a teacher of religion would be pleased to have for his auditors. They consisted partly of curiosity-seekers who were more interested in the personality of the preacher than in what he had to preach, partly of the representatives of the cranky and fraudulent elements . . . who thought they had found in the Swami a proper tool to forward their interests.[90]

His public addresses were fairly well attended, but his audience declined appreciably, and he was forced to work mainly through private classes or through addressing smaller organizations or clubs.[91] Even in England—the country to be Vedantized within a decade as per his prediction—his audience included mostly the elites and "fashionable ladies with pretensions to culture, and others, half-educated, to whom the oracular is always irresistible."[92]

Actually he could boast of only a few converts. He made two *sannyāsīs* in New York: a middle-aged Russian Jew and an erstwhile journalist, Leon Landsberg, who became Swami Kripananda, and Marie Louise, who was rechristened Swami Abhayananda—"a lady who is said to be French by extraction, American by domicile, Saiva by faith, Vaishnava in neck ornamentation, Vedantic by philosophical persuasion and a Sannyasin in her mode of life."[93] Both Kripananda and Abhayananda became disillusioned with their Vedantic fervor and parted company with the Swami and his society. Kripananda had been distressed by "the committee of petticoats" that distanced him from his guru, and Abhayananda's enthusiasm for "making propaganda, preaching, teaching, talking, writing on Hinduism" eventually fizzled out.[94] Two of Vivekananda's intimate friends and admirers, Mary Hale and Josephine MacLeod, "resisted his discipleship."[95] Even his most famous Western disciple, Sister Nivedita, who dedicated her life to social service in India after having been initiated as a *naiṣṭhika brahmacāriṇī* at the Belur Math, did not feel herself a religious convert. She was quoted as insisting in a New York newspaper of 27 June 1900:

It is wholly a mistake to suppose that I have renounced either my nationality or my religion in becoming a sister of the order. Christianity is the
nursery in which my spiritual thought was trained. In acquiring the larger
lessons of life that come when the world opens to us, we do not renounce
the valuable teachings of the nursery.[96]

Nevertheless the Swami did not hesitate to inform his friend Priyanath Singha that he had initiated over three thousand Westerners into
discipleship. They were all "initiated . . . with Mantras" and permitted
"to utter Pranava (OM)," because they exhibited their *sattvika* nature
and thus qualified to be regarded as Brahmin.[97]

Dr. Wilbert White, secretary to the College Young Men's Christian
Association of Calcutta, sought the opinion of forty prominent
Americans on the *Indian Mirror* editorial (referred to above) regarding Vivekananda's impact on the prospect of Christianity in the
United States. His respondents, one and all, expressed their appreciation of the Swami's work but denied the claim made by the *Mirror*.
These responses flatly contradict Vivekananda's claims of spiritual
conquest of the West. A perusal of a few select responses is in order.
Dr. Lyman Abbott, editor of *The Outlook* (New York), wrote that
"the report that Swami Vivekananda has made hundreds of converts
in America surpasses in its exaggeration anything I remember ever to
have seen in the American press, given as it is to exaggeration. I do
not know, nor have I heard of a single such convert." Dr. James
Angell, president of the University of Michigan, observed that "the
likelihood of America's abandoning Christianity and adopting either
Hinduism or Mohammedanism is, I think, rather less than the probability that the Ganges will reverse its current and run up into the
Himalayan mountains."[98] In a similar vein, Professor George P. Fisher
of Yale University quipped that "the prospect of the spread of Hinduism in this country to a degree to attract any notice is about as great
as the likelihood that the Himalayas will sink down into the earth
and become level ground."[99]

Dr. Charles W. Elliott, president of Harvard University, considered
the *Indian Mirror* editorial "simply silly so far as it undertakes to
describe Vivekananda's performances in America," and Dr. Richard
T. Ely of the University of Wisconsin commented that neither Hinduism nor Islam "answer[s] our needs in America."[100] John W. Foster,
an erstwhile secretary of state of the United States, observed that the
Mirror editorial "sounds very absurd to all intelligent people in this
country."[101] In a similar vein, George Gates, president of Iowa College, maintained that "the impression that any significant movement

toward Hinduism has arisen in America, is the most arrant nonsense."[102]

Dr. John H. Barrows, chairman of the General Committee that organized the World's Parliament of Religions, to which Vivekananda presented his maiden speech on Hinduism, reminded his audience in an address in India:

> People going to America from the Orient are easily liable to misunderstand the interest and courtesy with which they are received. Curious to hear all truth the American people listen eagerly to lectures on the Vedanta philosophy or on Esoteric Buddhism, and continue to go to their own churches, cherish their own Christian work as before.[103]

Barrows quite emphatically told a correspondent of the *Chronicle* in California on 10 May 1897:

> What I particularly object to in Vivekananda is his ridiculous and exaggerated statement about the influence of Hindu speakers in England and America. He is a man of brilliant and pleasant qualities, but he seems to have lost his head. I could never tell whether to take him seriously or not.[104]

His point was shared by Dr. David Jordan, president of the Zealand Stanford Junior University, Palo Alto (California), in his response to White's query:

> . . . there is naturally a growing interest in knowing the Hindoo point of view and in knowing what the best Hindoo sages have thought. This interest, however, is largely among those who have not the slightest intention of casting away the Christian religion for any of the dream philosophies that come from the Orient.[105]

It was, in fact, a Chicago lawyer who provided the most succinct response to White's letter. Luther Laften Mills, attorney-at-law, wrote:

> The statement that many hundreds of converts from Christianity to Hinduism have been made in America by Swami Vivekananda is without foundation in fact; and a person making it in this country would be pleasantly ridiculed for his ignorance or criticized for his exaggeration. This distinguished man, in the Parliament of Religions in the year 1893, delivered an address which was kindly received because of his fine personality and his manifest sincerity; and he subsequently made several public utterances to our people. A few curious minds may have been attracted by what he said, to a study of his religious faith. But no appreciable

impression has come upon the American mind from him, or his doctrines, . . . America is a Christian nation; its founders were Christians; Christianity is an essential element in the fibre of its being.[106]

Finally we ought to note that the World's Parliament of Religions, while proclaiming its avowed object of letting each system of religion "stand by itself" with a view to presenting "to the world the substantial unity of many religions," and while recognizing the "kinder spirit" of the "Oriental friends" vis-à-vis "some Western warrior . . . [who] uttered his war-cry," was basically an assembly organized and led by well-intentioned and well-informed American Christians. As the president of the Parliament Charles Bonney declared, "the Parliament of Religions has emancipated the world from bigotry, and henceforth civil and religious liberty will have a larger and easier sway." He, however, defined "relgious liberty" in purely Christian terms in his address to the Evangelical Alliance: "liberty of mind and conscience and heart to seek out God, and find Him and worship Him without any human restraint in the sacred relation which exists between the soul and its Creator." Continuing his concern for Christian religion, Bonney declared in the same address that the final and the most appropriate object of the Alliance was "to promote every kind of Christian work" and concluded: "This occasion, following the Parliament of the World's Religions, is nothing less than a Parliament of the Churches of Christendom."[107]

The Chicago Parliament was truly an enlightened Christian affair, and its avowed object was to remind Christians everywhere of the efficacy and sheer morality of respecting the plurality of faiths all over the world. Neither President Bonney nor Chairman Barrows ever recognized the alleged world conquest that Vivekananda and his enthusiastic admirers and devotees were proclaiming proudly and loudly. In fact Bonney does not seem to have addressed the Asian religious group (at least his addresses in this regard, if any, have not been printed) though he spoke to various Christian denominational organizations as well as the Jewish Congress. Thus one must concur with Swamiji's brother-biographer Bhupendranath Datta's conclusion:

It is not a fact that America became converted to orthodox Hinduism or that the life of the American converts started being regulated by the neo-Smritis. . . . On this issue lots of nonsense came to be inculcated among the credulous Ramakrishnaites of Bengal.[108]

As Veysey has shown, the Vedanta movement, despite its rigorous discipline and superb organizational technique, remained "numerically tiny, appealing only to an unrepresentative handful of persons. It was an elite movement within its own realm." In fact federal census figures show only 340 members in 1906, 190 in 1916, 200 in 1926, reaching 628 in 1936 to around 1200 in the early 1970s.[109] Though the Vedanta movement can now boast of 22,000 members with 12 independent centers and their subcenters, convents, and monasteries, the majority of them still belong to the class of the affluent and the affable.[110] As Chattopadhyaya informs us, on an average "there are about fifty to one hundred active members for every centre. Through the mostly secular institutions of education and medical services in India, the movement influences a part of the westernized Indians and intelligentsia, particularly in the eastern and southern Indian states."[111]

Conclusion

I

THE entire corpus of Vivekananda literature wholeheartedly agrees on the Swami's phenomenal spiritual conquest of the West. However an often overlooked fact is that he himself came to the painful realization that he had failed in his mission. This is ironic, especially when we note that he had always been nonchalant and confident about his capabilities: "Do you know why I am so intelligent?" he once asked Yogananda and answered the question himself:

> I hail from a family of nuts. . . . You folks are calculating to the core—always weighing things. Could you accomplish a truly great task if you remained so scheming? We, on the other hand, are somewhat nutty and do not care for any calculations. We just do the thing. If we succeed, well and good. If not, we couldn't care less.[1]

In the euphoria of his sudden celebrity status immediately following the Chicago Parliament, Swamiji "beat his own drums by inflating his popularity in his numerous letters to his followers and friends in India."[2] However by 1897 he had become cautious about giving public explanation for his foreign mission. For example he told a reporter of the *Madras Times* that he had gone there just "to get experience" and "to compare notes," because his "idea as to the key-note of our national downfall is that we do not mix with other nations—that is the one and the sole cause."[3] But only two days later, in a public address in Madras, he declared: "I did not go to America . . . for the Parliament of Religions. . . . I travelled twelve years all over India, finding no way to work for my countrymen, and that is why I went to America. . . . Who cared about this Parliament of Religions?"[4] Less than a year after his first visit to the United States, Vivekananda gave away the real motive of his American travel in a letter to one of his disciples in Madras: "America is the best field in the world to carry on any idea, so I do not think of leaving America soon. And why? Here I have food and drink and clothes, and everybody so kind, and all this for a few good words!"[5] He told Mary Hale that he spent all his energy in the United States, "so that the Americans may learn to be broader and more spiritual."[6] He seems to have shed his evangelical illusions altogether in later years. In 1900 he brusquely told an inquiring woman in San Francisco: "Madam, I am not teaching religion. I am selling my brain for money to help my people."[7] He further declared: "If you are beggars, you can have aims. I have no aims, no want, no purpose. I come to your country and lecture—just for fun. No other meaning."[8] Seven years earlier he had confided to Haripada Mitra that he had gone to the United States "not to have fun nor to achieve fame, but to find a way to help our poor."[9]

All the available evidence suggests that from around 1897 a feeling of despondence began to cast its spell on the mind of the untiring *karmayogī*, who had been, to borrow the expression of his first disciple Sharatchandra Gupta, "lunatic-like, he was so busy!"[10] A number of factors may have contributed to this feeling, one of the most important no doubt being his failing health. His chronic diabetic condition,[11] so long ignored and uncared for, his weak heart and generally fragile health, his obesity, joined by bouts of asthma and lumbago, together with his atrocious eating and smoking habits had begun to take their toll. He was becoming irascible, emotional, and mercurial. Some time in 1901, he lamented to Chakravarti: "You can see the state of my health. None of you have come forward to help me in my work. Tell me, what could I achieve all by myself? This body is a product of Bengal. What more work can it do?"[12] A chronic patient of dyspepsia, Swamiji believed that this disease came easily to the Bengalis who were naturally sentimental![13]

Some of the monastic disciples devoted to the late Paramahamsa felt scandalized by the Swami's close association with the feudal princes of India—men such as the Maharajas of Khetri, Ramnad, Mysore, Junagad, Alwar, Bhunj, and Bhinga or, nearer his home state of Bengal, the Rajas of Uttarpara, Shobhabazar, and Dharbhanga. He actually wanted Akhandananda and Brahmananda to accept Raja Ajit Singh's hospitality but was disappointed with both. Akhandananda could not linger at the court of Khetri because of his indiscretion (involvement in local politics) resulting in the Raja's disaffection. Brahmananda's monastic conscience prevented him from accepting a monthly allowance from Singh as per Vivekananda's suggestion. The Swami had done his best to flatter and placate his royal disciple in a letter of 1897 with a view to using the latter's resources for his work, even though he was aware that Ajit Singh was but a petty chieftain given to drinking.[14] The Swami's discontented cohorts of Belur Math founded a dissident organization called *Garīb Ramakrishna Sabhā* (Ramakrishna Association of the Poor) in 1889. The renegade monks

caused Vivekananda great irritation as the news of this internal dissension, which had been going on since his return to India in 1897,
reached the public. As early as 18 January 1899, Shachindranath
Basu, manager of the Mahisadal Raj Estate, had written to Shubhananda about this schism.[15]

Professor Niranjan Dhar has persuasively argued that the Vedantic
thought served as a prop for maintaining the hegemony of the British
over India and that of the native feudal landlords and chiefs over the
people. To begin with the Upanishads, which served as the foundation
of the Vedanta, were called *Rājavidyā* (royal learning), because the
Upanishadic speculations on the regime of the Universal Soul were
conceived by the ancient Indian Kshatriya kings such as Pravahana
Jaibali, Pratardana, Janasruti, Brhadratha, Pautrayana, Chitragangay-
ani, and Sabatjynara in the image of their vision of universal empire.[16]
The British government in India sought to keep the common people
passive and the elites loyal and to this end encouraged the other-
worldly Vedantic spiritualism on the one hand and created a new
landed aristocracy through the devise of Permanent Settlement
(1791) on the other. The British interest in the Vedanta as the authentic religion for the Hindus commenced with the governor-generalship
of Warren Hastings and with the founding of the Asiatic Society in
1784. It reached its apogee during the regime of Lord Wellesley as
the governor-general of India and following the founding of the Fort
William College in 1800 in Calcutta. The resurgence of the Vedanta
was an attempt to turn the tide of discontent in India, as occasioned
by the peasants' revolt of 1783 in Rangpur, the uprisings of 1789
in Bankura and Bishnupur, and the Chuar rebellion of 1795–99 in
Midnapur, among others. The feudal landlords of British India were
partners of British imperialism in exploiting the agricultural laborers.
Quite expectedly the zamindars (landlords) of Bengal opposed the
Sepoy Mutiny of 1857 and even petitioned the British government
through their accredited organization, the British Indian Association,
to introduce Permanent Settlement throughout the country as a bul-
wark of defense of the British Empire.[17] It is thus not surprising that
the Swami, as an exponent of the Vedanta, would receive enthusiastic
support from the Rajas and Maharajas of India of his day.

II

As has already been noted in the chapter 4, the Swami was acutely
aware of the sham that lay behind his assuming the monk's mantle. A

bon vivant through and through, he could yet unhesitatingly proclaim before a bunch of young initiates:

A monk's real goal is: *ātmano mokṣārthaṁ jagaddhitāya ca* ["liberation of the soul for the welfare of the world"]. . . . Never believe those who say that they want to be in the world and attain knowledge of the Brahman at the same time. That kind of talk is the consolation of the crypto consumers. . . . That's the raving of a lunatic, contrary to the Scriptures. There is no emancipation without renunciation."[18]

His guru Ramakrishna had compared a monk's running after money with a Brahmin widow's spoiling her *vrata* (austere life) by taking on a low caste lover.[19] Even Vivekananda himself admitted in a letter to Sara Bull that "according to Manu, collecting funds even for a good work is not good for a Sannyasin. I have begun to feel that the old sages were right."[20] He probably realized that he had violated the very monastic injunction he had inflicted on his brother monks and disciples that "the ochre robe was a symbol of supreme duty [*mahā-kārya*] and not for comfort and pleasure [*bhoger janya nahe*]."[21] However his monastery at Belur with all its imported furniture and European devotees, disciples, and visitors, was considered by the municipality of Bali territory of Howrah that had jurisdiction over Belur, as Vivekananda's personal retreat (originally the house at Belur *was* the garden retreat [*bāgānbāḍī*] of Nilambar Mukhopadhyay) and not a Math and hence imposed a heavy municipal tax on the property. Fortunately for the monks, the timely intervention of the American consul in Calcutta (whose wife was a devotee of Vivekananda), who testified that Swamiji was the greatest of the *sannyāsīs,* and the furniture, gifted to him, were sacred relics, the municipality lost the case in the court of law and Belur Math retained its tax-free status as a holy shrine.[22] More important, Vivekananda knew that his career as a monk *had* brought him and his family financial comfort, higher education for his brothers, and fame, love, and respect of the multitude for himself. Toward the end of his life, he did manifest a desire to return to his family, now free from financial straits.[23] This ambivalence of the ailing monk caused him great anguish.

Finally as we have seen, since the arrival of Margaret Noble in Calcutta, Vivekananda appears to have encountered a serious crisis in his emotional and ascetic life. The letters and the reported conversations between the guru and his *mleccha śiṣyā* are full of erotic innuendos and imageries, while they harp on "sacrifice," "service," and "struggle" ad nauseam. They suggest a psychic revolution and struggle of the troubled and ailing young monk contending with the multiple problems of maintaining, indeed elevating, his reputation in the West. Then his impassioned perorations to the youths on the efficacy of a healthy body and mind sadly contrasted with his personal physical condition. The mundane responsibilities of running a spiritual organization with branches all over India and a few in the West—of which he had been the prime mover—were becoming too complicated and vexing to handle. His post-Amarnath days were also marked by a peculiar, though somewhat tragic, ambivalence of attitude toward Nivedita, whom he had trained, indeed tamed, into the life of a *sannyāsinī* with meticulous care, but whose feminine appeal he could not entirely ignore in spite of his desperate attempts. The result of this combined physical and mental torture was a transformation of his personality.

The process of this transformation, or dissolution, of the Swami's personality can be discerned mostly from his written statements. In his earlier years, he had desired to "burst on society like a bomb, and make it follow . . . [him] like a dog."[24] At another time he had declared: "No rest for me! I shall die in harness! I love action! Life is a battle, and one must always be in action, to use a military phrase."[25] In May 1896 he had written to Mary Hale from London, mocking his *gurubhāi* who had just arrived from India: "Poor man!—a typical Hindu, with nothing of that pluck and go which I have; he is always dreamy and gentle and sweet! . . . I will try to put a little activity into him."[26] But his letter of 12 December 1899 to Sara Bull shows him as mellowed down a bit: "The present looks very gloomy indeed; but I am a fighter and must die fighting, not give way—that is why I get crazy at the boys. I don't ask them to fight, but not to hinder my fight."[27] Nivedita thought of a couple of reasons for her master's frustration: his "growing consciousness of bodily weakness, conflicting with the growing clearness of a great purpose"; and "the terrible effort of translating what he had called the 'super-conscious' into the common life."[28] In Kashmir the militant monk was transformed into a helpless little child. In her letter of 13 October 1898, the Sister wrote:

> He simply talks, like a child, of the "Mother"—but his soul and his voice are those of a God. . . . To him at this moment "doing good" seems horrible. . . . "Patriotism is a mistake. Everything is a mistake"—he said when he came home. . . . "Swamiji is dead and gone" were the last words I heard him say.[29]

Interestingly enough the Swami claimed identification with Shiva and affiliation with Kali. Shiva, the "erotic ascetic," is the ethyphallus god who is a "renouncer." Appropriately Shiva invaded the Swami's brain. Kali, on the other hand, is the destroyer and conqueror of "men"—she is the terrible but lovable female, "mother"—Ramakrishna's Mother of the Universe and psychic protectress. Vivekananda turned into a childlike devotee of the Mother. His sick and suffering male physique, deprived of the love of an erotic woman, needed the nursing of the Mother, while his repressed male psyche sought succor in Shiva. Ultimately both gods failed the Swami.

Vivekananda was gradually overcome by a gnawing sense of nothingness and extinction. His fantastic vision of Hindu India holding the beacon of light for the entire human race remained a distant ideal. In 1895 he asserted boldly in a letter to his monastic brother: "Was I ever an orthodox, a traditional, or a ritualistic Hindu? I do not pose as one."[30] Three years later he wrote an acquaintance that "Advaitism is the last word of religion and . . . I believe it is the religion of the future enlightened humanity."[31] However, he could not assure himself that he had in fact succeeded in preaching an enlightened Hinduism to the Indians. In his address at the Victoria Hall, Madras, he confessed to his affiliation with traditional ritualistic Hinduism: "Take a thousand idols more if you can produce Ramakrishna Paramahamsa through idol-worship, and may God speed you! Produce such noble natures by any means you can. Yet idolatry is condemned! Why? Nobody knows."[32] At Kambakonam in southern India, sometime in February 1897, the triumphant Vedantic hero and the "conqueror of the West" proclaimed:

Ours is the true religion . . . because it teaches that God alone is true . . . because, above all, it teaches renunciation and stands up with the wisdom of ages to tell and to declare to the nations who are mere children of yesterday in comparison with us Hindus: "Children, you are slaves of the senses. . . . Give it all up, renounce the love of the senses and of the world; that is the way of religion."[33]

Two years later he was even more vocal in proclaiming the glory of traditional Hinduism. In an eloquent essay titled "Modern India" published in Bengali in the *Udbodhan* in 1899, Swamiji exhorted his readers to announce: "The Indian is my brother, the Indian is my life, India's gods and goddesses are my God."[34] In March 1901 he admitted in a public lecture in Dacca that he belonged to the ancient sect that believed in the soteriological merits of the Ganges water.[35] This is no declaration of religious syncretism, nor was it an erudite and elegant exposition of the superior merits of Hinduism as argued by the *Hindu-kula-śiromaṇi*, Rajnarain Basu, over a generation ago.[36] On the other hand, it is a disarmingly candid confession of a religious leader's cultural assumptions at the end of a life that had been buffeted by the crosscurrents of various influences and experiences—Western as well as Eastern.[37] Even a cursory glance at his various pronouncements proclaiming the glories of the Hindus and their religion will suffice to note his racial and religious chauvinism which he often masked by his rhetoric of patriotism and eclecticism.[38]

We need also to recall in this connection Swamiji's confession that when he traveled all over India preaching the gospel of the Vedanta to the people, he got nothing but their ridicule. Hence he decided to preach enlightened Hinduism, that is, Vedanta, to a free people like the Americans, to whom it would be "comprehensible."[39] He naturally prescribed a continuation of conventional Hinduism for his own country which had failed to pay heed to his Vedantic messages. Professor Ghatak has rightly observed that the Swami preached no new view of Hinduism in the West; the burden of his sermons there comprised the various strands of orthodox Hinduism.[40] In his letter to the Vedic scholar Shailendranarayan Ghosal, the famous Trotskyite revolutionary Saumendranath Tagore observed that

Swamiji is a totally split personality and his *dicta* are rent by contradictions. The Swami attempted the imposible reconciliation of Advaitism with idolatry. The lethargic hearts, that had been aroused by the jolts of Rammohan and Vidyasagar, were now assured by him that there is truth even in fetishism. The unenlightened felt secure in the belief that there are as many venues as there are views and languished in comfortable somnolence.[41]

From 1900 onward the Swami was quite vocal about his desire for peace and quiet. "What a mass of namby-pamby nonsense we create round ourselves!" he wrote to Sister Christine from San Francisco on 4 March 1900. "I don't want to work. I want to be quiet, and rest."[42] About a week later, he wrote to Brahmananda:

Kindly pray to the Mother that I do not have to shoulder all this trouble and burden any longer. Now I desire a little peace—it seems there is no more strength left to bear the burden of work and responsibility—rest and peace for the few days that I shall yet live. . . . No more lectures or anything of that sort. Peace! . . . But there is only this sorrow that the work of *gurudev* is not progressing; there is this regret that I have not been able to accomplish anything of his work.[43]

The Vivekananda of 1898–1902 was a far cry from the dashing and debonair monk of 1894 who had declared in a letter to his *gurubhāis* that "work, work, work" was his motto,[44] or who had dreamed in 1895 of creating "a new order of humanity"[45] and had proclaimed proudly and loudly: "I shall work incessantly until I die, and even after death, I shall work for the good of the world."[46] He seems to have discovered another aspect of his self in his letter to an American friend written in the early spring of 1900: "I am free. I am Mother's child. She works, She plays. . . . We are Her automata. She is the wirepuller."[47] A few days earlier, he had written to an anonymous American friend: "My boat is nearing the calm harbour from which it is never more to be driven out. Glory, glory unto Mother! I have no wish, no ambition now."[48] However, he still strove to exert himself to conclude his unfinished business. Just six months before death, Swamiji met his friend Brahmabandhav Upadhyay at the pond of Hedua in north Calcutta and confessed to him "in piteous tone" [*kātar svare*]: "Brother, I'm not going to live. . . . I am in a haste to complete the final arrangements of my math."[49] In fact it was Goodwin who had found out as early as 1897 that the Swami's chances for success in India were pretty slim. He was lionized and deified by the Indians because of his publicized success in the West. The Indians, Goodwin felt, would never change their ways of life even though they would applaud Swamiji for criticizing them for their superstition. For all his rhetoric and bombast, Vivekananda had failed to make a dent in the attitudes and habits of his own countrymen.[50]

III

Swami Vivekananda was a dreamer and a visionary who had once boasted that he could "create a better world."[51] But he was never a systematic planner. He even admitted that he "never planned anything" but had "taken things as they came."[52] He unhesitatingly confessed to his admirer, Durgacharan Nag: "Mr. Nag, I can't figure out what I am in fact doing or not doing. I act on momentary impulses and so can't tell whether I'm doing good or bad."[53] Haripada Mitra reminds us that "it was not his habit to think over the whole matter earlier. . . . In fact, he himself would not know what he would be talking."[54] "Plans! Plans! That is why you Western people can never create a religion! Religion was never never [*sic*] preached by planners," he thundered at Nivedita when she dared to proffer her guru some practical suggestions.[55] His dreams were vast: he wanted a new India socially progressive, politically stable, and economically autarchic. He also wanted a global spiritual renaissance that would "move and lift the massive tamas-ridden thought of the world" and "introduce a new path"[56] with the help of dedicated and determined ascetic workers. An admirer of the Swami called him a "realistic dreamer" (*vāstav–vādī svapnadraṣṭā*).[57] Whatever that epithet in mellifluous oxymoron means, Vivekananda was anything but a realist. Quite naturally in trying to achieve his multiple objectives, the "cyclonic Hindu," ever "impatient of delay, of obstacles and opposition,"[58] lived three lives in one only to face disappointments caused by factors beyond his control. "This is the world, hideous, beastly corpse," the disillusioned monk complained to Mary Hale. "Who thinks of helping it is fool!"[59] In fact the Swami may have always harbored a negative attitude toward the world and have been skeptical about its amelioration in spite of his public pronouncements of creating a holy and wholesome global community. As he confided to Goodwin on 8 August 1896:

> "A good world," "a happy world," "social progress" are equally intelligible as "hot ice," "dark light," etc. If it were good it would not be the world. The soul foolishly thinks of manifesting the Infinite in finite matter—the Intelligence goes through particles—and at last finds out its error and tries to escape.[60]

Underneath the razzle-dazzle of fame and apotheosis, Swami Vivekananda appears to be a tragic, even pathetic, victim of self-imposed repression as well as self-induced renown. The last phase of his life, especially the last five years (1897–1902), reveals the inner struggles of the mature young man trying desperately to cope with his deteriorating health and the dynamics of the conflict between natural manhood and the forced holy manliness of his ascetic life. His disorientation resulted in a change of personality and behavior. Contrary to his character and style, the Swami was seen as brooding, withdrawn, and introspective by his brother monks who were puzzled but thought that he was preparing for his death now that he had accomplished his life's mission.[61]

He had become acutely aware of his impending end, and this consciousness was manifest in his frequent allusions to it. Psychologically speaking this awareness of death in the prime of life could also be one of failure—the death of his carefully cultivated asceticism. The Swami was at his best when taking up the role of a militant Hindu evangelist and social reformer. This gesture of ascetic militancy had been his principal tool for projecting the image of a spiritual superman and at the same time compensating for the psychic loss of his natural manhood. But his pronouncements during the last five years of his life registered his disenchantment with his earlier successful career and a wish to return to the state of his late mentor Ramakrishna—the state of an infant—he had hitherto disdained. Thus the

Paramahamsa style of repression—a total denial of manhood by being a *puer aeternas*—was to be his ultimate support at a time when his physical and psychic existence faced a peril. Hence his emulation of his Master's behavior—which he had mocked shortly after the latter's death.[62]

Ramakrishna had discovered a solution to his inner crisis through androgyny and ecstatic devotionalism (*madhur bhāv* and *bhakti*) by castrating himself psychically and symbolically sacrificing his wife through the *soḍaṣī pūjā*.[63] The Master's life was lived in successful delusion—he became a *bhagavān* ("god"). His great disciple, on the other hand, ended his career on a note of despondency and defeat, acknowledging the utter futility of work and regressing into a behavior of which he had never approved. He ended his life not in delusion—he was too educated and intelligent for that—but in disillusionment. What the Swami failed to achieve in life—fulfillment of human wants, that is, a man's natural needs in a normal setting—he sought to achieve by dying a hero's death in harness—a kind of crucifixion.

IV

Nevertheless even though he despaired of his exertions for the benefit of the world and even though most of his prophetic predictions still remain to be fulfilled, the posterity seems to have confirmed Vivekananda's bold assertion, echoing Ramakrishna's prophesy about himself,[64] made in a lecture in Detroit: "Wait for a few days and you will see that the very heart of India will be astir, her every vein will be electrified and the people of India will embrace me in their celebration of conquest."[65] The Swami's exploits in the West were interpreted as his conquest of the West by his cohorts, admirers, and devotees back home. In numerous letters to his disciples in Bengal and Madras, he exhorted them to convene a mass meeting to pass a resolution that they endorsed his interpretation of Hinduism in the West and get that resolution published in the leading American newspapers. He particularly suggested that the leading citizens of the country, the chiefs and Rajas, should especially be encouraged to participate in these meetings.[66] The upshot of the entire affair—Vivekananda's popularity in the West and massive propaganda in India—certainly stirred many minds at home. The Swami, as the conqueror of the Christian missionaries and the propagator of Hindu faith in the Christian West, was seen as the liberator of Mother India from her bondage.

That his popularity multiplied a million times in the mind of the imaginative and sentimental Bengali could be illustrated by a couple of examples. Durgacharan Nag and Saracchandra Chakravarti literally worshipped Vivekananda as the living Shiva.[67] On reading the glowing accounts of the Swami in newspapers and hearing his praise from numerous people, Girish Ghosh exclaimed deliriously:

> What is happening! It seems the days of the miracles have returned. Miracles had happened centuries ago and now it is happening right in front of our eyes! All this transcends reasoning and rationality. . . . Could anybody accomplish so much without the support of a miraculous power?[68]

Having said this Ghosh turned toward the direction of Dakshineshwar and began to shout "Jai Ramakrishna" time and again. Swami Yogananda's octogenarian father felt dizzy with excitement on hearing that a disciple of Sri Ramakrishna was lecturing in America and earning great renown and respect from the people there. Shaking his head and hands wildly, old Chaudhury, who could not read English and had no clue as to what the Swami was lecturing about, told Ramakrishnananda:

> O Bhiteswar (Ramakrishnananda's nickname), what is this! This Naren has surpassed everybody. He can no longer be counted among ordinary people, he now belongs to the rank of Shankar and the Buddha. Wow! Shankar and the Buddha have resurrected![69]

A veteran lawyer named Gobindachandra Ghosh suddenly assumed a terrible persona like a flaming fire (*pradīpta hutāśan*) as soon as he heard Vivekananda's name and besides himself with rage began to kick the walls of the building of the Oxford Mission with great force, shouting: "I kick the missionaries like this and when Naren returns he will wipe them out."[70]

Admittedly the Swami failed to shake the foundations of Christianity, but he succeeded in making Hinduism known and acceptable in the Christian West. No doubt his version of Hinduism and Vedanta was far from authentic,[71] and he was "more the advocate than the scholar, "but his oratorical and organizational skill, coupled with his charismatic personality, led to the coming in of Ramakrishna movement in America. Though, according to Agehananda Bharati, Vivekananda's Hinduism is "a special brand of simplified belief-system" articulated by the English-speaking Swami, it "has become the official Hindu belief-system" both in India and abroad.[72] And "this was an impressive achievement" for which he "clearly deserves credit as the founder of American Hinduism and pioneer Asian teacher who paved the way for all Eastern teachers who have followed."[73] As for his own country, as an Indian sociologist noted some twenty years ago, "Vivekananda himself has become an ideal for millions in India" for having transformed the "elitist escapist" orientation of Hinduism into an engine for social development, thereby redirecting the individual Hindu's vocation from "self-directed mukti to an other-directed altruism." This reformulation—or better still, reformation—of *sanātana* Hinduism has provided at least a theoretical framework for "India's only possible processes of social change."[74]

Vivekananda's reputation as a magnificent patriot owed largely to the most effective propaganda campaign mounted by Nivedita. Following his death the Sister cut off her connections with the Ramakrishna Order and plunged headlong into the Indian nationalist movement, inspiring the youths with her speeches and writings.[75] In the diary of Barindrakumar Ghosh, we note that from 1902 to 1908 she was busy publishing excerpts from Swamiji's speeches in the *Bal Bharat* (*Young India*) of Madras, its most sensational issues being the ones reproducing his speeches under such titles as "Unfurl the Banner of Love: Vivekananda's Trumpet Call to the Young Men of India" (December 1907), "Vivekananda, the Real Pioneer of the New Movement" (January 1908), "Shivoham' (I am He): I Never Had Death nor Fear: Strengthening Is the Great Medicine for the World's Disease" (February 1908).[76] She took great care to create a Vivekananda medallion depicting the Swami as the symbol of Indian nationalism and even consulted the famous French jeweler René Lalique.[77] It was the Sister's favorite painter Nandalal Bose of Santiniketan, who popularized, visually, the divinity of Ramakrishna and Vivekananda. Bose wrote: "For the artists Swamiji's ideal was the backbone of art; without it all art was uninspiring and lifeless. Swamiji stood for the realization of the aesthetic path through that of knowledge."[78]

However most probably Vivekananda had not foreseen the exact extent of his legacy as he remained suspended between the Scylla of *nivṛtti* (ascetic withdrawal) and the Charybdis of *pravṛtti* (worldly involvement), because his chosen vocation demanded an emphasis on the former while his later realizations following his contact with the Western world prompted him on to a secular national developmental program, necessitating the espousal of the latter. This dilemma of the Swami has been explained away by an admiring scholar as "an exemplification of his Practical *Vedanta*" through "two distinguishable sets of guises: one other-worldly ['an instrument of God, a disciple . . ., a devotee, a sannyasi and a yogi']; the other, this-worldly ['a *kṣatriya,* a bodhisattva, and a guru']."[79] Be that as it may, he has not only been lionized and canonized by scholars, devotees, and admirers but in fact has been one of those rare personalities to make a quick leap from history into legend.

Yet interestingly enough even to this day, especially in the decade of the nineties, when Vivekananda's devotees, admirers, and even scholars are at pains to proclaim his undying influence on modern India, there are, inadvertently but inevitably, occasional voices of despair and concern in respect of his achievements. The two handsome and massive anthologies, *Vivekananda since Chicago* and *Mahimā Tava Udbhāsita,* through harping on the versatile genius of Swamiji—his stupendous scholarship, cosmic compassion, heroic patriotism, and militant social activism (the acme of such apotheosisis reached in Swami Atmasthananda's truly obsequious panygeric "Eta Baḍa Mahā-puruṣ, Ekādhāre Eto Guṇ" in the latter), yet remain somewhat ambivalent as to his continuing influence. An eminent scholar of Hinduism has titled his brief essay in *Vivekananda since Chicago* "Swami Vivekananda: Where Are You When We Need You?"[80] Even the editor of this commemorative volume has found the current young generation of Indians quite impervious to Vivekananda and Vedanta and suggested ways to modernize and adapt the Swami's "radicalism" (that is, "going to the root of national and human problems and finding their discovery of the human soul, the *atman*") and project "a new image of Vivekananda" by telling the indifferent and heedless Indian youths that "not few great minds of the West today share his faith in the philosophy of Vedanta as the spiritual foundation of a new civilization."[81] Indeed as Professor Ashin Dasgupta has pointed out in his review of *Vivekananda since Chicago,*

> granted that Swamiji was an extraordinary individual, who had often inflamed [the mind] with his [superb] Bengali, but have the Indians become civilized thereby? And what has happened to his grand program of service to the *daridranārāyaṇ?* He is no longer present, but the godly Indian poor are in the legion.[82]

Admittedly Vivekananda conceived of an India with "Vedanta brain and Islam body"[83] and in fact envisioned a world united by an awareness of oneness. The reality, however, is that the fin de siècle India, indeed the entire world, is torn asunder by communalism, petty provincialism masquerading as nationalism, and religious fundamentalism and its offspring fanaticism. Nevertheless Vivekananda still occupies the idealized world of the admiring scholars who, contrary to the canons of scholarship, unhesitatingly display their paranoia for any voice of scholarly dissent or any critical examination of the hallowed profile of their beloved Swamiji, who has been transformed into a veritable *stupor mundi*.[84] Although it is necessary to exercise due caution in our historical approach to the life of a religious personality,[85] it is time we rescued the human and historical Vivekananda from the Swamiji of the legend immortalized in his most popular description inscribed on a marble plaque on the portals of his ancestral home in Calcutta: "a saint and a philosopher of modern India who consecrated his life to the service of humanity." Swami Vivekananda emerges from a century-old gilded cage of myth and mystification not as the herald of a brave new world of spiritual humanism but as a tragic figure whose brief but tumultuous public life was spent contending with multiple tensions and conflicts—much less attractive but probably more authentic, and eminently human.

Appendix: Biographical Abstracts

Abhedananda, Swami (1866–1939): monastic name of Kaliprasad Chandra who had been a young devotee and later a disciple of Ramakrishna. He was a Vedanta enthusiast and hence nicknamed Kali Vedanti by his monastic brethren. He lectured in London for some months in 1896 and thereafter spent several years in the United States (1897–1920).

Adbhutananda, Swami (d. 1920): a native of Bihar, his premonastic name was Rakhturam. He had been an erstwhile domestic servant in the household of Ramchandra Datta and later became a devotee of Ramakrishna and was called Latu (or Leto) by the Master. Illiterate but extremely devoted and kindhearted, the Swami was admired and loved by all his brother monks, as well as by friends and acquaintances.

Advaitananda, Swami (*ca.* 1828–1902): monastic name of Gopalchandra Ghosh and the senior-most disciple of Ramakrishna. He was nicknamed Budo Gopal for he was even older than the Master and "Hutko" Gopal because he used to disappear from and reappear at Ramakrishna's community from time to time. He is reported to have distributed *geruā* cloth to his *gurubhāis* even before they were initiated ritually as *sannyāsīs*.

Akhandananda, Swami (1864–1937): monastic name of Gangadhar Ghatak (Gangopadhyay), a disciple of Ramakrishna and a *parivrājak* monk who traveled extensively in northern India, including as far as Tibet, and devoted himself to social welfare work.

Allan, Edith: she and her husband Thomas of San Francisco became Vivekananda's disciples during the Swami's second visit to the United States. It was Tom Allan who, on his own admission, acted "like a crazy man" after having heard Vivekananda's lecture on the similarity between Vedanta philosophy and Christianity and thought the Swami was "not a man, . . . [but] a god." Both Edith and Tom became Hindu and adopted the Hindu name of Viraja and Ajoy, respectively.

Ansell, Ida: a devotee of Vivekananda and his stenographer and secretary in San Francisco during the Swami's second visit to the United States. Her transcription of Swamiji's sixteen lectures are included in the *CW*.

Atulananda, Swami (1870–1966): monastic name of Cornelius J. Heijblom of Amsterdam. He met Vivekananda in the fall of 1899 in New York and at the age of 30 had a conversion experience. He became a monk of the Ramakrishna Order in 1923 at Belur. He is the author of the famous book titled *With the Swamis in America.*

Barrows, John H. (1847–1902): a minister of the First Presbyterian Church of Chicago, Rev. Barrows was the organizer of the World's Parliament of Religions. He is the author of *The World's Parliament of Religions* (1893). Though initially he was favorably disposed to Vivekananda, he later became disenchanted with the Swami for his anti-Christian speeches and sermons.

Basu, Balaram (1842–90): Ramakrishna's householder disciple and a wealthy Bengali landlord from Orissa. He became one of the Master's *rasaddārs* and was noted for his generosity toward all the devotees, disciples, and admirers of Ramakrishna.

Basu, Rajnarain (1826–99): a prominent member of Adi Brahmo Samaj, an educator by profession, and a prolific writer of immense erudition, Rajnarain was a diehard supporter of traditional Hindu beliefs and practices. He was highly critical of the activities of the Hindu College teacher Henry Louis Vivian Derozio and his Young Bengal movement. He made a strong ideological defense of Vedantism in *Vedantic Doctrines Vindicated* (1845).

Bhattacharya, Yajneshwar: nicknamed Fakir, Bhattacharya was a private tutor to Balaram Basu's son Ram. He became quite intimate with Balaram's *gurubhāis,* especially with Vivekananda, who used to call him Fakruddin Ahmed.

Brahmananda, Swami (1863–1922): monastic name of Rakhalchandra Ghosh, one of Ramakrishna's most favorite disciples. Brahmananda was held in high esteem by Vivekananda and became the first president of the Ramakrishna Math and Mission in 1902 following Vivekananda's death that year.

Bull, Sara C. Thorp alias Mrs. Ole Bull (1850–1911): premonastic name of Sister Dhiramata, who hailed from Wisconsin and her father was the Hon. Joseph C. Thorp, a rich lumberman and state senator. She married the Norwegian violinist Ole Bull from whom she separated later. While a resident of Cambridge, Mass., Sara was introduced to Vivekananda by Emma Thursby, the famous singer from New York, and she remained the Swami's lifelong devotee.

Calvé, Emma: the famous prima donna of the Paris Opera, Emma met Vivekananda on 28 November 1899 at Chicago. She became an ardent devotee of the Swami and even took him with her during her Oriental tour. Swamiji considered the Madame a "'great woman'—a giant pine struggling against a cyclone."

Chakravarti, Saracchandra (1868–1942): Vivekananda's great admirer and householder disciple from eastern Bengal. He was initiated by the Swami in 1897 and authored the widely read diary *Swami-Śisya Samvād* covering the last five years of his guru's life. He was often addressed endearingly as *bāngāl* by the monks of the Belur Math.

Chattopadhyay, Bankimchandra (1838–94): the famous Bengali novelist, essayist, nationalist, and intellectual, who, reportedly, had scandalized Ramakrishna in 1884 by boldly declaring that man's duties consisted in "eating, sleeping, and mating." His poem was later adopted as the national anthem by the government of independent India.

Datta, Ramchandra (1851–99): one of the most influential householder disciples of Ramakrishna and an elder cousin of Swami Vivekananda. Datta was one of those devotees who had declared Ramakrishna's divinity and authored the Master's first full-blown biography *Śrīśrīramakrishna Paramahamsadever Jīvanvṛttānta* in 1890. He was also the first individual to build a temple for the regular worship of his Master's relics at his retreat called Yogodyan at Kankurgachhi on the northeastern suburb of Calcutta. Datta was the person who persuaded the reluctant Narendranath to visit Ramakrishna's home at Dakshineshwar.

Deussen, Paul (1845–1919): the famous Sanskritist from Kiel who wrote *Systems of the Vedanta* and *Algemeine Geschichte der Philosophie*. He also translated the *Vedānta Sūtra with Shankara's Commentary* as well as the *Sixty Upaniṣads*. Vivekananda met him in September 1896 at his residence and was profoundly impressed by the erudition of this German Vedanta scholar.

Devamata, Sister (d. 1942): monastic name of Laura Glenn, daughter of well-to-do parents and a graduate of Vassar College. She attended Vivekananda's lectures in New York in 1895–96 and became an active Vedanta worker, assisting Abhedananda and finally taking initiation from Paramananda in 1909. She lived in India for two years (1907–9).

Dharmapala, Anāgarika (1864–1933): born David Hewivitarane, was a leader in the Buddhist revivalist movement of Ceylon. A reformer and a promoter of lay participation in religion (his prefix *anāgarika* stands for a lay ascetic), Dharmapala promulgated a set of two hundred rules for the laity combining elements of Buddhist asceticism with bourgeois morality gaining the upper hand in the society of late nineteenth-century Ceylon. He worked untiringly to restore the principal Buddhist sites and shrines in India, including Bodhgaya, and founded the Mahabodhi Society in 1891, which aimed at revitalizing and promoting Buddhism in dialogue with modern thought. He joined the American Theosophist Col. Henry S. Olcott (who visited Ceylon in 1880) in his struggle against Christian missionary domination of Ceylonese educational system. He developed a National Trust Scheme that led to the establishment of Buddhist colleges in Ceylon. His celebrated book, *The Return to Righteousness,* became a manifesto of Ceylonese nationalist discourse. He was perhaps the most acclaimed and appreciated speaker at the World's Parliament of Religions, Chicago (1893).

Dutt, Michael Madhusudan (1824–73): perhaps the most brilliant poet of nineteenth-century Bengal and originator of a new rhyme in Sanskritized Bengali, the *amṛtākṣar chanda.* He visited with Ramakrishna sometime in 1884–85.

Fincke, Martha B.: met Vivkenanda when she was a student at Smith College, Northampton, where he lectured on 15 April 1894. She is the author of "My Memories of Swami Vivekananda," *Prabuddha Bharata* (September 1936).

Gargi, Sister: monastic name of Marie Louise Burke, the celebrated author of the six–volume *Swami Vivekananda in the West: New Discoveries.* She is presently attached to the Vedanta Society of Northern California.

Ghosal, Sarala: granddaughter of Devendranath Tagore, she was the editor of *Bharati,* and a progressive social worker. Though she was requested by Swamiji to go to the West and preach Vedanta, she remained somewhat skeptical of his socialist-humanist rhetoric.

Ghosh, Girishchandra (1844–1912): an influential playwright, novelist, and stage director of Calcutta in the late nineteenth century. A householder disciple of Ramakrishna, Girish, along with Ram Datta, had declared the Master to be an *avatāra.* He was an intimate friend of Vivekananda.

Ghosh, Purnachandra (1871–1913): one of the six direct disciples of Ramakrishna who were declared as *īśvarakoṭis* (somewhat like the *bodhisattvas*) by the Paramahamsa; the other five were Vivekananda, Brahmananda, Premananda, Yogananda, and Niranjanananda. Next to Vivekananda and Brahmananda, Purna was perhaps the most favorite young man of the Master who literally doted on him. Ghosh, however, never became a monk but remained a successful householder with an abiding interest in the Ramakrishna Order. He was elected to the post of secretary of the Vivekananda Society of Calcutta in 1907.

Ghosh, Tulsiram (b. 1856): elder brother of Baburam (Premananda) and brother-in-law of Balaram Basu. Because of his connections, he was closely acquainted with Ramakrishna and his flock.

Goodwin, Josiah J. (1870–98): the young Englishman who joined the Vedanta Society of London as a stenographer and was the transcriber of Swamiji's speeches and sermons in the United States. He also edited and proofread the transcripts. On Vivekananda's insistence Goodwin came to India and was initiated as a *brahmacārī* by Swamiji sometime in February 1897. He died in south India on 2 June 1898.

Goswami, Nityagopal: a lecturer of Jagannath College, Dacca, Nityagopal heard of Ramakrishna from his friend Vijaykrishna Goswami, a Brahmo devotee of the Paramahamsa. He met the Master sometime in 1884 and devoted the rest of his life to preaching his message.

Gupta, Mahendranath alias ŚrīM (1854–1932): served as headmaster in several Calcutta schools, and by the time he met Ramakrishna (February 1882), he had become headmaster of the Shyambazar branch of the Vidyasagar Institution. A householder disciple of the Master, ŚrīM is the celebrated diarist who wrote *Śrīśrīramakrishnakathāmṛta* in five parts (*bhāgas*), published during 1902–32.

Gupta, Nagendranath (1861–1940): writer and journalist and a younger cousin of Mahendranath Gupta (ŚrīM). He is the author of *Reflections and Reminiscences* (1947)—a work of much firsthand information on Ramakrishna and Vivekananda.

Hale, Mary: eldest daughter of George and Mary Hale of Chicago, patrons of Vivekananda. Mary was a close friend of the Swami, who corresponded with her often.

Hansbrough, Alice Mead: one of the famous Mead sisters of South Pasadena, Alice heard Vivekananda's lectures on 8 December 1900 and was instantly converted to Vedanta. She later helped found the Vedanta Society of Pasadena and Los Angeles.

Hazra, Pratapchandra (*ca.* 1846–1900): hailed from a neighboring village to Kamarpukur (Ramakrishna's native village) called Mahmudpur and, in spite of his critical attitude, a devotee, of Ramakrishna. Hazra was quite idiosyncratic, even somewhat eccentric, in his habits, though he was an intelligent individual. Narendranath admired him and was his intimate friend, Ramakrishna's disapproval notwithstanding.

Leggett, Francis H.: Francis Leggett and his wife Betty (Josephine MacLeod's sister) were wealthy aristocrats of New York. He became Vivekananda's disciple and generous patron. Francis became president of the Vivekananda Society of New York in 1898. The Leggetts invited the Swami to Paris in 1900.

MacLeod, Josephine (1858–1949): a devotee, though not a disciple, of Vivekananda, MacLeod claimed she was Swamiji's "friend." She admired him and was indeed very affectionate to him and helped him financially. She herself was quite a cultivated, high-spirited, and flamboyant woman whom the Swami admiringly addressed as Tantine or Jo Jo. The correspondence between Nivedita and Josephine throws interesting light not only on the personality and behavior of Swami Vivekananda but also on the two women who sort of competed for their guru's attention and affection.

Majumdar, Devendranath (1844–1911): was a devotee of Ramakrishna but was refused initiation into *sannyās* by the Master. Nevertheless Majumdar continued in his devotion and later built a temple for his guru—Śrī Ramakrishna Archanālay—in central Calcutta.

Mitra, Haramohan (b. *c.*1862): a classmate of Vivekananda and a devotee of Ramakrishna, Mitra regularly provided financial support to the Holy Mother after his guru's death.

Mitra, Pramadadas: an affluent property holder of Benares and a Sanskrit scholar who helped Vivekananda with advice on the scriptures and who acted as his host and patron in Benares and other nearby places in north India.

Mitra, Surendranath (1850–90) alias Sureshchandra Mitra: a devotee of Ramakrishna. It was at his residence that Narendranath was invited to sing a few songs in honor of his guest Ramakrishna and met the latter for the first time.

Mozoomdar, Protap Chunder (1840–1905): Brahmo scholar whose article on Ramakrishna in the *Theistic Quarterly Review* (October-December 1879) was one of the earliest to proclaim the purity of the Paramahamsa among readers. He had been to the United States in 1883 as a lecturer of Vedanta as well as Brahmoism prior to his participation in the World's Parliament of Religions in Chicago in 1893 as a member of the selection committee. It is Mozoomdar who accepted Vivekananda's late application without a letter of invitation and allowed him to participate in the Parliament by classifying the Swami as a representative of the Hindu monastic order.

Mudaliar, Singaravelu: an assistant professor of Christian College, Madras, turned a devotee of Vivekananda, who nicknamed him Kidi (bird) for his vegetarian habits.

Müller, Friedrich Max (1823–1900): the famous German Sanskrit and Vedic scholar of Oxford whom Vivekananda met in May 1896. Max Müller wrote a biographical article on Ramakrishna ("A Real Mahatman," *Nineteenth Century,* 1886) and later *The Life and Sayings of Sri Rāmakrishna* (1898). He was critical of Vivekananda's interpretation of Ramakrishna's teachings as Vedantic.

Nag, Durgacharan (1846–99): a resident of Dhaka, Durgacharan became an admirer of Brahmoism at an early age. He met Ramakrishna in 1882 and became an ardent devotee of the Master as well as of the Holy Mother.

Niranjanananda, Swami (1862–1904): monastic name of Nityaniranjan Ghosh, a disciple of Ramakrishna and a close associate of Vivekananda.

Noble, Margaret (1867–1911): premonastic name of Sister Nivedita. A native of Ireland and a school teacher at Wimbledon, Margaret met Vivekananda in London in 1895, and became his devotee and later, in Calcutta, his disciple. She was initiated as a *naisthika brahmacārinī* with the monastic name of Nivedita (meaning the dedicated). She was the spirit behind a girls' school later named Nivedita Girls' School. After Swamiji's death in 1902,

Nivedita parted company with the Ramakrishna Order and devoted herself to the work of national and social regeneration in India, until her death at Darjeeling in 1911.

Okakura, Tenshin (Kakuzō) (1862–1913): was a Japanese art critic and founder of the Institute of Japanese Fine Art (Nihon Bijutso-in). Josephine MacLeod met him in Japan and arranged for his visit to India in 1902. Okakura later became Curator of Far Eastern Art at the Museum of Fine Arts in Boston, Massachusetts.

Pal, Bipinchandra (1858–1932): a member of the Sadharan Brahmo Samaj and an acute observer of his time, Pal authored, among others, an immensely interesting and informative autobiography, *Memories of My Life and Times* in two volumes (Calcutta: Modern Book Agency, 1932–50).

Paramananda, Swami (1884–1940): monastic name of Sureshchandra Guha-thakurata and nicknamed Basanta by Brahmananda. He joined the Ramak-rishna Order at the age of sixteen and was trained by Ramakrishnananda and initiated as a monk by Vivekananda in January 1902. In 1908 he came to the United States where he successfully taught and preached Vedanta until his death. He was one of the most popular and successful monks of the Ramakrishna-Vivekananda Order in the West.

Perumal, Alasinga: a lecturer of a Madras college and an ardent devotee of Vivekananda, Alasinga was responsible for collecting funds for sending the Swami to the Chicago Parliament of Religions. Thereafter he helped his guru with books and articles on Hinduism for the latter's study abroad. He devoted himself to social work in his state.

Premananda, Swami (1861–1918): monastic name of Baburam Ghosh, brother-in-law of Balaram Basu, and a disciple of Ramakrishna. He was an ardent follower of the Paramahamsa and somewhat skeptical of Viveka-nanda's interpretation of the Master's spiritual messages. He later reconciled himself to Swamiji's ways.

Ramabai Saraswati, Panditā (b. 1858): called *Panditā* by Maharaja Jatindra-mohan Tagore, Ramabai was born in Maharastra into a Chitapavan brahmin family. Inspired and guided by her father, Anant Shastri Dangre, a Sanskrit scholar, she herself became a fine Sanskritist and subsequently professor of Sanskrit at the Ladies' College, Cheltenham, England, in 1883. She visited

America in 1886 and published *The High Caste Indian Women* in 1887. She successfully raised funds to establish a school for widows in India, and in the 1880s she founded the Arya Mahila Samaj in Poona. Her later conversion to Christianity annoyed the Hindus.

Ramakrishna (1836–86): monastic name of Gadadhar Chattopadhyay (though he was never initiated ritually into *sannyās*), a native of Kamarpukur village in Bengal and a semiliterate priest of the Kali temple at Dakshineshwar owned by Rani Rasmani (1793–1861), the widow of an influential landlord of Calcutta. He is noted for his ecstatic behavior and eclectic religious outlook (*yata mat, tata path,* that is, "as many views, so many venues" for reaching God), which was later publicized by Vivekananda as a genuine Vedantic view. He was admired for his sermons in simple vernacular Bengali, and he acquired a celebrity for his spiritual performances, including, notably, his ecstatic dancing and getting into a trance (*samādhi*). Many young men became his devotees, and some twelve of them, including Vivekananda, espoused monastic life and founded the Ramakrishna Order after his death.

Ramakrishnananda, Swami (1863–1911): monastic name of Shashibhusan Chakravarti and a disciple of Ramakrishna. As a college student, he had been attracted to the Brahmo Samaj and in fact came to know about the Paramahamsa through the Brahmo press. He was a close associate of Vivekananda and solely responsible for the daily rituals at Baranagore Math. When the Math shifted to Alambazar, his responsibilities increased, and his preoccupation at the monastery prevented him from undertaking pilgrimages. A shrewd judge of men, Vivekananda acknowledged in a letter that Shashi "is the only faithful and true man there." He went to Madras in 1897 at the behest of Swamiji and organized the Order in Madras and Bangalore. He returned to Calcutta due to an attack of tuberculosis and died in August of that year.

Rhodehamel, Frank S.: was one of the students in Vivekananda's Vedanta classes in Oakland. Like Ida Ansell he, too, took notes of the Swami's lectures. His notes of Vivekananda's lectures "The Vedanta Philosophy and Christianity" (*CW,* VII) are especially significant.

Roy, Raja Rammohan (1774–1833): started the Brahmo movement as a reformist, enlightened, and unitarian version of Hindu religion. He hailed from a wealthy landlord family and was quite supportive of British administration in India. Though he is reputed to be instrumental of the abolition of widow burning of the Hindus—the notorious Suttee practice—actually he came to support the abolition after the British government had in fact passed a legislation against the custom on 4 December 1829.

Sanyal, Vaikunthanath (1857–1937): a devotee of Ramakrishna and the author of *Śrīśrīramakrishna Līlāmṛta* (1936) which provides, inter alia, intimate details of the Master's longing for Narendranath. This work also provides Sanyal's profile of Ramakrishna's other devotees.

Saradamani (1853–1920): wife of Ramakrishna and also known as the Holy Mother or Śrīmā. Though married to the Master, she never had any conjugal relations with her husband on his own choice but was a companion to him and looked after him as well as his male devotees and admirers. Reportedly sometime in 1872, Ramakrishna worshiped her as Goddess Kali as part of his *tāntrik sādhanā*. She was regarded as *Saṅghajananī*—the mother of the Ramakrishna Order founded by Vivekananda. Sister Nivedita was very fond of the Holy Mother.

Saradananda, Swami (1865–1927): monastic name of Sharatchandra Chakravarti, Ramakrishna's disciple. He visited England and the United States in 1896 to carry on Vivekananda's Vedantic mission there. He was appointed secretary to the Ramakrishna Mission by Swamiji. He was not only a deft organizer who founded the Order on a sure footing, but more famously, he was the author of the magisterial life of Ramakrishna—*Śrīśrīramakrishnalīlā-prasaṅga* (1909–19), later translated by Swami Jagadananda into English as *Ramakrishna the Great Master*.

Seal, Brajendranath: a brilliant student of philosophy and a senior colleague of Narendranath at the General Assembly's Institution. He later became a renowned philosopher and wrote on Vivekananda in the *Prabuddha Bharata* (April 1907), parts of which are always quoted by Swamiji's biographers to prove his intellectual prowess as witnessed by a great contemporary.

Sen, Adharlal (1855–85): one of Ramakrishna's most intimate householder disciples and *rasaddārs,* Adhar had been a distinguished student of the University of Calcutta and a skeptic, until his meeting the Paramahamsa of Dakshineshwar in March 1883. Though a civil servant (deputy collector of Chittagong in Eastern Bengal, now Bangladesh), he published a number of treatises in Bengali. His brilliant life came to a sudden end following his death from an injury caused by fall from horseback.

Sen, Akshaykumar (1854–1923): nicknamed "*śāṅkcunnī*" or goblin by his friend and *gurubhāi* Narendranath, Sen was a devotee of Ramakrishna and wrote the Paramahamsa's biography in verse: *Śrīśrīramakrishnapuṅthi* (1901); it was highly praised by Vivekananda.

Sen Keshabchandra (1838–84): a Brahmo leader and the organizer of the Brahmo Samaj of India (1868) and later of the splinter association called New Dispensation or Navavidhan. Ramakrishna met Sen in 1875, and both admired each other. Keshab publicized Ramakrishna's spiritual behavior and recognized the Master as a Paramahamsa in his *Paramahaṁser Ukti* (1878).

Sevier, Captain John H. and Charlotte: the English couple who became Vivekananda's disciple. They founded the Advaita Ashrama at Mayavati, a hillside estate, some fifty miles from Almora. Even after the Captain's death in October 1900, Mrs. Sevier continued to work at Mayavati.

Shankaracharya (*ca.* 788–820): also known as Shankara, the most powerful exponent of Advaita Vedanta, he was born in the village of Kalati or Karati in Kerala State of India. Modern researchers place his life during 650–775. He was a man of prodigious learning who also was a prolific writer of Hindu philosophy and metaphysics (vide *Śaṅkara-Granthāvalī*, 10 vols.). Shankara's original contribution lies in his organization of the Hindu monastic order (as spelled out in his *Mahānuśāsana*) and in his teaching that stressed cultivation of wisdom as the way to reach the pinnacle of religious life. He either died at Kanchi or in the Himalayas where, according to one tradition, he undertook his last journey.

Shastri, Shivanath (1847–1919): a Brahmo devotee of Ramakrishna and author of *History of the Brahmo Samaj*, 2 vols. (1912) and *Men I Have Seen* (1919), which provide interesting information on the Master's behavior.

Shivananda, Swami (1854–1934): monastic name of Taraknath Ghosal, one of Ramakrishna's disciples. He was an indefatigable Ramakrishna enthusiast till the last day of his life.

Shubhananda, Swami (?1875–1926): monastic name of Charuchandra Das of Calcutta, an admirer of Vivekananda, and a social worker of Benares (where his parents relocated after retirement), who later organized the Kashi Sevashram under the auspices of the Ramakrishna Mission in 1903. He was initiated into *sannyās* by Brahmananda in 1921 and died in 1926 at Kankhal in the Himalayas, having reportedly been drowned accidentally in the Ganges River.

Shuddhananda, Swami (1872–1938): monastic name of Sudhirchandra Chakravarti, who met Vivekananda at the Alambazar Math in April 1897 and was initiated into *sannyās* in May. He became the assistant editor of the Ramakrishna Order's official organ *Udbodhan* which was first published in 1899. He supervised the publication of Vivekananda's writings and speeches and assumed full leadership of the *Udbodhan* from 1902. He was appointed a trustee of the Belur Math in 1903. He rose to the rank of secretary and, from 1927 through 1934, president, of the Ramakrishna Math and Mission.

Singh, Raja Ajit (1861–1901): ruler of Khetri, Rajasthan, and a devotee of Vivekananda. He financed the Swami's voyage to America, bought him the silk robe and turban that later became the Swami's most familiar monastic outfit, and even suggested for the latter the famous monastic name of Vivekananda.

Sturdy, Edward (b. 1861): an Englishman, born in Canada, Sturdy grew to manhood in New Zealand, where he became interested in Theosophy, led by Madame Helena P. Blavatsky, and in Hinduism. In 1885 he became a fellow of the Theosophical Society of New Zealand. He visited Madras and Almora to read the *Bhāgavadgītā* and practice *sādhanā*. He invited Vivekananda to England in 1895 and helped the Swami's Vedanta work there. He later dissociated with Swamiji.

Subodhananda, Swami (1867–1932): monastic name of Subodhchandra Ghosh and also nicknamed as Khoka Maharaj in the Ramakrishna Order. He was one of the direct disciples of Ramakrishna. He was appointed one of the trustees of Belur Math by Vivekananda.

Tagore, Devendranath (1817–1905): a member of the aristocratic Tagore family of Jorasanko area of north Calcutta. He was the organizer of the Brahmo movement and founder of the Brahmo Samaj. He is the father of the poet Rabindranath. Ramakrishna met the great patriarch of the Tagore clan and was much impressed by him. Devendranath, on the other hand, found the Master somewhat clumsy socially.

Tagore, Rabindranath (1861–1941): poet, patriot, essayist, novelist, storywriter, lyricist, and humanist, and the first Indian to win the Nobel Prize for Literature in 1913 for his *Gītāñjali* (*Song Offerings*). Narendranath used to sing some of Rabindranath's spiritual songs at Keshab Sen's Samaj, though he condemned Tagore as a purveyor of "erotic venom" in society.

Trigunatitananda, Swami (1865–1915): monastic name of Saradaprasanna Mitra, a disciple of Ramakrishna. He traveled to the States in 1903 and worked with the Vedanta Society of California at San Francisco and Los Angeles until his death in 1915.

Turiyananda, Swami (1863–1922): monastic name of Harinath Chattopadhyay, a disciple of the Paramahamsa. He was a close friend of Swamiji and accompanied him to the West during his second voyage. He founded the Shanti Ashrama in the San Anton Valley near San Jose.

Virajananda, Swami (1873–1951): monastic name of Kalikrishna Basu, an admirer and an indefatigable devotee of Vivekananda. He was drawn to the Ramakrishna Order following his acquaintance with Mahendranath Gupta. He met Vivekananda in 1897 at the Alambazar Math, and within a few days, he was initiated into *sannyās,* rising eventually into the ranks by first becoming the general secretary of the Ramakrishna Math and Mission in 1934 and subsequently becoming its president during the last years of his life.

Waddedar, Harinath (1878–1960): premonastic name of Swami Sadashivananda. Vivekananda met him in Benares in 1901 and initiated him into discipleship that year. He was later initiated as a monk in 1902 by Swami Brahmananda at the Ramakrishna Math in Benares. He preached the messages of Ramakrishna and Vivekananda in various regions of India for forty years.

Wright, John Henry (1852–1908): a professor of Greek at Harvard University and subsequently the dean of Harvard Graduate School and a friend of Kate Sanborn, Vivekananda's hostess at Massachusetts. Wright studied Sanskrit and classical philosophy for two years at Leipzig. He admired Vivekananda and gave him a strong letter of recommendation to present to the organizers of the World's Parliament of Religions. According to Marie Burke, "in short, Professor Wright acted as a sort of *deus ex machina,* without whose timely intervention Swamiji might never have attended the Parliament at all" (*Prophetic Mission,* I, 20).

Yogananda, Swami (1861–99): monastic name of Yogindranath Ray Chaudhuri (or Raychaudhuri), Ramakrishna's disciple and a dedicated devotee of the Holy Mother. He hailed from the illustrious Chaudhuri family of Dakshineshwar. After Ramakrishna's death Yogen became the caretaker of the Master's widow, Saradamani, and was initiated into *sannyās* by her. Along with Premananda, Yogananda once questioned Swamiji's refusal to regard the Master as an incarnation.

Notes

Preface

1. Ronald Hyman, *Nietzsche: A Critical Life* (New York: Oxford University Press, 1980), 9.
2. See the interesting journalistic war between Arun Shourie ("Myths about the Swami," *Sunday,* Calcutta, 31 January–6 February 1993 and 7–13 February 1993) and the secretary of the Communist Party of India, A. B. Bardhan ("Rejoinder," *Sunday,* 28 March–3 April 1993). This journalistic duel over the genuineness of Swamiji's statements echoes the controversy between Jaladhar Sen and Dinendrakumar Roy in 1935–36 (see *SAS,* 305–66).
3. *The Statesman* (Calcutta), 20 August 1992.
4. "Homage" by Dr. Chakravarti Rajagopalachari, the first governor-general of Independent India, in Rameshchandra Majumdar, ed., *Swami Vivekananda Centenary Volume* (Calcutta: General Printers & Publishers, 1965), xiii.
5. "The Sāi Bābā Movement: Approaches to the Study of Indian Saints," *The Journal of Asian Studies,* 33, no. 4 (1972): 863.
6. See *RPP.*
7. See Swami Nikhilananda, *The Gospel of Sri Ramakrishna* (1942; reprint, New York: Ramakrishna-Vivekananda Center, 1984), vii. See also *KM.*
8. Jeffrey J. Kripal, letter to author (10 June 1994).
9. *With the Swamis in America and India,* ed. Pravrajika Brahmaprana (Calcutta: Advaita Ashrama, 1988), 275.

Introduction

1. Prophetic Mission, I, 87.
2. Reminiscences of A. Srinivasa Pai, *REM,* 108.
3. Confession of Margaurite Cook to Sara Bard Field (Mrs. Charles Erskine Scott Wood), *Prophetic Mission,* I, 305.
4. Ibid., 486.
5. Cited in Pravrajika Brahmaprana, "Swamiji and His Western Women Disciples," *Prabuddha Bharata,* May 1989, 236.
6. *KSV,* 6–7.
7. Reminiscences of Martha B. Fincke, *REM,* 132.
8. *Prophetic Mission,* I, 88.
9. Atulananda, *With the Swamis in America,* 60.
10. Reminiscences of Sister Christine, *REM,* 148, 219.
11. Brahmaprana, "Swamiji and His Women Disciples," 236.
12. Reminiscences of Ida Ansell, *REM,* 374.
13. *New Gospel,* I, 389–90.

14. *Lawrence American and Andover Advertiser,* 18 May 1894, *Prophetic Mission,* II, 69. Emphasis in original.

15. Ibid., 336.

16. Remark of an old lady from Sydenham, London, *World Teacher,* II, 162–63.

17. Reminiscences of Sister Devamata, *REM,* 124. Emphasis in original.

18. Reminiscences of Josephine MacLeod, *REM,* 244. Emphasis in original.

19. See Swami Lokeshwarananda, ed., *Cintānāyak Vivekananda,* rev. 2d ed. (1395 B.E.; reprint; Calcutta: Ramakrishna Mission Institute of Culture, 1397 B.E.); Nemaisadhan Basu, ed., *Śāśvata Vivekananda* (Calcutta: Ananda Publishers Pvt. Ltd., 1992); Rabindrakumar Dasgupta, ed., *Swami Vivekananda: A Hundred Years since Chicago: A Commemmorative Volume* (Belur: Ramakrishna Math & Mission, 1994); Pravrajika Vedantaprana, ed., *Mahimā Tava Udbhāsita: Dharmasabhā. Śatavarsa Smārakgrantha* (1994; second printing. Dakshineshwar: Sri Sarada Math, 1995).

20. George Williams, "Swami Vivekananda: Archetypal Hero or Doubting Saint?" in *Religion in Modern India,* ed. Robert D. Baird, (New Delhi: Manohar, 1981), 197.

21. The Brahmo Samaj movement, inaugurated by Raja Rammohan Roy, was a reformist, enlightened, and unitarian vision of Hindu religion. The real organizer of the movement was Maharsi Devendranath Tagore, the scion of the house of Tagore of Jodasanko, Calcutta, and father of the poet Rabindranath. In 1868 Keshabchandra Sen separated from Tagore's Adi Brahmo Samaj, and thereafter the Brahmo movement was split into the Adi Brahmo Samaj and the Brahmo Samaj of India under Sen. A further schism took place in 1878 after Keshab, in violation of Brahmo canons, had married his underage daughter off to a wealthy aristocratic family of Cochbihar. Now the Brahmo Samaj of India was split into Keshab's New Dispensation (*Navavidhān*) and a new splinter group called Sadharan Brahmo Samaj. In spite of these internal dissensions, the Brahmo movement did act as a dike against the rushing waves of Christian evangelism in India, especially Bengal. A readable account of Sen's career is Meredith Borthwick, *Keshub Chunder Sen: A Search for Cultural Synthesis* (Calcutta: Minerva Associates [Publishers] Pvt. Ltd., 1978). The best history of the Brahmos remains David Kopf, *The Brahmo Samaj and the Shaping of the Modern Indian Mind* (Princeton: Princeton University Press, 1979).

22. Williams, "Vivekananda: Hero or Saint?" 221.

23. Ronald Bainton, *Here I Stand: A Life of Martin Luther* (1950; reprint, New York: American Library, 1977); Erik Erikson, *Young Man Luther: A Study in Psychoanalysis and History* (New York: W. W. Norton, 1958); Narasingha P. Sil, "Luther, Erikson, and History: A Strange Encounter," *Quarterly Review of Historical Studies* 22, no. 3 (1982).

24. *VAC.*

25. *Vivekananda Anya Cokhe:Ekti Samīkṣā—Āro Kichu Vitarka* (Salt Lake, Calcutta: Utsa Mānus, 1989).

26. Surath Chakravarti, "Svami Vivekananda Banām Brahmo Narendranath O Chicago Dharmasabhā," *Tattvakaumudī,* 16 Māgh 1400 B.E., 16 Jyaistha 1401 B.E., 16 Āsād 1401 B.E.; idem, "Chicago Dharmasabhā (1893): Kichu 'Myth' O Apapracār," *Dharmatattva,* Vaiśākh-Jyaistha 1399 B.E.—Vaiśākh-Āsād 1400 B.E.; idem, "Chicago Dharmasabhāy Pratapcandra Majumdar O Svami Vivekananda (Apapracārer Svarūp Udghātan)," *Dharmatattva,* Māgh 1400 B.E.; idem, *Chicago Parliament of Religions (September 1893): A Short History* (Calcutta: Navavidhan Publication Committee, 1993); idem, *Vivekananda, Brahmo Samaj and Chicago Parliament, 1893* (Calcutta: Navavidhan Publication Committee, 1994).

27. Vivekananda Vitarka ("Pāṭhaker Pratikriyā" and "Lekhaker Nivedan"), *VAC*, 95–102.

28. *CB*, I, 52. Dr. Pratap Chunder Chunder, an erstwhile professor of ancient Indian history and culture at the University of Calcutta, observed that Vivekananda "was first and foremost a *Karmayogī*" who "combined in himself *buddhi, viveka* and *karma*." Cited in Thomas Bryson, "The Hermeneutics of Religious Syncretism: Swami Vivekananda's Practical Vedanta" (Ph.D. dissertation, University of Chicago, 1992), 55.

Chapter 1. Narendranath's Childhood and Education

1. See *LP*, I (Pūrvakathā O Vālyajīvan), 89, 94–96; *BJG*, I, 3; *SVV*, 11, 19.
2. *LP*, I (Pūrvakathā O Vālyajīvan), I, 68–69.
3. *LSV*, I, 11.
4. *SVV*, 10–11.
5. *VJG*, I, 2; *SVB*, 9.
6. *LSV*, I, 2, 4. Durgaprasad became a wandering ascetic (*pravrājika*) at twenty or twenty-two (*SVV*, 4).
7. *CB*, I, 40; *VJG*, I, 6.
8. *Swami Vivekananda on Himself* (Calcutta: Vivekananda Centenary, 1963), 5.
9. *CB*, I, 33.
10. *VJG*, I, 4.
11. *CB*, I, 41.
12. *LP*, I (Pūrvakathā O Vālyajīvan), 92, 106; (Sādhakbhāv), 44.
13. *VJG*, I, 10.
14. *LP*, I (Pūrvakathā O Vālyajīvan), 88, 93, 113; Akshaykumar Sen, *Śrīśrīramak-rishnapuṅthi*, 10th ed. (Kalikātā: Udbodhan Kāryalāy, 1392 B.E.), 21–22.
15. *LP*, I (Pūrvakathā O Vālyajīvan), 112–13, 128–34.
16. Ibid., 141; *LSV*, I, 34.
17. Reminiscences of Kamakhyanath Mitra, *REM*, 336.
18. *SVV*, 19, 73.
19. *VJG*, I, 14.
20. *SVV*, 73.
21. *VJG*, I, 47.
22. *LoSV*, I, 5.
23. Ibid., II, 186.
24. Narasingha P. Sil, "Illiterate Genius?" chap. 8 in *RPP*.
25. *KM*, III, 59 (diary of 27 December 1883).
26. *LP*, I (Pūrvakathā O Vālyajīvan), 116–17; Sen, *Ramakrishnapuṅthi*, 19, 21–22.
27. *CB*, I, 57; *BJG*, I, 11.
28. *CB*, I, 52.
29. Mahendranath Datta, *Śrīśrīramakrishner Anudhyān*, ed. Dhirendranath Basu, 6th ed. (Calcutta: Mahendra Publishing Committee, 1396 B.E.), 89.
30. *CB*, I, 53. He translated Spencer's *On Education* and Thomas à Kempis's *The Imitation of Christ* into Bengali. See Bhupendranath Datta, *Swami Vivekananda Patriot Prophet: A Study*, rev. ed. (Calcutta: Navabharat Publishers, 1993), 88, 286 n. 8.
31. *CB*, I, 53. Most probably he read a survey of Western philosophers such as Friedrich Uberweg, *History of Philosophy: From Thales to the Present Time*, trans.

George S. Morris, 2 vols. (New York: Charles Scribner's Sons, 1885) which Kali
Vedanti attempted to read. *VJG*, I, 99. For a succinct account of Naren's studies, see
Tim Bryson, "Calcutta and Cultural Convergence: Swami Vivekananda as Sycretist,"
Calcutta, Bangladesh, and Bengal Studies: 1990 Bengal Studies Conference Proceedings,
ed. Clinton Seely (East Lansing, Mich.: Michigan State University, 1991), 9–28.
See also Rabin Pal, "Swamijīr Adhyayaner Jagat," Vedantaprana, ed. *Mahimā Tava
Udbhāsita,* 398–405.

32. *VJG*, I, 103.

33. *CW*, I, 479. Vivekananda's language was quite obscure at times, due perhaps
to his literal translation of some rhetorical Bengali expressions. Here "die game,"
apparently a nonsensical phrase, means, most probably, "to engage in the game of
death [*marankhelā* or *maranlīlā* in Bengali]. He must have read the Bengali writings
of Michael Madhusudan Dutt while in college and borrowed the latter's interpretations of the character of Satan.

34. Mahendranath Datta, *Srīmat Saradananda Swamijīr Jīvaner Ghatanāvalī*
(Calcutta: Mahendra Publishing Committee, 1355 B.E.), 104.

35. *CB*, I, 59.

36. *VJG*, II, 127.

37. Ibid., I, 69.

38. *World Teacher,* II, 285.

39. *CB*, I, 328.

40. *RBM*, I, 54.

41. Tapan Raychaudhuri, *Europe Reconsidered: Perception of the West in Nineteenth
Century Bengal* (Delhi: Oxford University Press, 1988), 8 (see also ch. III, 103–218).

42. *CB*, II, 1443.

43. Professor Dhar has provided Narendranath's mediocre scores at the En-
trance, F.A., and B.A. examinations. *CB*, I, 106 n. 20.

44. Reminiscences of Nagendranath Gupta, *REM,* 3.

45. *CB*, I, 51.

46. Bryson, "Hermeneutics of Religious Syncretism," 93–94.

47. Brajendranath Seal, "An Early Stage of Vivekananda's Mental Development," *Prabuddha Bharata,* 12 (April 1907): 64–65.

48. Bandyopadhyay's article in the *Prabāsī* (Māgh 1317 B.E.), transcript by Surath Chakravarti.

49. Vivekananda's letter to Sister Nivedita, 3 June 1897, *CW*, VI, 399. Just a
year earlier he had written to Mary Hale, ridiculing a brother monk who "is always
dreamy, gentle, and sweet." Vivekananda's letter, May 1896, *LV*, 293.

50. *VJG*, I, 97. He must have been encouraged by Ramakrishna's loving comments about him: "See this boy . . . [men like him] belong to the class of the *nityasiddha* [ever-realized]. . . . They come to this world to educate people." Cited in *MJD,*
258. Vivekananda succeeded in making himself a cultural model. Devendradas
Chaudhury's brief study of the Swami as a student has every chapter concluding
with a section on morals (*nītikathā*) exhorting young children of Bengal to emulate
Swamiji's life. See *Vivekanander Chātrajīvan* (Chittagong: Kohinoor Press, 1338 B.E.

51. Vivekananda's letter to Mary Hale, 22 March 1900, *CW*, VIII, 503.

52. Tapan Raychaudhuri, "Muslims and Islam in Swamiji's Vision of India—A
Note" in Dasgupta, ed. *Vivekananda since Chicago,* 322–28.

Chapter 2. Narendranath and Ramakrishna

1. *Vivekananda on Himself,* 23.
2. *VAC*, 13–14.

3. Nivedita's address at the Gaiety Theater, Bombay, 26 September 1902, published in the *Mahratta,* 5 October 1902, *VIN,* 399. According to Swami Gambhirananda, Narendranath asked Maharṣi Devendranath: "Sir, have you seen God?" and received a response from the Brahmo leader: "Your eyes are perfectly like those of a *yogī.*" He also asked Ramakrishna the same question, not when he met the Paramahamsa for the first time, but some time after he had been to Dakshineshwar. *RBM,* II, 17, 24.

4. *VJG,* I, 15.

5. Datta, *Ramakrishner Anudhyān,* 25.

6. *VJG,* I, 15.

7. *LP,* II (Divyabhāv O Narendranath), 110, 111.

8. Ibid., 115 (also 112).

9. *KM,* V, 133 (diary of 22 February 1885).

10. *LP,* II (Divyabhāv O Narendranath), 194.

11. *RPP,* ch. IV (see, especially, 59).

12. *KM,* II, 130 (diary of 29 September 1884).

13. Reminiscences of Tulsiram Ghosh, elder brother of Swami Premananda (Baburam Ghosh), *SAS,* 250. Narendranath's expression is cited in its English original, as reported by Ghosh.

14. The entire paragraph is taken (with slight modifications) from *RPP,* 60.

15. *LP,* II (Divyabhāb O Narendranath), 115. For a detailed treatment of Ramakrishna's homoeroticism see Jeffrey J. Kripal, *Kālī's Child: The Mystical and the Erotic in the Life and Teachings of Ramakrishna* (Chicago: University of Chicago Press, 1995) and idem, "Kālī's Tongue and Ramakrishna: 'Biting the Tongue' of the Tantric Tradition," *History of Religions,* 34, no. 2 (1994).

16. *LSV,* I, 90.

17. *KM,* IV, 230 (diary of 15 July 1885).

18. *LSV,* I, 76–78; *RBM,* I, 19–22.

19. *LSV,* I, 76–77, 87–88, 92; *KM,* IV, 228 (diary of 15 July 1885); Swami Nikhilananda, *Vivekananda: A Biography,* 2d ed. (Calcutta: Advaita Ashrama, 1971), 26–27.

20. Chandrashekhar Chattopadhyay, *Śrīśrīlātumahārājer Smṛtikathā,* 5th ed. (Kalikātā: Udbodhan Kāryālay, 1400 B.E.), 85.

21. *LP,* II (Divyabhāv O Narendranath), 214.

22. Ibid., 217.

23. Ibid., 21–22.

24. Ibid., 222.

25. Datta, *Saradananda Swamijīr Ghatanāvalī,* 13.

26. *KM,* I, 136 (diary of 25 June 1884).

27. *KM,* II, 114 (diary of 21 September 1884).

28. *MJD,* 249.

29. *LP,* I (Pūrvakathā O Vālyajīvan), 104–10 (Sādhakbhāv); VI (Vyākulatā O Pratham Darśan) and VII (Sādhanā O Divyonmattatā). See Timothy A. Jensen, "Madness, Yearning, and Play: The Life of Sri Ramakrishna" (Ph.D. dissertation, University of Chicago, 1976), 81–86. Note, especially, Dr. Jensen's observation: "What Ramakrishna above all sought to do through his Kālī *sādhana* was to replace his paternal loss with a maternal gain" (85).

30. *LP,* II (Divyabhāv O Narendranath), 221.

31. *LSV,* I, 115: "The inner history of Naren's conversion and illumination is too subtle to be described: the Guru brought about these in an inscrutable manner."

32. Sudhir Kakar, *The Inner World: A Psycho-Analytic Study of Childhood and Society in India* (Delhi: Oxford University Press, 1978), 179–80.

Chapter 3. From Narendranath to Vivekananda

1. Nikhilananda, *Vivekananda,* 26–27.

2. *CB,* I, 40, 115.

3. Ibid., 116. Dhar's date of Naren's first meeting with the Master as 5 March 1882 may not be correct. See Swami Prabhananda, *First Meetings with Sri Ramakrishna* (Mylapore: Sri Ramakrishna Math, 1987), 183–86 and 195–97, nn. 8–12.

4. *VJG,* I, 19.

5. *CB,* I, 116.

6. He visited Dakshineshwar on 2 March, 25 June, and 14 September 1884, though he met Ramakrishna at Suresh Mitra's home sometime in August and at Adhar Sen's home on 6 September.

7. *CB,* I, 154–57.

8. *RBM,* I, 30.

9. *RPP,* 57–61.

10. *LSV,* I, 90; *KM,* IV, 230 (diary of 15 July 1885); III, 159 (diary of 9 September 1885); *CB,* I, 136.

11. *LP,* II (Divyabhāv O Narendranath), 208. For *medhānādī,* I have provided part dictionary meaning (the primary meaning of *medhā* is intelligence and of *nāḍī* vein or artery) and part cultural meaning (Bengalis often refer to the development of intellect as "*māthā khule yāwā,*" that is, "the head [or the brain] being opened up").

12. *CB,* I, 145.

13. *LSV,* I, 141; *CB,* I, 146–47. A possible psychological explanation of Narendra's vision of his "double"—albeit tentative—would be that it was the materialization of his split consciousness caused by the gradual breakdown of his Western rationality and its replacement with another kind of "rationality" he had absolutely no idea about.

14. *LSV,* I, 148.

15. Ibid., 92.

16. Report of Vaikunthanath Sanyal, ibid., 130.

17. Ibid., 140–41.

18. Ibid., 137. Ramakrishna of course reminisced about his meeting Goddess Kali in the inner sanctum of the temple because of his *Vyākulatā* (intense longing) and because he had threatened the Merciful Mother with suicide. *LP,* I, 113–14 (Sādhakbhāv).

19. *CB,* I, 148.

20. Swami Abhedananda, *Āmār Jīvankathā* (Kalikātā: Ramakrishna-Vivekananda Math, 1964), 84–85, cited in Swami Prabhananda, *Śrīramakrishner Antyalīlā,* 2d ed., 2 vols. (Kaliakātā: Udbodhan Kāryālay, 1396–1401 B.E.), II, 33 (see also 32 n.2). For Vivekananda's brief career as a school teacher see Swami Nityatmananda, *ŚrīM-Darśán,* 15 vols. (Calcutta: Presidency Library, 1367–81 B.E.), IV, 55.

21. Ibid., II, 34.

22. *VJG,* I, 19.

23. Ibid., 19–20.

24. *MJD,* 239. We should, however, note that their wearing *geruā* cloth was more like *dressing up* as monks. For the Bengalis the stereotypical image of a *sannyāsī*

was that of an ochre robed upcountry man (Hindi speaker) carrying a pair of tongs and a rug made of deer skin. Naren reportedly told Gopal in Hindi, on 16 January 1886, after having visited Ramakrishna in that outfit: "Get yourself a deer skin and a pair of tongs" (*Le leo. Hiran* ["*Harin*"] *kā camdā aur cimtā le leo*). Ibid.

25. Ibid., 249. However, Swami Abhedananda denied the experience in his autobiography, *Āmār Jīvankathā*, 104–5.

26. *VJG*, I, 21–22.

27. Ibid., 22–23.

28. Ibid., 30.

29. Ibid., 25.

30. *RBM*, I, 37–38. This episode is probably based on Vivekananda's personal testimony. About a decade later, his disciple and personal secretary Josiah J. Goodwin informed Sara Bull in a letter (23 May 1897) that "he evidently learnt of the incident either from the Swami himself, or from one of the direct disciples of Paramahamsa Ramakrishna." *LSV*, I, 182.

31. *LSV*, I, 183. It is quite possible that the entire episode was a fabrication. The report of Swamiji's *sādhanā* in different faiths, his receiving the Master's special powers, and his obtaining from the latter the mandate to assume leadership of Ramakrishna's flock was intended to legitimize his spiritual leadership. It is on record that a few years ago he had refused Ramakrishna's offer to transfer his supernatural powers to him because he had wanted to realize God first. *LP*, II (Divyabhāv O Narendranath), 196. And, on his own admission, he had not realized God even after his Master's death. Mahendranath Gupta records Narendra's confession: "It seems God does not exist. No matter how much I pray, I don't get any response." *KM*, II, 246 (diary of 7 May 1887).

32. Swami Prabhananda, *More About Ramakrishna* (Calcutta: Advaita Ashrama, 1993), 237.

33. *VJG*, I, 126.

34. *LSV*, I, 188.

35. Swami Gambhirananda, *History of Ramakrishna Math and Ramakrishna Mission*, 3d ed. (Calcutta: Advaita Ashrama, 1983), 31.

36. *VJG*, I, 32–33: "Well, we householders need a place for relaxation after our daily hard labor for earning money," Mitra said. He contributed Rs. 30.00 for a few months and then raised his monthly contribution to Rs. 100.00.

37. Ibid., 63, 135.

38. Ibid., 55 (see also 35).

39. Kalikrishna Basu provided a graphic description of the homely and spare Math. "Swami Virajananda," *SPP*, 53–54.

40. Gambhirananda, *Ramakrishna Math and Mission*, 39.

41. Apparently the mantra for the *Virajā Hom* had been procured by Kali (Abhedananda) from a monk of the Puri Order of Shankaracharya at Gaya. Ibid., 51. Ô

42. See Swami Chetanananda, "Vivekananda: On the Way to Chicago," ed. Dasgupta, *Vivekananda since Chicago*, 13–14. See also Beni S. Sharma, *Swami Vivekananda: A Forgotten Chapter of His Life* (Calcutta: Oxford Book & Stationary Co., 1963), chs. III and IV; *CB*, I, 401–2.

43. Chakravarti, "Vivekananda Banām Narendranath," *Tattvakaumudī*, 16 Jyaistha 1401 B.E., 23.

44. *KM*, II, Appendix, 246 (diary of 7 May 1887).

45. Ibid., 260 (diary of 8 May 1887).

46. Cited in Chakravarti, "Vivekananda Banām Narendranath," *Tattvakaumudī*,

16 Jyaiṣṭha 1401 B.E., 26. The typos in the quotation as it is printed in Chakravarti's article have been corrected here.

47. Cited in ibid., 27.

48. Cited in ibid., 16 Āsād, 1401 B.E., 36.

49. Shivanath Shastri, *The Mission of the Brahmo Samaj* (1910), 92, cited in Ibid., 40.

50. David Kopf, "The Reinterpretation of Dharma in Nineteenth-Century Bengal: Righteous Conduct for Man in the Modern World" in Rachel van M. Baumer, ed. *Aspects of Bengali History and Society* (Honolulu: University of Hawaii Press, 1976), 96.

51. David Kopf, "The Universal Man and the Yellow Dog: The Orientalist Legacy and the Problem of Brahmo Identity in the Bengal Renaissance" in ed. Baumer, *Aspects of Bengali History,* 74.

52. Ibid.

53. Ibid., 41.

Chapter 4. Vivekananda the Worldly Monk

1. Vivekananda's reply to the address of welcome at Madurai, 2 February 1897, *CW,* III, 174; Vivekananda's address "Vedanta and Its Application to Indian Life" in Madras, 13 February 1897, ibid., 242.

2. Diary of 1898, *SSS,* 160–62.

3. An anonymous correspondent's letter in *The Amrita Bazar Patrika* (Calcutta), 21 April 1898. Surath Chakravarti, letter to author, 4 November 1994.

4. *SSS,* 212.

5. Ibid., 45.

6. Cited in *World Teacher,* II, 288.

7. I thank Rajagopal Chattopadhyaya for sharing his manuscript with me during my visit to Calcutta in December 1995.

8. *VJG,* II, 113–25, 147–50; I, 179–82.

9. *VJG,* II, 151.

10. Ibid., 104.

11. Vivekananda's letter to Alasinga, 11 February 1893, *CW,* VIII, 291. This letter is cited (albeit with a wrong date: 21 February in place of 11 February) in Rajagopal Chattopadhyaya, "'Parivrājak' Vivekanander Bhārat Bhrāman 1886 theke 1893," *Utsa Mānus* (September–October 1995). Chattopadhyaya argues convincingly that Swamiji's famous photograph as the saffron-clad, clean-shaven *parivrājak* with a long walking stick, standing tall against a picture perfect background was probably taken inside a studio. Ibid., 234.

12. *VJG,* I, 184.

13. *SVV,* 12.

14. *CB,* I, 35.

15. *LP,* II (Divyabhāv O Narendranath), 123.

16. Sara C. Bull's letter to Lady Henry Somerset, 22 August 1895, *World Teacher,* I, 195.

17. *New Gospel,* II, 125. Emphasis in original.

18. Shankariprasad Basu, *Sahāsya Vivekananda,* 5th ed. (Calcutta: Navabharat Publishers, 1991), 275.

19. Vivekananda's letter to Alasinga, 20 August 1893, *LV,* 138.

20. *LoSV,* I, 192.

21. Correspondence between Sturdy and Nivedita as well as Sturdy and Viveka-nanda in the fall of 1899, *New Gospel,* I, 76–97; Vivekananda's letter to Sturdy, November 1899, *CW,* VII, 519.

22. "On Fanaticism," *CW,* V, 242.

23. Vivekananda's letter to Edward Sturdy, 14 September 1899, *LV,* 393.

24. Shankariprasad Basu, "Lahore Tribune Patrikāy Vivekananda-Saṁvād evaṁ Vivekananda O Sampādak Nagendranath Gupter Samparka-Kathā," ed. Vedanta-prana, *Mahimā Tava Udbhāsita,* 247. Narendranath had to quit his meditation at Buddhagaya, because he could not digest foods obtained through begging. *RBM,* I, 266.

25. Vivekananda's sermon in Pasadena, California, 27 January 1900, *CW,* VII, 89.

26. *LV,* 393.

27. *VJG,* II, 118.

28. Diary of 1898, *SSS,* 156.

29. Vivekananda's lecture in London, 23 November 1895, *CW,* VII, 227.

30. Vivekananda's conversation with T. J. Desai in London, 1896, *VJG,* II, 118–19.

31. Vivekananda's letter to Sturdy, November 1899, *CW,* VII, 518. Emphasis in original.

32. *LoSV,* II, 56–57.

33. "Swami Virajananda," *SPP,* 78.

34. Cited in *MJD,* 298.

35. *CW,* VIII, 489.

36. Vivekananda's letter of 7 March 1900. Ibid., 496.

37. Chitragupta, *Ādālate Vipanna Vivekananda* (Kalikātā: Yogmāyā Prakāśanī, 1993), 102.

38. Reminiscences of Josephine MacLeod, *REM,* 242.

39. Sharma, *Vivekananda: Forgotten Chapter,* 154.

40. *New Gospel,* I, 71.

41. Vivekananda's letter to Sara Bull, 17 January 1900, *CW,* VIII, 490.

42. *SVV,* 60–61.

43. *VAC,* 29.

44. Vivekananda's letter to Nivedita, 25 August 1900, *PAT,* 744. Part of this letter reproduced in *CW,* VI, 435, is missing.

45. *LP,* II (Divyabhāv O Narendranath), 67–68.

46. Cited in Wendell Thomas, *Hinduism Invades America* (New York: Beacon Press, Inc., 1930), 87.

47. *LoSV,* I, 98–100.

48. Diary of 1898, *SSS,* 114–16, 120.

49. Vivekananda's letter to Mitra, 14 July 1889, *PAT,* 7.

50. *VAC,* 18.

Chapter 5. Vivekananda on Hinduism and the Hindus

1. Rev. Hugh R. Haweis, *Travel and Talk,* 2 vols. (London: Chatto & Windus, 1896), I, 74, reprinted in the *Indian Mirror,* 28 November 1893, *VIN,* 4.

2. *Prophetic Mission,* II, 350.

3. Cited in Kopf, "Orientalist Legacy and Brahmo Identity in Bengal Renais-sance," *Aspects of Bengali History and Culture,* 54.

4. *Prophetic Mission,* II, 155.

5. Vivekananda's lecture reported in the *Detroit Tribune,* 11 March 1894, *Prophetic Mission,* I, 416.

6. *Brooklyn Standard Union,* 27 February 1895, *Prophetic Mission,* II, 291.

7. *CB,* II, 845.

8. Vivekananda's conversations with the audience at Harvard, 25 March 1896,*CW,* V, 309.

9. *CB,* II, 1084.

10. *Brooklyn Standard Union,* 27 February 1895, *Prophetic Mission,* II, 291.

11. *Boston Evening Transcript,* 17 December 1894. Ibid., 239.

12. Scraps of conversation with Vivekananda reported in the *Detroit Tribune,* 1 April 1894, *Prophetic Mission,* I, 445–46.

13. *CW,* V, 466.

14. *LoSV,* II, 163.

15. John N. Farquhar, *Modern Religious Movements in India* (1915; reprint, New Delhi: Munshiram Manoharlal, 1967), 200.

16. Cited in *World Teacher,* I, 493. Emphasis in original.

17. "East and West," *CW,* V, 534. This is entirely contrary to historical facts. One only needs to take notice of the *Aśvamedha* ritual of the Hindu kings. Kautilya's *Arthaśāstra* is a living testimony (admittedly discovered after Vivekananda's death, in 1905) to the iniquities and corruptions in society for which he prescribed elaborate rules and regulations. His discussion of warfare and diplomacy also speaks volumes on the military aspirations of the Hindu conquerors (*vijigīṣu*). See Narasingha P. Sil, *Kautilya's Arthāśāstra: A Comparative Study,* 2d rev. ed. (New York: Peter Lang Publishers, 1989), 80–81. The *Bhāgavadgītā* rationalized and justified violence. Lord Krishna urged Arjuna to battle against his kins at the field of Kurukshetra: "Die and you win heaven. Conquer, and you enjoy the earth" (*Hato vā prāpyasi svargaṁ jitvā vā bhoksyase mahīm*). *Bhagavad Gita: The Song of God,* trans. Swami Prabhavananda and Christopher Isherwood (1944; reprint, Hollywood: Vedanta Press, 1987), 42 (Canto II, Verse 37).

18. Vivekananda's lecture "The Soul and God" delivered in San Francisco, 23 March 1900, *CW,* I, 496.

19. *NWV,* 26.

20. Reminiscences of Basu, *SAS,* 185.

21. Excerpts from the typescript of an article by Mary T. Wright, *Prophetic Mission,* I, 32–33.

22. *Chicago Inter Ocean,* 21 September 1893. Ibid., 124.

23. *Detroit Free Press,* 14/15 February 1894. Ibid., 308.

24. Vivekananda's lecture on Indian women at the Shakespeare Club, Pasadena, 18 January 1900, *New Gospel,* I, 272. The woman, however, responded to the Swami's outburst by calling him a liar.

25. *Detroit Tribune,* 15 February 1894. Ibid., 310.

26. *Detroit Free Press,* 16 February 1894. Ibid., 312. To poke fun at the bishop, Burke makes a childish pun with his surname Ninde which sounds like the Bengali word *nindā,* meaning slander.

27. Datta, *Ramakrishner Anudhyān,* 8.

28. "East and West," *CW,* V, 471.

29. Ibid., 471–72.

30. *Prophetic Mission,* I, 31. Emphasis in original.

31. Vivekananda's letter to Mary Hale, 30 October 1899, *CW,* VIII, 476.

32. *CB,* I, 543.

33. Sister Nivedita, *The Master as I Saw Him*, 12th ed. (Calcutta: Udbodhan Office, 1977), 45. Nivedita's version of the Swami's story differs somewhat from that of his brother Mahendranath, who recounts Vivekananda's nightly lecture in London in which he told his audience how during the time of the Mutiny an old Hindu monk at Prayag (Allahabad) was fatally stabbed by a Muslim and how the dying sage, while bleeding profusely, forbade the Hindu sepoys from killing the murderer, whom they had apprehended, by saying with a smile: "Do not harbor any ill-will against him. He, too, is my Lord, my beloved." *LoSV*, III, 232.

34. Haweis, *Travel and Talk*, I, 74 reprinted in the *Indian Mirror*, 28 November 1893, *VIN*, 4.

35. Abhijit Dutta, *Nineteenth Century Bengal Society and the Christian Missionaries* (Calcutta: Minerva Associates [Publications] Pvt. Ltd., 1992), ch. VI and 215–18.

36. Vivekananda's paper read on 19 September 1893, *CW*, I, 20. The United States overturned the Hawaiian Kingdom in 1893.

37. Letter to the editor of the *Indian Social Reformer*, 1 June 1895, *VIN*, 427.

38. Letter to the editor of the *Indian Mirror*, 21 February 1897. Ibid., 155. Emphasis in original.

39. G. C. Banerji, *Keshab Chandra and Ramakrishna* 2d ed. (Calcutta: Navavidhan Publication Committee, 1942), 130.

40. Letter to the editor of the *Indian Mirror*, 25 February 1897. Ibid., 157.

41. Vivekananda's reply to welcome at Tr ɔlicane Literary Society, Madras, 9 February 1897, *CW*, IV, 346.

42. Ray Ellis, "In Search of Swamiji," in ed. Dasgupta, *Vivekananda since Chicago*, 120.

43. *DBN*, 103.

44. Pravrajika Vajraprana, *"My Faithful Goodwin"* (Calcutta: Advaita Ashrama, 1994), 80–82.

45. Vivekananda's letter to Subrahmanya Iyer, 3 January 1895, *CW*, IV, 372–73. It ought to be noted that Swamiji was writing to a very cast conscious brahmin of Madras and hence elevated caste with his specious argument that caste is identified and recognized by Hindu astrology "and we can rise by giving it full sway again." Ibid., 373. See also Kopf, "Reinterpretation of Dharma in Nineteenth-Century Bengal," 90.

46. Report of Vivekananda's sermon in the *Chicago Inter Ocean*, 21 September 1893, *Prophetic Mission*, I, 124.

47. Discussion at the Graduate Philosophical Society, Harvard University, 25 March 1896, *CW*, V, 307. Rajnarain Basu had argued in favor of retaining the caste system in an article in the *Tatvavodhinī Patrikā* in 1874. Kamalkumar Ghatak, *Hindu Revivalism in Bengal: Rammohan to Ramakrishna* (Calcutta: Minerva Associates [Publications] Pvt. Ltd., 1991), 49–50.

48. "East and West," *CW*, VIII, 537. A rather uncritical, though well written, essay is Jayashree Mukherjee's "The Institution of Caste in the Eyes of Ramakrishna and Vivekananda," *Quarterly Review of Historical Studies* (Calcutta), 27, no. 2 (1987).

49. Vivekananda's lecture at the Twentieth Century Club, 28 March 1896, *CW*, V, 311. Note here the Swami's indirect praise for the British rule of India to his English audience.

50. Vivekananda's lecture reported by the *Brooklyn Standard Union*, 8 April 1895, *CW*, II, 516.

51. *CB*, I, 22.

52. *CW*, V, 309.

53. *VJG*, II, 168.

54. Vivekananda's lecture "My Plan of Campaign" at Victoria Hall, 6 February 1897, *CW*, III, 211. See also Vivekananda's letter of 3 March 1894 to Singaravelu Mudaliar. *LV*, 70.

55. For a reliable account of the Indian caste system, see Rev. Krishnamohan Banerjee's *An Essay on Hindu Caste* (Calcutta 1851) discussed in Dutta, *Bengal Society and Christian Missionaries*, 114–15. Vivekananda must have derived the basic facts on the caste system from this work but interpreted them in his own way.

56. Dutta, *Bengal Society and Christian Missionaries*, 221–22.

57. *VIN*, 164.

58. Vivekananda's lecture "The Future of India" at the Harmston Circus Pavilion, Madras, 14 February 1897, *CW*, III, 298.

59. *VJG*, I, 8. Vivekananda also considered the Africans ugly, as is evident in his scornful remark on the Bengali in London, who in Western outfit looked like Negroes (*kāfrī*). *Sahāsya Vivekananda*, 183. He was also quite contemptuous of their character and habits. Vivekananda's letter to Ramakrishnananda, 1894, *PAT*, 239–40.

60. Vivekananda's letter to Mary Hale, 1 November 1896, *LV*, 318.

61. Dinanath Ganguli's letter to the *Indian Mirror*, *VIN*, 155.

62. "Future of India," *CW*, III, 293–95.

63. Ibid., 297–98. Vivekananda's attitude to castes was influenced by that of his *guru* Śrī Ramakrishna, who believed that one need not hasten the abolition of the caste system and observed: "When the fruit is ripe it falls from the tree itself. To wrench the unripe fruit is not good." Sajanikanta Das and Brajendranath Bandopadhyay, ed., *Samasāmayik Dr̥stite Śrīramakrishna Paramahaṁsa* (Calcutta: General Printers & Publishers Pvt. Ltd., 1375 B.E.), 31.

64. Report in the *Detroit Evening News*, 25 March 1894, *Prophetic Mission*, I, 444–45.

65. Report of the Swami's lecture in the *Chicago Daily Inter-Ocean*, 23 September 1893, *CW*, VIII, 198.

66. Report in the *Evening News*, Massachusetts, 29 August 1893. Ibid., 48.

67. Lecture on Indian women, 17 December 1894, *Prophetic Mission*, II, 416.

68. Diary of Mary Wright, 1893, *Prophetic Mission*, I, 35.

69. Report of *Daily Eagle*, New York, 7 February 1895, *CW*, II, 514. It is quite possible that Vivekananda had a vague understanding of Horace Hyman Wilson's essay "On the Supposed Vaidik Authority for the Burning of Hindu Widows and on the Funeral Ceremonies of the Hindus," published in the *Journal of the Royal Asiatic Society*, 16 (1854), reprinted with a rejoinder from Raja Radhakanta Dev, in *Essays and Lectures Chiefly on the Religion of the Hindus*, II, 270–309. See H. H. Wilson, *Essays and Lectures Chiefly on the Religion of the Hindus*, ed. Reinhold Rost, 2 vols. (London: Trübner, 1861–62).

70. Scraps of conversation with Vivekananda reported in the *Detroit Tribune*, 1 April 1894, *Prophetic Mission*, I, 447.

71. Report in the *Daily Tribune*, 8 May 1894, *Prophetic Mission*, I, 390.

72. Vivekananda's lecture on Indian women at Cambridge, Massachusetts, 17 December 1894, *Prophetic Mission*, II, 421.

73. *KM*, II, 49 (diary of 4 June 1883), 97 (diary of 5 April 1884).

74. *Prophetic Mission*, II, 417.

75. *KM*, IV, 240 (diary of 9 August 1885).

76. Bryson, "Hermeneutics of Religious Syncretism," 340.

77. "Modern India," *CW*, IV, 479–80.

78. Vivekananda's lecture "The Sages of India" at Victoria Public Hall, Madras, 11 February 1897, *CW*, III, 256.

79. Vivekananda's lecture "Women of India" at the Shakespeare Club, Pasadena, 18 January 1900, *CW*, VIII, 58.

80. Ibid., 61.

81. We get the reference to Vivekananda's sister's tragic death in his letter to Sara Bull. Letter of 12 December 1899, *LV*, 405–6.

82. Reminiscences of Shachindranath Basu, *SAS*, 184–85.

83. *VAC*, 82.

84. Report in the *Daily Gazette*, 29 August 1893. Ibid., 468. The Swami must have derived his insight from Bankimchandra's satirical essay on "traditional" and "new" women—"Prācīnā evaṁ Navīnā"—in which the author had contrasted the women of two different generations and lambasted the "new women" as lazy, luxurious, and delinquent in housekeeping. He may have deliberately presented the analysis from the hegemonic masculine viewpoint and thus subsequently published three fictional letters from women who, as readers, felt that his conclusions were gender biased. Vivekananda either ignored Bankim's subtle autocritique, or he was innocent of those fictional letters published by Bankim. See Partha Chatterjee, *The Nation and Its Fragments: Colonial and Postcolonial Histories* (Princeton: Princeton University Press, 1993), 135.

85. Interview with Vivekananda published in the *Prabuddha Bharata*, December 1898, *CW*, V, 231.

86. Padma Khastgir, "Vivekananda's Ideas on Womanhood" in ed. Dasgupta, *Vivekananda since Chicago*, 351.

87. Papiya Chakravarti, "Nārīvāder Paripreksite Swami Vivekanander Nārī-Bhāvanā" in ed. Basu, *Śāśvata Vivekananda*, 137.

88. *VAC*, 82.

89. Vivekananda's letter, 24 January 1894, *CW*, V, 28–29.

Chapter 6. Vivekananda's Humanitarian and Social Thought

1. See, for example, Ramendranarayan Sarkar, "Swami Vivekananda O Ganacetanā," in ed. Lokeshwarananda, *Cintānāyak Vivekananda*, 337–49.

2. Datta, *Patriot-Prophet*. See also my review of this work in *The Statesman* (Calcutta), 29 January 1994.

3. Santwana Dasgupta, "Swami Vivekanander Samājdarśane Rāstranaitik O Arthanaitik Cintā" in ed. Lokeshwarananda, *Cintānāyak Vivekananda*. The writer's concluding remark reveals her conviction in the Swami's achievements: "Not just for the present, even in the days to come, those striving to recover their human rights will have to turn to Vivekananda's thoughts and speeches for inspiration and guidance" (439).

4. Vivekananda's letter to Ramakrishnananda, 27 April 1896, *PAT*, 455; *VAC*, 26.

5. For a discussion of this subject, see Kripal, *Kālī's Child*, ch. 3.

6. *KM*, III, 169 (diary of 9 May 1885).

7. *KM*, I, 50–51 (diary of 27 October 1882).

8. "Hermeneutics of Religious Syncretism," 339.

9. *VAC*, 35 (see also the section "Vivekananda O Maitrībhāvanā," 33–46).

10. *PAT*, 258–59.

11. Vivekananda's letter to Akhandananda, March/April 1894. Ibid., 242.

12. Vivekananda's letter to Miss Sarala Ghosal, 24 April 1897. Ibid., 534.

13. Vivekananda's letter to Akhandananda, 5 June 1897. Ibid., 559.

14. Vivekananda's letter to Haridas Viharidas Desai, November 1894, *CW*, VIII, 331.

15. Vivekananda's letter to Mr. Mitra, 28 December 1893. Ibid., 100. Four years later, in Madras, the Swami would appeal to the Brahmins to "work hard to raise the Indian people by teaching them what they know, by giving out the culture that they have accumulated for centuries." "Future of India," *CW*, III, 297.

16. Cited in Nivedita, *Master*, 21–22.

17. Reminiscences of Shuddhananda, *SPP*, 7–8.

18. Cited in Dasgupta, "Vivekanander Samājdarśan," 92.

19. "Memoirs of European Travel," *CW*, VII, 327.

20. Vivekananda's lecture at the Shakespeare Club, Pasadena, 27 January 1900, *CW*, VIII, 86.

21. Vivekananda's letter to Sarala Ghosal, 24 April 1897, *PAT*, 534.

22. Reminiscences of Turiyananda, *SAS*, 1.

23. Reminiscences of Manmathanath Gangopadhyay. Ibid., 112.

24. Vivekananda's letter to Chakravarti, 3 July 1897, *PAT*, 563.

25. Reminiscences of Surendranath Datta, *SAS*, 231. See also reminiscences of Manmathanath Gangopadhyay. Ibid., 100.

26. Reminiscences of Swami Achalananda. Ibid., 55.

27. Diary of 1902, *SSS*, 242. See also *VUG*, 163.

28. *World Teacher*, I, 347.

29. Swami Jagadishwarananda, *Śrīramakrishna Pārsad-Prasanga* (1357 B.E.; reprint, Belur: Śrīramakrishna Dharmacakra, 1398 B.E.), 4.

30. Vivekananda's letter to Indumati Mitra, 24 May 1893, *PAT*, 65.

31. Cited in Nachiketa Bharadwaj, "Bhārater Navajāgaraṇ: Rammohan Theke Vivekananda," ed. Lokeshwarananda, *Cintānāyak Vivekananda*, 751.

32. Vivekananda's letter to Ramakrishnananda, Summer? 1898, *PAT*, 164.

33. *LoSV*, II, vi: cited from Mahendranath Datta, *Guruprāṇ Rāmcandrer Anudhyān* (Calcutta: Mahendra Publishing Committee, 1958), 76.

34. Diary of 1898, *SSS*, 143.

35. Reminiscences of Priyanath Sinha, *SAS*, 148–49.

36. Diary of 1898, *SSS*, 143.

37. Vivekananda's letter to Margaret Hale, 20 June 1897, *CW*, VIII, 406.

38. Vivekananda's letter to Brahmananda, 1895, *PAT*, 287.

39. Vivekananda's letter to Alasinga, August 1895, *CW*, V, 92; Vivekananda's letter to Mary Hale, 1 February 1895, 70. Emphasis in original.

40. Rita Rudra, "Swami Vivekananda's Concept of Man" (Ph.D. dissertation, Claremont Graduate School, 1974), 183.

41. Datta, *Patriot-Prophet*, 71–72.

42. Vivekananda's letter to Alasinga, 28 May 1894, *CW*, V, 3.

43. Vivekananda's letter to Shuddhananda, 11 July 1897, *PAT*, 575.

44. Vivekananda's letter to Akhandananda, 21 February 1900. Ibid., 696.

45. Vivekananda's letter to Brahmananda, 10 July 1897. Ibid., 572.

46. Vivekananda's letter to Akhandananda, March/April 1894. Ibid., 241–42.

47. Vivekananda's letter, 24 January 1894, *CW*, V, 29.

48. E. Chelishev, "Swami Vivekananda—the Great Indian Humanist, Democrat and Patriot" in Harish C. Gupta, ed. *Swami Vivekananda Studies in Soviet Union* (Calcutta: Ramakrishna Mission Institute of Culture, *ca.* 1987), 210.

49. *World Teacher,* II, 435.

50. *CW,* V, 67. Emphasis in original.

51. Vivekananda's letter to Alasinga, 6 May 1895, cited in *World Teacher,* II, 436: For part of this letter see *CW,* V, 79–83. By this time the Swami had made some money through organized lectures.

52. *Selected Writings by Brahmananda Keshav,* preface by Surath Chakravarti (Calcutta: 150th Birth Anniversary Committee, 1990), 4–5.

53. *LV,* 117–18. Emphasis in original.

54. *Prophetic Mission,* I, 81.

55. *New Gospel,* II, 79.

56. Vivekananda's letter, 9 July 1897, *LV,* 350. Swami Satprakashananda has called Swamiji a *Bodhisattva.* See his *Swami Vivekananda's Contribution to Present Age* (St. Louis: The Vedanta Society of St. Louis, 1978), 108.

57. Diary of 1898, *SSS,* 168. Ramakrishna had said: "I would indeed feel blessed if by assuming a thousand births I can liberate one single person." Cited in Swami Prabhananda, "Reflections on Swami Vivekananda's Doctrine of Service," ed. Dasgupta, *Vivekananda since Chicago,* 404. See also *LP,* I (Sādhakbhāv), 312–13.

58. Cited in F. R. Allchin, "The Social Thought of Swami Vivekananda," Swami Ghanananda and Geoffrey Parrinder, ed., *Swami Vivekananda in East and West* (London: The Ramakrishna Vedanta Centre, 1968), 92.

59. *CB,* II, 941. This behavior of the Swami appears to be an imitation of Ramakrishna's alleged vicarious suffering on his back at the sight of a boatman being hit on the back. Rameshchandra Majumdar, *Śrīramakrishner Ātmakathā* (Nava Barrakpur: Sri Sri Ramakrishna Trust, 1987), 83.

60. Reminiscences of Akhandananda, *SAS,* 16.

61. Reminiscences of Nagendranath Gupta, *REM,* 16.

62. Diary of 1897, *SSS,* 60–62. We need to recall in this context that Girish the dramatist had proclaimed the divinity of Ramakrishna and his wife Saradamani in similar fashion. *RPP,* 71; Narasingha P. Sil, "Saradamani the Holy Mother: The Making of a Madonna," *Asian Culture Quarterly* 21, no. 2 (1993): 75 and nn. 27–28.

63. Reminiscences of Swami Vijnanananda in Jagadishwarananda, *Ramakrishna Pārṣad-Prasaṅga,* 26. It may very well be that the Swami suffered from breathing difficulty due to asthma, and this asthma attack resulted in his moaning, which was taken for "loud wailing."

64. Gambhirananda, *Ramakrishna Math and Mission,* 87.

65. Cited in Swami Prabhananda, "Swami Vivekānander Āloke Dāridryamocan Samasyā," ed. Basu, *Śāśvata Vivekananda,* 83.

66. Vivekananda's letter to Leggett, 6 July 1896, *LV,* 296.

67. *VJG,* I, 104.

68. Conversations of Subodhananda, Jagadishwarananda, *Ramakrishna-Pārṣad-Prasaṅga,* 182.

69. *CB,* I, 104.

70. Vivekananda's letter, 1 October 1897, *CW,* VIII, 429.

71. *KSV,* 42–43.

72. Communication from Biswajit Das, Akashvani, Calcutta A, *Anubhav* program at 8:15 A.M. (20 December 1995).

73. *CB,* II, 941.

74. *VAC,* 66.

75. Allchin, "Social Thought of Vivekananda," 92.

76. Nivedita's letter to Josephine MacLeod, *ca.* 1899, *LSN,* I, 150.

77. Vivekananda's letter to Mary Hale, 1 November 1896, *CW,* VI, 381. See

also V.K.R.V. Rao, *Swami Vivekananda: The Prophet of Vedantic Socialism* (New Delhi: Ministry of Information & Broadcasting, 1979); Arun K. Biswas, *Vivekananda and the Indian Quest for Socialism* (Calcutta: Firma KLM Pvt. Ltd., 1986); Satindranath Chakravarti, "Swami Vivekananda O Socialism," ed. Lokeshwarananda, *Cintānāyak Vivekananda,* 320–36; Swami Someshwarananda, "Natun Pṛthivīr Sandhāne Karl Marx O Swami Vivekananda." Ibid., 793–833; idem, "Vivekananda O Bhārate Samājtantrī Āndolan," ed. Basu, *Śāśvata Vivekananda,* 69–81; Dietmar Rothermund, "Vivekanander Cintāy Aitihyavād O Samājvād" [Bengali translation from German original]. Ibid., 150–55; Santwana Dasgupta, "Samājtāntrik Deśe Vivekanander Vāṇī." Ibid., 204–29; Hiren Mukherjee, "The Glory That Was Vivekananda," ed. Dasgupta, *Vivekananda since Chicago,* 582–86.

78. Vivekananda's lecture "Buddhistic India" at the Shakespeare Club, Pasadena, 2 February 1900, *CW,* III, 516.

79. Vivekananda's lecture "Women of India," *CW,* VIII, 63, 65.

80. *World Teacher,* II, 383.

81. Vivekananda's lecture "Vedanta and Privilege" in London, undated, *CW,* I, 426.

82. Dr. Bhupendranath Datta, *Swami Vivekananda* (1961; 3d ed. Calcutta: Navabharat Publishers, 1400 B.E.), 3.

83. *Vivekananda and Socialism,* 102 (see also ch. I).

84. E. N. Komarov, "Modern Views of Vivekananda in the Context of Enlightenment Ideology of India" and R.B. Rybakov, "Bourgeois Reformation of Hinduism," ed. Gupta, *Vivekananda Studies in Soviet Union.*

85. Vivekananda's letter to Akhandananda, 21 February 1900, *PAT,* 696.

86. Vivekananda's letter to Alasinga, 1895, *CW,* V, 74.

87. "Future of India," *CW,* III, 289.

88. Cited in *VUG,* 168.

89. Reminiscences of Haripada Mitra, *REM,* 36.

90. *VAC,* 47–52.

91. Cited in Benoy K. Roy, *Socio-political Views of Vivekananda* (New Delhi: People's Publishing House, 1970), 34–35.

92. Ibid., 63–64.

93. Sanat Mukhopadhyay and Manju Datta, *Vivekananda Parikar Kiranchandra Datta O Tatkālīn Samāj (1876–1960)* (Kalikātā: Kiran Niketan, 1396 B.E.), 49–50.

94. "East and West," *CW,* V, 475.

Chapter 7. Secrets of Vivekananda's Popularity

1. *Prophetic Mission,* I, 83–84. The sentence claiming uniqueness for Sanskrit is omitted from Swamiji's address on 11 September 1893 as it appears in *CW,* I, 3–4, *Vivekananda: The Yogas and Other Writings,* rev. ed. (New York: Ramakrishna-Vivekananda Center, 1984), 183, and in ed. Dasgupta, *Vivekananda since Chicago,* Appendix A.

2. Vivekananda's letter to Alasinga, 2 November 1893, *CW,* V, 21.

3. *Prophetic Mission,* I, 81.

4. Lewis P. Mercer, *Review of the World's Religious Congresses of the World's Congress Auxiliary of the World's Columbian Exposition, Chicago, 1893* (Chicago: Rand, McNally & Co., 1893), 44. Emphasis added.

5. Ibid., 32. Emphasis in original.

6. *Prophetic Mission,* II, 95.

7. *Boston Daily Globe*, 24 March 1894, *World Teacher*, II, 61.

8. *World Teacher*, I, 486.

9. Vivekananda's letter to Sara Bull, 12 December 1899, *LV*, 405–6.

10. "Swami Virajananda," *SPP*, 76.

11. Reminiscences of Miss MacLeod, *REM*, 228.

12. Pravrajika Prabuddhaprana, *The Life of Josephine MacLeod: Friend of Swami Vivekananda* (Dakshineshwar: Sri Sarada Math, 1990), 286.

13. Ibid., 12. M. Rolland perhaps justifiably observed that Josephine had little concern for "the God of Vivekananda" but "was very intimate with Vivekananda . . . looking after him and entertaining him." She "never tires of pointing out his beauty, his charm, the power of attraction which was radiating from him." R. Rolland, "Journal 1915–1943," *Inde* (1960), cited in ibid., 208, 210.

14. Cited in *World Teacher*, II, 162–63.

15. *LoSV*, I, 21.

16. Vivekananda's letter, 1895, *PAT*, 413.

17. Emma Calvé, "My Life," tr. Rosamond Gilden, *Saturday Evening Post* (9 September 1922) cited in *New Gospel*, II, 396.

18. Reminiscences of Swami Shuddhananda, *REM*, 319.

19. Rev. H. M. Morey of Michigan commented on Vivekananda's "half-truths," which "may sometimes do the work of lies and slanders." The Reverend said that Vivekananda "has told a truth or a half-truth in such a way as to justify the claim of the rabbi [*sic*] that it is a 'delusion' to send missionaries to India." Report of *Detroit Tribune*, 26 February 1894, cited in *Prophetic Mission*, I, 385–86.

20. Vivekananda's speech "My Life and Mission" at the Shakespeare Club, Pasadena, 27 January 1900, *CW*, VIII, 82. The source of this piece of information appears to be nonexistent.

21. Sevak Ramchandra (Datta), *Śrīśrīramakrishnaparamahaṁsadever Jīvanvṛttānta* (1297 B.E. Eighth ed. Kalikātā: Udbodhan Kāryālay, 1402 B.E.), 32. This edition is (at places) a slightly emended version of the 1950 edition now out of print.

22. "My Master," 1896, *CW*, IV, 175.

23. Datta, *Jīvanvṛttānta*, 10–11.

24. *Prophetic Mission*, I, 28.

25. Cited in Banerji, *Keshab Chandra and Ramakrishna*, 295.

26. *LSV*, I, 328.

27. Reminiscences of Haripada Mitra, *REM*, 46.

28. *LoSV*, 153–54.

29. Diary of November 1898, *SSS*, 100

30. Vivekananda's lecture, 5 October 1893, *CW*, III, 479.

31. *Swami Vivekanander Vāṇī O Racana Sankalan* 6th ed. (Kalikātā: Udbodhan Kāryālay, 1400 B.E.), 335.

32. *New Gospel*, II, 58–59: Vivekananda delivered three lectures on 20, 23, and 27 March 1900: "Nature and Man," "Soul and God," and "The Goal."

33. Ibid., 218. Vivekananda's lecture on the *Gītā* at the home of Dr. Milburn H. Logan, San Francisco, 29 May 1900. Emphasis in original.

34. Conversation of November 1898, *SSS*, 105.

35. *New Gospel*, II, 57–58.

36. *LSV*, I, 428.

37. Amalendu Bose, "Vivekananda: Lord of Language" in *The Other Harmony* (Calcutta, 1977), 70, cited in Vishwanath Chatterjee, "The Living Voice" in ed. Dasgupta, *Vivekananda since Chicago*, 88.

38. Reminiscences of Calkins, *REM*, 387.

39. *LoSV*, II, 49 (see also 45, 182–83, 185).

40. *LoSV*, I, 93.

41. Ibid., 170.

42. Datta, *Ramakrishner Anudhyān*, 124.

43. Rajagopal Chattopadhyaya, *World's Parliament of Religions, 1893. Participation from the Indian Subcontinent and the 1993 Parliament* (Calcutta: Minerva Associates [Publications] Pvt. Ltd., 1995), 28–29. For an almost desperate but feeble attempt to add something new to the already inflated evaluation of Vivekananda's exploits in Chicago, see Nemaisadhan Basu, "Samasāmayik Pāścātyer Dṛṣṭikone Chicago Dharmamahāsammelan O Swami Vivekanander Bhūmikār Tātparyer Mūlyāyan," *Udbodhan*, 96, nos. 5 & 6 (Jyaiṣṭha & Āṣāḍ, 1401 B.E.).

44. Vivekananda's letter to Ramakrishnananda, 25 September 1894, *PAT*, 191.

45. *Swami Vivekananda and His Guru with Letters from Prominent Americans on the Alleged Progress of Vedantism in the United States* (London and Madras: The Christian Literature Society for India, 1897), iv–vi.

46. *VIN*, 297.

47. Carl T. Jackson, *Vedanta for the West: The Ramakrishna Movement in the United States* (Bloomington: Indiana University Press, 1994), 29.

48. *Days in an Indian Monastery* (La Crescenta, Calif.: Ananda Ashrama, 1927), 326.

49. Laurence Veysey, *The Communal Experience: Anarchist & Mystical Communities in Twentieth-Century America* (1973; with a new Preface. Chicago: University of Chicago Press, 1978), 217–19 and n. 22.

50. *CW*, I, 373–74.

51. Ibid., 424.

52. Ibid., 448.

53. See Bryson, "Hermeneutics of Religious Syncretism," 305–6. Bryson cites Vinet's *Homiletics or the Theory of Preaching*, trans. Thomas H. Skinner, 3d ed. (New York: Ivison & Phinney, 1870), 22, 26, 29–32, 37, 227–28. See also K. Panchapagesan, "A Stylistic Study of Swami Vivekananda's Speech," *Prabuddha Bharata*, 90 (January 1985).

54. Manmohan Ganguly, *The Swami Vivekananda: A Study* (2d print. Calcutta: Contemporary Publishers, 1962), 72.

55. *LoSV*, II, 50. He would also be curious about the impact his sermon of a particular day made on the audience. Thus he would often inquire of Goodwin how he had fared and would, like a simple child, seek his devotee's interpretation of his sermon: "What is the meaning of it?" On being told the meaning, he would suggest that his sermons be written down together with Goodwin's interpretations. This harmless behavior of the Swami was an unmistakable imitation of Ramakrishna's making similar queries to ŚrīM. See *KM*, IV, 122 (diary of 3 August 1884).

56. "The Necessity of Religion." Lecture delivered in London sometime in summer 1896 and published by Edward Sturdy in December, *CW*, II, 63–64.

57. Burke tamely suggests that "Swamiji would not have disagreed with this principle" (Bentham's concept of the greatest good of the greatest neumber). *World Teacher*, II, 208.

58. *LoSV*, II, 93–94.

59. Ibid., 95.

60. Ibid., 93–94.

61. "Swami Vivekananda as a Speaker and Writer of English" in Asitkumar Bandyopadhyay, Shankari prasad Basu, and Shankar, ed., *Viśvavivek* (Kalikātā: Vāk Sāhitya, 1963), 451.

62. *Hinduism Invades America,* 111.

Chapter 8. Vivekananda's Ramakrishna

1. Diary of 1897, *SSS,* 3.
2. "My Life and Mission," *CW,* VIII, 79.
3. "My Master," *CW,* IV, 179, 187.
4. Vivekananda's lecture "Practical Vedanta" in London, 10 November 1896, *CW,* II, 245.
5. Datta, *Patriot-Prophet,* 143.
6. Ibid., 159.
7. Ibid., 177.
8. Vivekananda's letter to Mohammed Sarfraj Husain, 10 June 1898. *LV,* 380.
9. *KM,* II, 69 (diary of 26 September 1883).
10. *KM,* I, 505 (diary of 27 October 1882).
11. *CB,* II, 948.
12. *LSV,* I, 156.
13. "My Plan of Campaign," 1897, *CW,* III, 225.
14. *KM,* IV, 298 (diary of 21 February 1887).
15. See Reminiscences of Sisters Christine and Nivedita, Emma Calvé, and Edward Sturdy, *REM.*
16. *CW,* VI, 335. Vivekananda's letter to Ramakrishnananda (*ca.* 1895). See also "*Śrīśrīramakrishnapunthi Samvandhe Ācārya Śrīmat Swami Vivekanander Abhimat*" [Preface by Vivekananda] in Sen, *Śrīśrīramakrishnapunthi.*
17. Vivekananda's letter to Dr. Nanjunda Rao, 30 November 1894, *CW,* VI, 281.
18. Nivedita, *Master,* 255.
19. *LSV,* II, 354.
20. Vivekananda's letter to Shivananda, 1894, *PAT,* 255.
21. *KM,* I, 253 (diary of 27 October 1885).
22. *CB,* II, 1009; Dhar, *Vedanta and Bengal Renaissance,* 129.
23. *CB,* II, 947.
24. *VJG,* II, 130.
25. Vivekananda's letter, 20 June 1894, *CW,* VIII, 308–9.
26. Vivekananda's letter, 30 November 1894, *CW,* V, 54. Emphasis in original.
27. Sen originally composed *Bhagavān Śrīśrīramakrishna Paramahaṁsadever Caritāmrta* during 1894–1901. He publicly recited from one of its four parts, *Śrīśrīramakrishnapunthi,* for the first time in 1895 at Dakshineshwar on the occasion of Ramakrishna's birth anniversary. He sent a copy of this version of the *Punthi* to Vivekananda. Later on 25 November 1901, the *Punthi* was published, incorporating all the four parts of the *Caritāmrta.*
28. Vivekananda's letter, 1895, *PAT,* 414, 420.
29. Ibid., 414.
30. Vivekananda's letter to Ramakrishnananda, 24 June 1896, *PAT,* 464.
31. "East and West," *CW,* V, 505.
32. Vivekananda's letter to Ramakrishnananda, 1895, *PAT,* 421.
33. Cited in Narendranath's letter, 7 February 1889, *KM,* V, 287.
34. Vivekananda's letter, 14 April 1896, *PAT,* 449. The quoted lines are in Swamiji's own English.
35. Cited in *KM,* V, 287.

36. *CW,* V, 140.
37. Vivekananda's letter, 1895, *PAT,* 284. Datta's *Upadeś* was first published in 1884 and reprinted in 1886, and finally published as an expanded version together with a biographical sketch of the Master in 1892. See the 34th edition published by Mitra Brothers of Calcutta in 1398 B.E. (1–20).
38. Vivekananda's letter, 1895, *PAT,* 419.
39. Vivekananda's letter to a Madras disciple, 28 June 1894, *CW,* VIII, 314.
40. Ibid., 312.
41. *CW,* V, 53–54.
42. Vivekananda's letter, 3 March 1894, *LV,* 71. Emphasis in original. Puzzlingly enough *CW* omits this important letter.
43. Vivekananda's letter to his brother monks, 1894, *PAT,* 258.
44. The most "scandalous" biography of Ramakrishna containing the lurid details of his *sādhanā* as well as his suggestively sexual encounters with his patron Mathur was Datta's *Jīvanvṛttánta.* See Kripal, "Kālī's Tongue."
45. Vivekananda's letter to the brother monks, 1894, *PAT,* 162. It is on record that he hesitated to discuss Ramakrishna's life, confessing that he did not quite understand his guru. See *SSS,* 155.
46. *LP,* I (Gurubhāv—Pūrvārdha), 3.
47. The Pratham Bhāg ("First Part") of the *KM* was published on 11 March 1902 from the Udbodhan Office.
48. See Nikhilananda's Preface to the *Gospel of Ramakrishna.* See also Kripal, "Kali's Child."
49. Freda Matchett, "The Teaching of Ramakrishna in Relation to the Hindu Tradition and as Interpreted by Vivekananda," *Religion* 11 (1982), 1.
50. Ibid., 7.
51. *The Place of the Hidden Moon: Erotic Mysticism in the Vaiṣṇava-Sahajiyā Cult of Bengal* (1966; reprint with a new Foreword by Wendy Doniger. Delhi: Motilal Banarasidass Publishers, 1989), 250.
52. *CW,* V, 82 cited in Matchett, "Teaching of Ramakrishna," 8.
53. Ibid., 9.
54. Ibid., 9–10.
55. Ibid., 12.
56. Cited in Nikhilananda, *Vivekananda,* 193–94.
57. Vivekananda's letter, 1895, *PAT,* 284.
58. "My Master," *CW,* IV, 154–87.
59. See Frederick Max Müller, *Rāmakṛṣṇa: His Life and Sayings* (1899; reprint, New York: AMS Press, 1975), Introduction.
60. *CW,* IV, 267–68. Cf. Vivekananda's conversation with Sharat Chakravarti: "First we must raise the whole Hindu race in this way and then the whole world. That is the reason behind the Master's incarnation." *SSS,* 125. Vivekananda was wrong in making Ramakrishna a totally illiterate man. Perhaps the misstatement was made deliberately for rhetorical effect. In actuality, however, Ramakrishna could and did sign his name. He also, reportedly, copied a portion of Krittivasa's *Rāmāyaṇa.* See Swami Ramakrishnananda, *Sri Ramakrishna and His Mission* (Madras: Sri Ramakrishna Math, 1972), 14.
61. Vivekananda's conversation with Ranadaprasad Dasgupta, founder of the Jubilee Art Academy, Calcutta, *CW,* VII, 205.
62. Cited in Chattopadhyay, *Lātumahārājer Smṛtikathā,* 447. The English word "original" occurs in Bengali.
63. Cited in Datta, *Patriot-Prophet* (1954 ed.), 178.

64. See *RPP,* especially chs. 2 and 3. A typical sample of the popular image of Ramakrishna, which is universally held by devotees and admirers alike, is to be found in the statement made by independent India's first Prime Minister, Pandit Jawaharlal Nehru in 1949. Speaking on the occasion of the 114th-birth anniversary of the Master at the Ramakrishna Mission, New Delhi, Pandit Nehru declared that "men like Sri Ramakrishna Paramahamsa, men like Swami Vivekananda and men like Mahatma Gandhi are great unifying forces, great constructive geniuses of the world . . . not only in regard to the particular teachings that they taught, but their approach to the world and their conscious and unconscious influence on it is of the most vital importance to us." Pandit J. Nehru, *Sri Ramakrishna and Swami Vivekananda* (Mayavati: Advaita Ashrama, 1949), 13–14. The last sentence in the above quote must have been inspired by Vivekananda's characterization of the Paramahamsa: "He is the method, that wonderful unconscious method!" Nivedita, *Master,* 255.

65. *RPP,* chs. 7 and 8I. See also Kripal, introduction to *Kālī's Child.*

66. Very few scholars, since Max Müller's days, are prepared to regard Ramakrishna as a Vedantin. *RPP,* 97–98. Walter G. Neevel ("The Transformation of Sri Ramakrishna," ed. Bardwell L. Smith, *Hinduism: New Essays in the History of Religion* [Leiden: E. J. Brill, 1976]) argues that Ramakrishna's basic orientation was tantric. He is powerfully supported by Kripal ("Kālī's Child"). For a contrary view, see *RPP,* chs. VI–VIII. My *Ramakrishna Revisited: A New Biography* (unpublished) provides a detailed critique in this regard.

67. Swami Prameyananda, *Viśvacetanāy Śrīramakrishna* (Kalikātā: Udbodhan Kāryālay, 1987), 28. The journalists of Detroit called Vivekananda "cyclonic Hindu" for his eloquent and forceful lectures. Vivekananda's letter from Detroit to the Hale sisters, 15 March 1894, *CW,* VIII, 301.

68. Vivekananda's letter to Pramadadas Mitra, 26 May 1890, *PAT,* 46.

69. Brahmabandhav Upadhyay, "Who Was Ramakrishna?" *Sophia* 4, no. 9 (1897), cited in Anders Blichfeldt, "Tantra in the Ramakrishna Math and Mission," *Update,* 6 (1982), 37.

70. Cited in *CB,* II, 947.

Chapter 9. Vivekananda and Women

1. Vivekananda's letter, 25 September 1894. *PAT,* 193.

2. Vivekananda's letter to Ramakrishnananda, 19 March 1894. Ibid., 120.

3. Vivekananda's letter to Raja Ajit Singh, 1894, *CW,* VI, 248–49.

4. See Vivekananda's letter to Ramakrishnananda, 25 September 1894, *PAT,* 193; Vivekananda's letter to Manmathanath Bhattacharya, 5 September 1894, *CW,* VII, 475. This letter in its Bengali original is reproduced in a severely truncated and edited form in *PAT,* 184–85, with a cryptic footnote on 185 that it "was found later" (whatever that means).

5. Conversation of February 1898, *SSS,* 94. There is of course no evidence for this claim.

6. Vivekananda's letter to Alasinga, 2 November 1893, *LV,* 54–55.

7. Vivekananda's letter to his Madras disciples, 24 January 1894. Ibid., 63.

8. Cited in a report in the *Iowa State Register,* 3 December 1893, *Prophetic Mission,* I, 213.

9. Vivekananda's letter, 1894, *LV,* 76.

10. Cited in introduction, *VIN,* ix.

11. Report in *Framingham Tribune,* 25 August 1893, *Prophetic Mission,* I, 22.

12. Vivekananda's letter, 20 August 1893, *LV*, 39.

13. Vivekananda's lecture at the Detroit Opera House, 11 March 1894, *Prophetic Mission*, I, 416. Emphasis in original.

14. Vivekananda's address at a reception organized by Mrs. Potter Palmer of Chicago, 14 September 1893. Ibid., 98. Emphasis in original.

15. Report in the *Boston Daily Globe*, 24 March 1896, *World Teacher*, I, 61.

16. "Sayings and Utterances," *CW*, V, 413.

17. Diary of March–April 1897, *SSS*, 52.

18. Diary of 1902. Ibid., 250.

19. Vivekananda's lecture "The Women of India" at the Shakespeare Club, 18 January 1900, *New Gospel*, I, 272. Even though Alice Hansbrough replied to the woman "No, I haven't found that out yet," she herself, on her own admission, was often subjected to violent verbal abuse by the Swami. "He often scolded me," she wrote. "He was constantly finding fault and sometimes he could be very rough. 'Mother brings me fools to work with,' he would say; or, 'I have to associate with fools!' This was his favorite word in his vocabulary of scolding." In fact Vivekananda could be extremely unkind with that vocabulary. Once he told her: "You are silly, brainless fool, that's what you are." Ibid., II, 28.

20. "Sayings and Utterances," *CW*, V, 412. It is highly unlikely that "Swamiji—true to his inner vision of womanhood—never emanated even a gesture of prudishness or made his women followers feel they were an 'opposite sex.'" Brahmaprana, "Swamiji and His Women Disciples," 234.

21. Vivekananda's letter, 15 June 1897, *PAT*, 60.

22. Vivekananda's letter to Alasinga, 1 July 1895, *CW*, V, 86. Emphasis added.

23. Nivedita, *Master*, 175.

24. Sen's private diary, *CW*, V, 345.

25. *LSV*, II, 354.

26. Swami Pajnanananda, *Saṅgītpratibhāy Swami Vivekananda* (Kalikātā: Śrīramakrishna Vedanta Math, 1397 B.E.), 47.

27. Cited in Raychaudhuri, *Europe Reconsidered*, 225. The Sister was so influenced by her *guru* that she confided to Josephine: "Mr. Tagore's is not the type of manhood that appeals to me." Nivedita's letter, 15 October 1904, *LSN*, II, 686.

28. Vivekananda's letter to his monastic brethren, 25 September 1898, *PAT*, 198.

29. Reminiscences of Singha, *SAS*, 135.

30. An unpublished article by Mary Tappan Wright, *Prophetic Mission*, I, 34. Emphasis added.

31. Reminiscences of Turiyananda, *SAS*, 3.

32. Datta, *Saradananda Swamijīr Ghatanāvalī*, 66–67.

33. Vivekananda's letter, 25 July 1897, *CW*, VIII, 415. Emphasis in original.

34. Interview with Vivekananda published in the *Prabuddha Bharata*, December 1898, *CW*, V, 231.

35. *Prophetic Mission*, II, 336.

36. *CB*, I, 33.

37. *NWV*, 97–98. See also *World Teacher*, I, 230.

38. *CB*, I, 34.

39. Ibid., 35.

40. *VJG*, II, 164. The complimentary comment on Vivekananda's marksmanship was made by his devotee Kidi. Apparently Professor Shankari Basu agrees with Kidi and cites the remark of the latter with approval and great enthusiasm. *Sahāsya Vivekananda*, 26.

41. Basu, "Lahore Tribune Patrikāy Vivekananda," 246–47.

42. Reminiscences of Priyanath Singha, *SAS,* 296 n. 1

43. Ibid., 297n.

44. Vivekananda's letter, 27 August 1901, *LV,* 450.

45. Cited in Roma Chowdhury, "Sociological View of Swami Vivekananda and His Ideals of Social Reforms—Uplift of Women and Masses," ed., Majumdar, *Vivekananda Centenary Volume,* 432. Emphasis added.

46. "My Plan of Campaign," *CW,* III, 223–24.

47. Kopf, "Reinterpretation of Dharma in Nineteenth-Century Bengal," 90 (also 98 n. 28).

48. "My Plan of Campaign," *CW,* III, 224.

49. Reminiscences of Gangopadhyay, *SAS,* 112.

50. Dr. Beall's article was reproduced in the *Amrita Bazar Patrika,* Calcutta, 20 February 1897, *VIN,* 77.

51. *LSV,* II, 463.

52. Vivekananda's letter to Pramadadas Mitra, 3 March 1890, *PAT,* 35–36. He gave his disciple Chakravarti an entirely different reason for giving up on the Baba. He told Chakravarti that he dreamed the night before being initiated by Pavhari Baba that Ramakrishna was staring at him with a melancholy face. This dream reminded him that as the disciple of the Great Master he could not make anybody else his guru and he thus gave up the idea of taking initiation from the Baba. Diary of 1902, *SSS,* 238.

53. The two most recent contributions by women scholars are Chakravarti, "Nārīvāder Paripreksite Swami Vivekanander Nārī-bāvanā," 134–49; and Khastgir, "Vivekananda's Ideas on Womanhood," 343–51.

54. *Swamijir Vāni O Racanā,* VI, 388–89, cited in Pravrajika Muktiprana, "Nārī-jāgaran O Swami Vivekananda," ed. Lokeshwarananda, *Cintānāyak Vivekananda,* 293.

55. Cited in Khastgir, "Vivekananda's Ideas on Womanhood," 351.

56. Santwana Dasgupta, "The Chicago Lectures of Swami Vivekananda and His Unique Social Philosophy," ed. Dasgupta, *Vivekananda since Chicago,* 174. For Swamiji's lecture as reported in the *Chicago Inter-Ocean,* 23 September 1893, see *CW,* VIII, 198.

57. Vivekananda's letter, 27 April 1897, *LV,* 331.

58. Vivekananda's letter, 29 July 1897. Ibid., 363.

59. Robert P. Goldman, "Transsexualism, Gender, and Anxiety in Traditional India," *Journal of the American Oriental Society* 113, no. 3 (1993), 375–76. For an interesting study that finds similar attitudes to women in Christianity and Islam, see Frithjob Schoun, "The Problem of Sexuality," *Studies in Comparative Religion* 2, no. 1 (1977).

60. Prabhati Mukherjee, *Hindu Women: Normative Models* (New Delhi: Orient Longman Ltd., 1978), 12.

61. *Mahābhārata,* Anusaśāna Parva, ch. 38 cited ibid., 11.

62. Mukherjee, *Hindu Women,* 12. This phobia of female is, of course, true of human culture in general. It is a product, Gregory Zilboorg wrote some time ago, of man's primal frustration, his "phylogenetic awareness that his primordial role is 'highly specialized as no more than a temporary and ephemeral appendage to life' as a 'parasitic' fertilizer." "Masculine and Feminine: Some Biological and Cultural Aspects," *Psychiatry* 7 (1944), 257–96, cited in Ashis Nandy, *At the Edge of Psychology: Essays in Politics and Culture* (Delhi: Oxford University Press, 1980), 33.

63. Datta, *Saradananda Swamijir Ghatanāvalī,* 45.

64. Vivekananda's letter to Mary Hale, 9 July 1897, *LV,* 351.
65. Vivekananda's letter to Mary and Harriett Hale, 26 June 1894, *CW,* VI, 258–59.
66. *New Gospel,* II, 48.
67. *RPP,* 87, 145.
68. *New Gospel,* II, 47.
69. Report of Vivekananda's lecture in Boston reprinted in the *Indian Mirror,* 3 July 1894, *VIN,* 26.
70. "Modern India" (originally published in the *Udbodhan,* March 1899), *CW,* IV, 479–80.
71. Vivekananda's lecture "Women of India," *CW,* VIII, 58, 61.
72. Mukherjeee, *Hindu Women,* 13–14.
73. Ibid., 17. See also Susan S. Wadley, "Women and the Hindu Tradition," *Signs: Journal of Women in Culture and Society,* 3, no. 1 (1977). Even to this day, women of modern India have not been liberated from their age-old cultural stereotype. For a spirited discussion of their odyssey with the politics of the rising Hindu nationalism, see Sucheta Mazumdar, "Women, Culture and Politics: Engendering the Hindu Nation," *South Asia Bulletin* 12, no. 2 (Fall 1992), 1–24.
74. *VAC,* 81–82. See Sally J. Sutherland, "Sītā and Draupadī: Aggressive Behavior and Female Role-Models in the Sanskrit Epics," *Journal of the American Oriental Society,* 109, no. 1 (1989).
75. "East and West," *CW,* V, 506.
76. Vivekananda's letter to Bhattacharya, *CW,* VII, 474–75.
77. Vivekananda's letter to Ramakrishnananda, *PAT,* 192–93.
78. "East and West," *CW,* V, 466–67, 469, 502.
79. Nivedita's letter to Josephine MacLeod, 11 May 1899, *LSN,* I, 128.
80. Vivekananda's letter to the Hale sisters, 26 July 1894, *CW,* VIII, 317. See also Chakravarti, "Chicago Dharmasabhāy Majumdar O Vivekananda," 42–43.
81. *CB,* I, 16–17; Vivekananda's letter to Sara Bull, 11 April 1895, *CW,* VI, 303.
82. Charles S. J. White, "Indian Developments: Sainthood in Hinduism," Richard Kieckheifer and George Bond, ed. *Sainthood: Its Manifestations in World Religions* (Berkeley: University of California Press, 1988), 110. For a discussion of Shiva's eroticism, see Wendy D. O'Flaherty, *Śiva: The Erotic Ascetic* (Oxford: Oxford University Press, 1973).
83. Chakravarti, "Chicago Dharmasabhāy Majumdar O Vivekananda," 42. The Swami had some misgivings about Mrs. Bagley's lukewarm attitude toward him. Vivekananda's letter to John Henry Wright, 18 June 1894, *CW,* VII, 469.
84. The phrase "inly-pleased" is borrowed from Vivekananda's description in the *Chicago Advocate,* 12 September 1893 cited in *Prophetic Mission,* I, 87.

Chapter 10. Vivekananda and Nivedita

1. *Prophetic Mission,* I, 282 (see especially, 278–84).
2. Prabuddhaprana, *Josephine,* 217.
3. Reminiscences of Josephine MacLeod, *REM,* 228.
4. Prabuddhaprana, *Josephine,* 136.
5. Ibid., 157–58.
6. See *RPP,* 32.
7. Nivedita, *Master,* 165. Emphasis in original. During his second visit to the United States, Vivekananda proudly informed his listeners of his experience with

meditation. The thirty-seven-year-old monk declared: "It took me thirty years to learn it; thirty years of hard struggle. Sometimes I worked at it twenty hours during the twenty-four; sometimes I slept only one hour in the night; sometimes I worked whole nights; sometimes I lived in places where there was hardly a sound, hardly breath; sometimes I had to live in caves. Think of that." Vivekananda's lecture "The Powers of the Mind" in Los Angeles, 8 January 1900, *CW*, II, 22.

8. Ibid., 385. See also Nivedita's letter to Josephine MacLeod, 16 June/July? 1900, *LSN*, I, 365. This story with light parallels Ramakrishna's account of his experience with light. *RPP*, 86.

9. Nivedita, *Master*, 3–5. In the United States, Eloise Roorbach attended Vivekananda's sermons and observed: "His voice was so magnificent! It would roll out those Sanskrit verses and everyone in the audience would sit up and take notice. They didn't know a word of Sanskrit; I didn't either." Recorded conversations of Roorbach, 4 May 1950, *New Gospel*, II, 56.

10. *DBN*, 28.

11. Nivedita, *Master*, 9–10. Vivekananda's spiritual message was indeed practical rather than metaphysical. As she wrote, she ultimately accepted his message after having come to the realization that "all religions . . . have called a halt in the quest of pleasure. . . . All have striven to make man strong for death rather than for life. Where I think that the Swami perhaps differed from other teachers is his acceptance of any kind of mastery as a form of renunciation." Ibid., 18.

12. *DBN*, 28.

13. Ibid., 16, 24, 30.

14. Nivedita, *Master*, 27–28.

15. Ibid., 43.

16. Reminiscences of Reeves Calkins, *REM*, 387.

17. *DBN*, 51.

18. Nivedita, *Master*, 28. This is contrary to the generally believed story that it was Nivedita who wanted to come to India on her own.

19. *New Gospel*, I, 9.

20. *DBN*, 49.

21. Ibid., 53. Note the Swami's deliberate use of the verb "incarnated" instead of his usual "be born again and again."

22. Vivekananda's letter to Nivedita, 29 July 1897, *CW*, VII, 511–12. This sounds more like a man's promise to a woman after his heart! At least this is what the Hindi-speakers mean in its Hindi original: "*maradkī bāt, hāthinkā dānt.*

23. *DBN*, 63.

24. Ibid., 77.

25. Ibid.

26. Pravrajika Muktiprana, *Bhaginī Nivedita*, 6th ed. (Calcutta: Sister Nivedita Girls' School, 1992), 82–83.

27. Nivedita, *Master*, 32. Emphasis added.

28. Reminiscences of Sister Christine, *REM*, 148, 171.

29. Ibid., 169.

30. *LoSV*, II, 101. He, however, lectured elsewhere that "it is better to be an atheist than to be a pietist" because a pietist stood for a coward and a parasite. He further declared that "personal God is a big superstition." Ibid., pp. 33–34.

31. Ibid., 115–16, 202–3.

32. *CB*, II, 1066.

33. Vivekananda's review of Max Müller's *Rāmakrishna* in *Udbodhan*, 14 March 1899, *CW*, IV, 412.

34. *CB*, II, 1079. Emphasis in original.

35. Nivedita's letter to Josephine MacLeod, 28 June 1899, *LSN*, I, 172.

36. Nivedita's letter to Josephine MacLeod, 1 May 1899. Ibid., 129: Emphasis in original.

37. *NWV*, 161.

38. Reminiscences of Shuddhananda, *REM*, 324. We cannot substantiate Swamiji's "cat on a hot tin roof" experience.

39. Vivekananda's letter to Marie Halboister, 25 July 1897, *CW*, VIII, 414. Emphasis in original.

40. *CB*, II, 1079. Vivekananda's distrust of the householder was so acute that he even declared in Boston: "If Bhagavan (God) incarnates Himself as a householder, I can never believe Him to be sincere." "The Sannyasin and the Householder," *CW*, V, 261.

41. *DBN*, 99.

42. *NWV*, 80. Emphasis in original.

43. Ibid., 66–67.

44. Nivedita, *Master*, 99.

45. Ibid., 102.

46. *NWV*, 151.

47. Nivedita, *Master*, 103. Emphasis in original. Vivekananda told Sharat Chakravarti: "Shiva has been sitting inside my head for twenty-four hours a day, as it were, after I had a *darśan* of Amarnath." He then told him that he had performed tremendous *tapasyā* at Amarnath and Kshir Bhavani and then ordered the befuddled disciple to prepare a smoke for him. Diary of November 1898, *SSS*, 98.

48. *NWV*, 127.

49. Nivedita's letter, August 7, 1898, *LSN*, I, 18.

50. *DBN*, 128.

51. Bangiya Sahitya Parisad Library (Calcutta), MS. No. 69/2 (no pagination or signatures). I thank the Parisad Librarian, Dr. Aruna Chatterjee, and the library museum curator, Mr. Habul C. Das, for allowing me to read the extremely fragile manuscript. Recently the Ramakrishna Mission has photographed (the leaves are too brittle to be xeroxed) the entire manuscript.

52. Nivedita's letter to Hammond, *LSN*, I, 18.

53. See n. 30 above.

54. Nivedita, *Master*, 106.

55. *KM*, II, 8 (diary of 16 October 1882). The Master also declared that "a heroic man is one who lives with a woman without making love to her" [*ye bīrpuruṣ, se 'ramanīr sange thāke, nā kare raman'*]. Majumdar, *Ramakrishner Ātmakathā*, 242.

56. Nivedita, *Master*, 109.

57. Ibid., 110–13.

58. Ibid., 111.

59. *LP*, II (Divyabhāv O Narendranath), 209.

60. Swami Akhandananda, *Smṛtikathā*, 4th ed. (Kalikātā: Udbodhan Kāryālay, 1983), 193.

61. *SSS*, 132–33.

62. Vivekananda's letter to Brahmananda, 1895, *PAT*, 274.

63. Vivekananda's letter to Ramakrishnananda, 11 April 1895. Ibid., 309.

64. Basu, *Sahāsya Vivekananda*, 24.

65. Reminiscences of Abhedananda, *SAS*, 58.

66. Reminiscences of Alice Hansbrough, *New Gospel*, I, 359.

67. "East and West," *CW*, V, 473.

68. *VUG*, 6 n. 3. V. Subramanya of Madras called him *Pahalwan* Swami. *LSV*, I, 368.
69. *VUG*, 85 n. 2.
70. He in fact wrote to his patron Raja Ajit Singh from the sea on his way to the United States from Japan that his sea travel had cured him of his chronic diarrhea. See *VJG*, III, 2.
71. *VJG*, I, 49, 61, 85, 135; Vivekananda's letter to Brahmananda, 20 May 1897, *PAT*, 546.
72. *VJG*, I, 165.
73. *VJG*, II, 118.
74. Sil, "Saradamani," 75.
75. *VJG*, I, 14.
76. *LoSV*, I, 91.
77. Ibid., 35.
78. *VJG*, I, 112–13.
79. Reminiscences of Singha, *SAS*, 157–58.
80. "East and West," *CW*, V, 488.
81. Basu, *Sahāsya Vivekananda*, 119.
82. Vivekananda's letter to Dr. Shashibhusan Ghosh, 29 May 1897, *PAT*, 547; letters to Brahmananda, 20 June and 13 July 1897, *PAT*, 561, 597; letter to Sara Bull, 19 August 1897, *PAT*, 591.
83. Vivekananda's letter to Indumati Mitra, 15 November 1897. *PAT*, 611.
84. Vivekananda's letter to Premananda, 24 November 1897. *PAT*, 613.
85. Vivekananda's letter to Josephine MacLeod, 18 April 1898. *PAT*, 629; same to same, 29 April 1898, *LV*, 378; letter to Brahmananda, 20 November 1898, *PAT*, 632.
86. *LSV*, II, 391.
87. Vivekananda's letter, 2 March 1898, *LV*, 376.
88. Vivekananda's letter, 20 November 1899, *PAT*, 673.
89. Ibid., 771.
90. *VUG*, 161.
91. Ibid., 6.
92. *LoSV*, I, 93.
93. Vivekananda's letter, 2 March 1898, *CW*, VI, 446.
94. Jonson's letter, 21 October 1899, *New Gospel*, I, 104–5. Nivedita worshiped the Swami's feet with flowers on 27 June 1899. Nivedita's letter to Josephine Mac-Leod, 28 June 1899, *LSN*, I, 173.
95. Correspondence between Sturdy and Nivedita as well as between Sturdy and Vivekananda in the fall of 1899. Ibid., 70–91. See also Vivekananda's letter to Sturdy, November 1899, *CW*, VII, 519.
96. *New Gospel*, I, 63.
97. Ibid., 70.
98. See ch. IV, n. 22 above.
99. Vivekananda's letter, 1 November 1899, *LV*, 398.
100. Vivekananda's letter, 24 January 1900. Ibid., 408–9.
101. Vivekananda's letter, 25 March 1900. Ibid., 416. Shankari Basu uses mellifluous prose to describe the Swami's sufferings. *Nivedita Lokmātā*, 4 vols. (Vol. I in 4 pts.) (Calcutta: Ananda Publishers Pvt. Ltd., 1375–1401 B.E.), III, 253–55.
102. Vivekananda's letter, 28 August 1900. Ibid., 433.
103. Vivekananda's letter to Nivedita, 26 May 1900. Ibid., 425–26.
104. Vivekananda's letter, 11 October 1897, *PAT*, 606.

105. Nivedita's letter to Josephine MacLeod, 7 February 1899, *LSN*, I, 50. Emphasis in original.

106. Reminiscences of Turiyananda, *SAS*, 7.

107. Vivekananda's letter to Nivedita, 25 August 1898, *CW*, VI, 417.

108. Nivedita's letter to Josephine, 7 February 1899, *LSN*, I, 48.

109. Nivedita's letter to Josephine, 21 May 1899. Ibid., 146.

110. Vivekananda's letter to Nivedita, 15 February 1900, *CW*, VI, 424.

111. Nivedita's letter to Josephine, 4 June 1900, *LSN*, I, 356.

112. Cited in Vivekananda's letter to Sister Christine, *LSV*, II, 451. This letter has been omitted from Swamiji's letters in *CW* and *LV*.

113. Nivedita's letter to Josephine, 5 July 1899, *LSN*, I, 174.

114. *New Gospel*, II, 286.

115. Nivedita's letter to Josephine, 1 July 1900, *LSN*, I, 368–71.

116. Vivekananda's letter to Nivedita, 28 March 1900, *CW*, VI, 430.

117. Ibid., 326. It is not clear why Vivekananda had to transform the attractive young woman into a monkey instead of into a mother or a sister, or why as a Vedantist, he had to conceive of monkey as a contemptible creature.

118. *DBN*, 223 (and also 222).

119. Vivekananda's letter, 25 August 1900, *CW*, VI, 435.

120. Nivedita's letter, 29 August 1900, *LSN*, I, 385.

121. Pravrajika Atmaprana, *Sister Nivedita of Ramakrishna-Vivekananda* (Calcutta: Sister Nivedita Girls' School, 1961), 133. This letter cannot be located in any of the published works of the Sister.

122. Nivedita's letter to Josephine, 29 August 1900, *LSN*, I, 386. Emphasis in original.

123. Nivedita's letter to Josephine, 24 June 1900. Ibid., 366. Capitals in original.

124. Nivedita's letter to Josephine, 21 August 1906. Ibid., 496.

125. Nivedita, *Master*, 221–22.

126. Anil Baran Ray, "Swami Vivekananda and the Indianization of a Western Disciple," ed. Dasgupta, *Vivekananda since Chicago*, 631.

127. Basu, *Nivedita Lokmātā*, II, 87.

128. Nivedita's letter to Josephine, 9 November 1902, *LSN*, I, 515–16.

129. Basu, *Nivedita Lokmātā*, II, 106 n. 23.

130. Nivedita's letter to Josephine, 1 October 1902, *LSN*, I, 510.

131. Nivedita's letter to Josephine, 9 November 1902. Ibid., 517.

132. Ibid., 487.

133. Nivedita's letter to Josephine, 21 December 1902. Ibid., 526.

134. See n. 3 above.

135. Cited in Nikhilananda, *Vivekananda*, 285.

136. Vivekananda's letter, 12 December 1899, *LV*, 406.

137. Diary of November 1898, *SSS*, 98; *LSV*, II, 389–90.

138. Vivekananda's letter, 12 March 1900, *PAT*, 702.

139. Vivekananda's letter, 22 March 1900. Ibid., 415.

140. Nivedita's letter to Josephine, 4 November 1899, *LSN*, I, 227–28. Burke feels that Swamiji "may have lost his power of meditation" but wonders "who can tell?" *New Gospel*, I, 134.

141. Cited in *DBN*, 207.

142. Barbara Foxe, *Long Journey Home: A Biography of Margaret Noble (Nivedita)* (London: Rider & Co., 1975), 54. This eminently readable biography, purportedly based on primary materials, suffers from a singular weakness due to its author's

idiosyncratic decision to eliminate footnotes. It also is very uncritical and frankly adulatory of its subject, and it totally bypasses the details of the Amarnath episode.

143. See a pioneering study arguing that Nivedita "was not a creature of Swami Vivekananda" by Niranjan Dhar, "The Noble Sister," *The Radical Humanist,* 17 December 1967, reprinted *in extenso* in idem, *Vedanta and Bengal Renaissance,* 85–89.

144. *LSV,* II, 449.

145. Nivedita's letter, 12 July 1905, *LSN,* II, 742–43. Emphasis in original.

146. Nivedita's letter to Josephine, 11 October 1902, *LSN,* I, 513. Emphasis in original.

147. Nivedita's letter to Brahmananda, 18 July 1902. Ibid., I, 482. See also Mukti-prana, *Nivedita,* 221–26.

148. Nivedita's letter, 25 May 1902, *LSN, I,* 468. Emphasis in original.

149. Nivedita's letter, 10 June 1901. Ibid., 432.

150. Nivedita's letter to Josephine, 13 January 1900. Ibid., 300.

151. Nivedita's letter, 18 January 1900. Ibid., 303.

152. Nivedita's letter, 24 August 1905, *LSN,* II, 754.

153. Vivekananda's letter, 22 March 1900, *CW,* VIII, 505. Note the Swami's deft play with the word "Vivekananda," which means "bliss of discrimination," but which he now claims "truly" means the absence of any discrimination (between good and evil). This letter seems to be a sincere confession of the Swami's regaining his true self through a transgression of the codes with which his public (artificial) self was constructed. The Swami's admirer, Professor Basu, of course, believes that this letter is a testimony to "the greatest drama of Advaita Vedanta." *Sahāsya Viveka-nanda,* 318.

Chapter 11. Vivekananda's Conquest of the West

1. *VJG,* III, 3. This letter does not appear in any of the published works by the Swami: *CW, PAT,* or *LV.*

2. Report in *Appeal-Avalanche,* Memphis, 22 January 1894, *Prophetic Mission,* I, 260. The idea of a polytechnic school must have been what Vivekananda hinted in his letter of 20 June 1894 to Haridas Desai: "Primarily my coming has been to raise funds for an enterprise of my own." *CW,* VIII, 306.

3. *Prophetic Mission,* I, chs. 6–8.

4. Cited in ibid., 315.

5. *World Teacher,* I, 485–86.

6. Nikhilananda, *Vivekananda,* 26–27.

7. Ibid., 29.

8. *CB,* I, 290–91.

9. Mozoomdar's letter to Professor Binayendranath Sen, 23 February 23 1897. Surath Chakravarti, letter to author, 4 November 1994. For Vivekananda's attack on Mozoomdar, see Chakravarti, "Chicago Dharmasabhā (1893): Myth O Apapracār."

10. Sturdy's letter to a friend in Calcutta, 22 October 1896, cited in a letter from Gaurhari Sen, Secretary of Chaitanya Library, to the editor of the *Indian Mirror,* 14 November 1896. Surath Chakravarti, letter to author, 4 November 1994.

11. Vivekananda's letter to Nivedita, 29 July 1897, *CW,* V, 512.

12. Letter from Janes to Sara Bull, 30 March 1909, *New Gospel,* I, 70.

13. Cited in *World Teacher,* I, 33–34, 37. There are some uncertainties regarding

the precise dating of Swamiji's and Mary Hale's letters, though presumably they were written in February 1895.

14. Vivekananda, *Inspired Talks; My Master and Other Writings*, rev. ed. (New York: Ramakrishna-Vivekananda Center, 1987), 6.

15. "The New Religions of America—Hindu Cults," *Forum* 77 (March 1927), 422, cited in *New Gospel*, II, 341.

16. Vivekananda's letter to Haridas Desai, 20 June 1894, *CW*, VIII, 309.

17. Vivekananda's letter, 21 September 1894, *CW*, V, 44.

18. *CW*, V, 81–82.

19. Vivekananda's letter to Alasinga, 6 March 1895, *CW*, V, 75.

20. *Prophetic Mission*, II, 379.

21. *CW*, V, 314.

22. Vivekananda's letter, 3 January 1895, *CW*, IV, 373.

23. Vivekananda's letter to Alasinga, 17 February 1896. Ibid., 104–5.

24. *Vivekananda: Yoga and Other Works*, 338–77. See also *Prophetic Mission*, II, 373.

25. "Future of India," *CW*, III, 290.

26. Gambhirananda, *Ramakrishna Math and Mission*, 87.

27. Vivekananda's notes (note # 39), *CW*, IV, 311.

28. Vivekananda's letter to Margaret Noble, 7 June 1896, *CW*, VII, 501.

29. *New Gospel*, II, 190.

30. For an interesting discussion of this problem, see Ursula King, "Indian Spirituality, Western Materialism: An Image and Its Function in the Reinterpretation of Modern Hinduism," *Social Action* 28 (January-March 1978).

31. Cited in Banerji, *Keshab Chandra and Ramakrishna*, 162.

32. *CW*, V, 226.

33. Ghatak, *Hindu Revivalism*, 42. See also Rajnarain Basu, *Hindudharmer Śresthatva* (Kalikātā: Jātīya Yantra, 1872); Dhar, *Vedanta and Bengal Renaissance*, 31–32, 143–44.

34. I thank Surath Chakravarti for supplying this quote from his personal research notes (23 December 1995).

35. For the Swami's other sources of insight—which he kept mostly concealed—see "Hermeneutics of Religious Syncretism," chs. 3 and 4. While preaching Hindu or Vedantic spirituality in the West, Vivekananda sought to incorporate the Western ideas and methods of organization, social activism, and service into Hinduism. As Ursula King has shown, "his encounter with Western 'materialism' became a transforming factor in Vivekananda's understanding of Hinduism and, on his return to India, influenced the dynamic organisation of a group of Hindu disciples." "Indian Spirituality, Western Materialism," 70. Swamiji, however, told a reporter of the *Sunday Times* in London that he never wished to "multiply organizations," because organizations "need individuals to look after them," and he being a *sannyāsī*, a renouncer, could only aim "to seek spiritual knowledge" and hence "cannot undertake this work." Vivekananda's interview in 1896, *CW*, V, 190. Yet he unhesitatingly declared in Madras next year that his "program of work here . . . [was] to start two institutions, one in Madras and one in Calcutta . . . to bring the Vedantic ideals into the everyday practical life of the saint or the sinner, of the sage or the ignoramus, of the Brahmin or the Pariah." Vivekananda's interview with the reporter of *The Hindu*, February 1897, *CW*, V, 217.

36. Vivekananda's letter to Ramakrishnananda, 1894, *PAT*, 239. The quoted sentence appears in Swamiji's own English in the letter written otherwise in Bengali

throughout. This sentence is omitted from the translated edition of Vivekananda's letters *(LV)*.

37. Mrinalini Sinha, *Colonial Masculinity: The "Manly Englishman" and the "Effeminate Bengali" in the Late Nineteenth Century* (Manchester: Manchester University Press, 1995), 15.

38. Among Swamiji's Yoga/Vedanta teachings in the West the following lectures are most significant. (i) "What is Vedanta?" at the hall of the Universal Brotherhood, New York, 1895; (ii) "The Vedanta Philosophy" at the residence of Amzi L. Barber, New York, 28 February and 7 March, 1895); (iii) Yoga classes at 228 W 39th Street, New York: Bhakti Yoga, 16 December 1895–17 February 1896; Jnana Yoga, 11 December 1895–12 February 1896; Karma Yoga, 13 December 1895–10 January 1896); Raja Yoga, 14 December 1895–22 February 1896; (iv) lectures on Vedanta at 39 Victoria Street, London: Practical Vedanta, 10–19 November 1896; Advaita Vedanta, 10 December 1896); (v) "The Vedanta Philosophy or Hinduism as a Religion" at the Blanchard Hall, Los Angeles, 8 December 1899); (vi) "The Claims of Vedantism on the Modern World" at the First Unitarian Church, Oakland, 25 February 1900); and (vii) "Vedanta Philosophy" at the Vedanta Society of New York, 10 June 1900. For a useful (though occasionally somewhat tenuous) discussion of "Practical Vedanta," see Bryson, "Hermeneutics of Religious Syncretism," 257–303.

39. The Swami's status as an incarnation of Shankaracharya was recognized not only by his American admirer Josephine MacLeod (as we have noted above) but also by the astute Indian politician and social reformer, Balgangadhar Tilak, who wrote in the *Keshari* that in the present time Swami Vivekananda was the second Shankara. Reminiscences of Kedarnath Bandyopadhyay, *SAS*, 235.

40. Govind C. Pande, *Life and Thought of Shankaracharya* (Delhi: Motilal Banarasidass, Publishers, 1994), 177. See also Anantanand Rambachan, "The Place of Reason in the Quest for *Moksha*—Problems in Vivekananda's Conceptualization of *Jnanayoga*," *Religious Studies* 22 no. 2 (1987), 279–88.

41. Pande, *Life and Thought of Shankaracharya,* 176–80.

42. Michael Comans, "The Question of the Importance of *Samādhi* in Modern and Classical Advaita Vedanta," *Philosophy East and West* 43, no. 1 (1993), 23.

43. Ibid., 24.

44. Bharati, *The Ochre Robe* (London: George Allen & Unwin Ltd., 1961), 129 cited in Bryson, "Hermeneutics of Religious Syncretism," 60.

45. M. Eliade, *Journey East, Journey West,* trans. Mac Linscott Ricketts (New York: Harper & Row, 1981), 191–92 cited in Bryson, "Hermeneutics of Religious Syncretism," 60.

46. Reportedly, Ramakrishna said: "Honestly speaking, I am not at all sorry that I haven't read the Vedanta or other scriptures." Diary of 22 February 1885, *KM*, V, 131.

47. *LP,* I (Sādhakbhāv O Gurubhāv—Pūrvārdha), 295–97.

48. "Rāmakrsna's Ecstasies: A Phenomenology of *Samādhi*," ch. 7 of *RPP*.

49. Vivekananda's letter, 1894, *PAT,* 255.

50. *RPP,* 116–17.

51. A. Rambachan, *The Limits of Scripture: Vivekananda's Reinterpretation of the Vedas* (Honolulu: Hawaii University Press, 1994), 136.

52. Bryson, "Hermeneutics of Religious Syncretism," 321.

53. *LoSV,* II, 165–66.

54. *Communal Experience,* 211.

55. Cited in *Vivekananda and His Guru,* ii. A review of this work in the *Indian Social Reformer* 27 February 1898, is reprinted *in extenso* in *VIN,* 449.

56. *Vivekananda and His Guru*, iii.

57. Vivekananda's letter to Ramakrishnananda, 1894, *PAT,* 236. The words in italics are in the Swami's own English.

58. Datta, *Patriot-Prophet,* 127.

59. Datta, *Ramakrishner Anudhyān,* 184. Apparently, he had known all along that he would be famous in Chicago. He is reported to have confided to Turiyananda in the Ramakrishna fashion: "The Parliament of Religions is being organized for this. My mind tells me so. You will see it verified in not-so-distant future." Cited in Swami Chetanananda "Vivekananda: On the Way to Chicago," ed. Dasgupta, *Vivekananda since Chicago,* 11.

60. Vivekananda's letter to Ms. Ghosal, 24 April 1897, *PAT,* 836.

61. *World's Parliament of Religion,* 24.

62. Vivekananda's letter to Alasinga, 2 November 1893, *CW,* V, 21.

63. Chattopadhyaya, *World's Parliament of Religions,* 29.

64. Vivekananda's letter to Alasinga, 2 November 1893, *CW,* 24.

65. Vivekananda's letter to Ramakrishnananda, 19 March 1894, *PAT,* 119.

66. Vivekananda's letter to Alasinga, 2 November 1893, *CW,* V, 24.

67. Vivekananda's letter to Ramakrishnananda, 19 March 1894, *CW,* VI, 252. The Bengali original as reprinted in *PAT* omits Swamiji's comment on Dharmapala's scholarship.

68. *LoSV,* I, 16. By contrast, Dharmapala referred to his Vedantic colleague at the Parliament as a "useful and noble-minded Sannyasi!" Dharmapala's letter to E. F. Sturdy, 27 November 1895, *VIN,* 84.

69. *World's Parliament of Religions,* 31.

70. Banerji, *Keshab Chandra and Ramakrishna,* 121–22.

71. Letter from J. J. Goodwin to Sara Bull, 22 January 1897, *LSV,* II, 170.

72. *Vivekananda and His Guru,* 4 (the entire editorial appears on 3–6). The *Mirror* editor Narendranath Sen was Vivekananda's admirer. On 12 December 1893, the paper reported, exaggeratedly, that "among those who created the greatest stir at Chicago was Swami Vivekananda, a Hindu. His utterances on Hinduism created widespread interests and some sensations even. The majority of his audiences heard of Hinduism for the first time from his lips." *VIN,* 8. On 31 January 1895, the *Mirror* had circulated a canard about the Swami's Temple Universal Society in New York. See *World Teacher,* I, 368–70. For a critical examination of Swamiji's propaganda, see Chakravarti, "Chicago Dharmasabhā: Myth O Apapracār."

73. "Swami Shuddhananda," *SPP,* 6; Reminiscences of Kumudbandhu Sen, *SAS,* 193.

74. Diary of 1898, *SSS,* 112.

75. *Vivekananda and His Guru,* iii.

76. Cited in Vajraprana, *"My Faithful Goodwin",* 82.

77. Reminiscences of Sadashivananda, *REM,* 411–12. See also *KSV,* 77–78.

78. Vivekananda's letter, 19 November 1894, *CW,* IV, 369.

79. Vivekananda's letter, 11 October 1897, *PAT,* 606.

80. Vivekananda's letter, 20 November 1899. Ibid., 673–74.

81. *RBM,* I, 41.

82. *VUG,* 19.

83. *New Gospel,* II, 320. Swamiji may have related his Chicago success story to his new acquaintance, Maxim, in Paris in 1900.

84. Datta, *Ramakrishner Anudhyān,* 187–88.

85. Reminiscences of Kamakhyanath Mitra, *REM,* 336.

86. "Swami Virajananda," *SPP,* 69.

87. Report of the *Indian Mirror, Vivekananda and His Guru,* xxviii.

88. Basu, *Sahāsya Vivekananda,* 26. See also *VJG,* II, 164. The complimentary comment on Swamiji's marksmanship was made by his devotee Kidi.

89. Swami Saradeshananda, *Śrīśrīmāyer Smṛtikathā,* 2d ed. (Kalikātā: Udbodhan Kāryālay, 1983), 31.

90. K's letter to the editor of the *Brahmavadin,* 15 February 1896, *VIN,* 480.

91. Ibid. See also Vivekananda's letter to Sara Bull, 8 December 1895, *CW,* VI, 352.

92. Report in the *Daily Graphic, Vivekananda and His Guru,* ix.

93. *VIN,* 454. Why Marie Louise preferred the male prefix of swami remains a mystery. She was, however, "a prominent member of the Manhattan Liberal Club" and "a fearless, progressive, advanced woman, whose boast it was that she was always in the forefront of the battle and ahead of her time." See the *New York Herald* report on her reprinted in the *Brahmavadin,* 29 February 1896.

94. *World Teacher,* I, 324–29, 339–40, 526–27.

95. Rudra, "Vivekananda's Concept of Man," 193.

96. Cited in *New Gospel,* II, 289.

97. Conversations and Dialogues, *CW,* V, 376–77.

98. *Vivekananda and His Guru,* 13.

99. Ibid., 18.

100. Ibid., 17.

101. Ibid., 18.

102. Ibid., 19.

103. Ibid., 14.

104. Cited in *LSV,* II, 263–64.

105. Ibid., 23.

106. Ibid., 25–26.

107. J. W. Hanson, ed., *The World's Congress of Religions: The Addresses and Papers Delivered Before the Parliament, and an Abstract of the Congresses Held in the Art Institute, Chicago, Illinois, U.S.A., August 25, 1893, under the Auspices of the World's Columbian Exposition* (Chicago: W. B. Conkey Co., 1894), 8, 11, 85, 73.

108. Datta, *Patriot-Prophet,* 125.

109. *Communal Experience,* 212.

110. Narasingha P. Sil, "Indian Religious Movements in the United States," *Asian American Encyclopedia* (New York: Marshall Cavendish Corporation, 1994), 668–70.

111. *World's Parliament of Religions,* 33.

Conclusion

1. *VJG,* I, 108.

2. Rajagopal Chattopadhyaya, *Swami Vivekananda in the West* (Calcutta: K. P. Bagchi, 1994); *idem,* "1893 Ār 1993 Sāler Dui Chicago Dharmasabhā Evaṁ Tanmadhye Bhāratīya Pratinidhitva" *Saṁvād Vicitrā,* New York, 16 January 1994, 14 and 1 February 1994, 18; "Chicago Dharmasabhāy Bhāratiya Pratinidhi: Ek Tathyanirbhar Vyavacched," 2 pts. *Utsa Mānuṣ* (May and June 1995). See also the works of Surath Chakravarti cited earlier.

3. Report in the *Madras Times,* 7 February 1897, *VIN,* 130.

4. Vivekananda's lecture at the Victoria Hall, Madras, 9 February 1897, *CW,* III, 226.

5. Vivekananda's letter of 28 June 1894, *LV,* 123. The Swami's claim that he

had traveled (prior to 1897) all over India for twelve years is unfounded. He actually traveled for six years (1887–93).

6. Vivekananda's letter, 9 July 1897, *CW*, V, 135.

7. Reminiscences of Alice Hansbrough, March 1900, *New Gospel*, II, 30.

8. Vivekananda's conversation with a member of the audience in San Francisco, 27 March 1900, *CW*, II, 471.

9. Vivekananda's letter to Mitra, 28 December 1893, *PAT*, 100.

10. Cited in Nivedita, *Master*, 55.

11. M. Rolland writes that the first symptom of diabetes appeared when Narendranath was very young. *VUG*, 6 n. 3.

12. Diary of 1901, *SSS*, 220.

13. Reminiscences of Swami Shuddhananda, *SAS*, 32.

14. *LoSV*, I, 131.

15. Swami Gambhirananda, *Yuganāyak Vivekananda*, 3 vols. (Kalikātā: Udbodhan Kāryālay, 1373 B.E.), III, 189n. cited in *VAC*, 13.

16. These kings are mentioned in the *Chāndogya Upaniṣad* cited in Dhar, *Vedanta and Bengal Renaissance*, 8.

17. Ibid., 27–28 (see the entire ch. 2: "British Imperialism at Work: Forces Behind the Vedantic Movement," 27–36).

18. Conversations dated 1897, *SSS*, 65–66.

19. *KM*, IV, 182 (diary of 2 October 1884).

20. Vivekananda's letter, 14 February 1895, *CW*, VI, 299.

21. Vivekananda's letter to Akhandananda, March or April 1894, *PAT*, 242. The same could be true for his most trusted *gurubhāi* Abhedananda [Tapan Mukherjee, "Kājaler Ghare Sannyāsī" (mimeo)] and his most favorite younger monk Paramananda (Veysey, *Communal Experience*). I thank Dr. Mukherjee for supplying me a copy of the draft.

22. *VAC*, Appendix: "Hindu Math nā Bāgānbāḍī?" 103–7.

23. Ibid., 20.

24. *VUG*, 18.

25. Cited in Nikhilananda, *Vivekananda*, 285.

26. *LV*, 293.

27. Ibid., 405.

28. Nivedita, *Master*, 32–33.

29. *LSN*, I, 24–25. The name of Nivedita's correspondent is not known.

30. Vivekananda's letter to Ramakrishnananda, *PAT*, 382.

31. Vivekananda's letter to Husain, *CW*, VI, 415.

32. "My Plan of Campaign," *CW*, III, 218.

33. *CW*, III, 180.

34. *CW*, IV, 480.

35. Cited in Chakravarti, "Vivekananda Banām Narendranath O Chicago Dharmasabhā," 42.

36. See ch. 11, n. 33 above.

37. Dr. Bryson competently analyzes the various intellectual influences on Vivekananda: traditional and contemporary Hindu texts, Brahmo Samaj, Christian missionaries, colonialists, Romantic Orientalists, Herbert Spencer, Ramakrishna and others. See "Hermeneutics of Religious Syncretism," 236.

38. See *Vivekanander Hindu Cetanā*, comp. Swami Hirananda and Sannyasini Tapomayi Puri (1988. Third ed. Jadavpur, Calcutta: Śrīsatyānananda Devāyatan, 1990). A recent document titled *Did Swami Vivekananda Give Up Hinduism?* (Ma-

dras: Sister Nivedita Academy, 1990) by "A Hindu" (G. C. Asnani) goes to a great length to prove proudly that Swami Vivekananda was a spokesman of Hinduism only.

39. *VJG*, III, 25.

40. Ghatak, *Hindu Revivalism in Bengal*, 89–90.

41. Tagore's letter to Ghosal, 1 Vaiśākh, 1365 B.E., Shailendranarayan Ghosal, *Vaidic Bhārat* (Kalikātā: Anandamohan Ghosal, 1397 B.E.), 192.

42. *LV*, 413; *CW*, VI, 428–29 (here the letter has been wrongly addressed to Nivedita. See *New Gospel*, I, 423, n. 31).

43. Vivekananda's letter, 12 March 1900, *CW*, VIII, 499. He also wrote to Miss Hale: "I do not want to work any more." Vivekananda's letter, 22 March 1900. *CW*, VIII, 503.

44. Vivekananda's letter to Ramakrishnananda, 22 October 1894, *PAT*, 205.

45. Vivekananda's letter to Alasinga, 6 May 1895, *CW*, V, 82.

46. *Vivekananda on Himself*, 183 (November 1895).

47. Vivekananda's letter, 12 April 1900, *LV*, 421.

48. Vivekananda's letter, 7 April 1900, *CW*, VIII, 513.

49. "Vivekananda," Bandopadhyay *et al.*, *Viśvavivek*, 93–94.

50. Goodwin's letter to Sara Bull, 14 April 1897, *World Teacher*, II, 490.

51. *CB*, I, 187. Narendranath said this to Hirananda Saukiram Advani on 22 April 1886, when the latter was visiting his guru, Ramakrishna Paramahamsa, lying in his deathbed.

52. Vivekananda's letter to Mary Hale, 9 July 1897, *LV*, 349.

53. Conversations of sometime in early 1899, *SSS*, 181.

54. Reminiscences of Mitra, *REM*, 46.

55. Nivedita, *Master*, 93–94.

56. *New Gospel*, II, 371.

57. Birendrakumar Bhattacharya, "Vivekananda: Nihsvārtha Sevār Vāṇī," ed. Basu, *Śāśvata Vivekananda*, 102.

58. *New Gospel*, II, 371.

59. Vivekananda's letter, 17 June 1900, *LV*, 428.

60. Cited in Nikhilananda, *Vivekananda*, 211. Just a month earlier the Swami had written to Francis Leggett that he was "beginning to see the Divine even inside the high and mighty Anglo-Indians." Vivekananda's letter, 6 July 1896, *LV*, 297.

61. Nikhilananda, *Vivekananda*, 336–37.

62. Premananda once told the Swami after his return from Kashmir: "We do not see any difference between Śri Ramakrishna and you." Cited in ibid., 284. For Narendra's making fun of his late Master's *samādhi* see *KM*, IV, 298 (diary of 21 February 1887).

63. *RPP*, chs. 3 and 10.

64. The Master told Saradamani: "I shall be worshipped in every house hereafter; I say this upon oath, so help me God." Cited in *RPP*, 169.

65. Cited in *RBM*, I, 73.

66. *VJG*, III, 82–83.

67. See *SSS*, 179–82, 112.

68. *VJG*, III, 101.

69. Ibid., 102.

70. Ibid., 78.

71. In fact in a celebrated legal action in the High Court of Calcutta in 1983, the Ramakrishna Order claimed that it represented a "minority religion, distinct from Hinduism." See Malcolm D. McLean, "Are Ramakrishnaites Hindus? Some Implications of Recent Litigation on the Question," *South Asia* 14, no. 2 (1991),

100. I thank Dr. McLean of the University of Otago for having kindly supplied me an offprint copy of his article.

72. Bharati, *Hindu Views and Ways and Hindu-Muslim Interface,* 18–19.

73. Jackson, *Vedanta for the West,* 33, 35.

74. Krishna P. Gupta, "Religious Evolution and Social Change in India: A Study of the Ramakrishna Mission Movement," *Contributions to Indian Sociology,* n.s., 8 (1974), 25, 48–49. See also idem, "Swami Vivekananda: A Case Study of the Hindu Religious Tradition and the Modern Secular Ideal," *Quest* 80 (1973).

75. For a judicious critique of the exaggerated credit ascribed to Nivedita's leadership role in the Indian nationalist movement see Haridas Mukherjee, "Sri Aurobindo, Sister Nivedita and The Bengal Revolutionaries," *Quarterly Review of Historical Studies* 32, nos. 1 and 2 (April–September 1992–93), 86–100. I thank Professor Mukherjee for supplying me an offprint copy of his paper.

76. Basu, *Nivedita Lokmātā,* III, 86–89.

77. Ibid., IV, 96.

78. Ibid., 201–27: "Nivedita O Nandalal.

79. Bryson, "Hermeneutics of Religious Syncretism," 285.

80. Article by Ninian Smart.

81. R. K. Dasgupta, "Swami Vivekananda and Our Younger Generation," ed. idem, *Vivekananda since Chicago,* 884–85.

82. A. Dasgupta, "Purāṇo Chicagor Karatāli," *Desh* 61, no. 22 (27 August 1994), 112.

83. Vivekananda's letter to Mohammed Sarfaraz Husain, 10 June 1898, *LV,* 380.

84. See, especially, Nemaisadhan Basu, "Swami Vivekananda: Praśna O Prasaṅga" in ed. Vedantaprana, *Mahimā Tava Udbhāsita.*

85. Edward C. Dimock, "On Impersonality and Bengali Religious Biography" in M. Nagatomi, B. K. Matilal, J. M. Masson and E. Dimock, ed., *Sanskrit and Indian Studies* (Dordrecht: D. Reidel Co., 1979), 237–42.

Glossary

Antaraṅga: belonging to the inner circle or "intimate."

Arjuna: one of the principal characters of the *Mahābhārata* and one of the five brothers belonging the Pandava clan fighting against the rival clan called the Kaurava at the battlefield of Kurukshetra.

Avatāra: meaning "descent," that is, the descent of God as an incarnation on earth. Also means incarnation of one God as another.

Bahiraṅga: belonging to the outer circle.

Bāṅgāl: literally "of Bengal" but especially designating the Bengalis of eastern Bengal (now Bangladesh). It could be a pejorative expression connoting a "country clod." Thus *bāṅgāl* often stands for a dumbo.

Bhāgavadgītā: literally means "song of the Lord," is a part of the *Mahābhārata*. It contains the kernel of the Upaniṣadic wisdom.

Bhairavī: a Tantric priestess or a shamaness who participates in numerous esoteric rituals. Ramakrishna reportedly practiced *Tantra* under a *bhairavī* called Yogeshwari.

Bhakta: a devotee or a lover of God.

Bhāv: is a Bengali word (*bhāva* in Sanskrit) capable of multiple meanings. Literally it connotes "mood," but in the mystic literature it stands for a "spiritual mood" or a state in which one is aware of the phenomenal world as waves of the Cosmic Mind. It is an expression popularized by Sri Ramakrishna.

Brahmacārī: a monastic initiate (fem. *brahmacārinī*) who has taken the vows of celibacy, nonviolence, poverty, and the like.

Brahmajnana: knowledge of *Brahman*.

Brahman: derived from the Sanskrit root *brih,* meaning "to be great," it is the Upanishadic concept of one Divine Being hidden in all beings, the Self within all beings. He is the Only One, free from qualities, and makes the one seed manifold. *Brahman* is also considered as the impersonal Spirit, the Divine Essence, the Absolute. The chief attributes to be linked with this name are *sat* (being), *cit* (awareness), and *ānanda* (bliss): *Saccidānanda* (utter reality, utterly conscious, and utterly beatific).

Brahmasūtra: see Vedanta.

231

Brahmin: the highest of the four Hindu castes, usually the caste of priests (not to be confused with *Brahman*).

Dakshineshwar: a village situated some four to five miles north of Calcutta and the site of the temple of *Bhavatārinī* ("Deliverer of the World"—an appellation of Goddess Kali), where Ramakrishna worked as a priest and later gathered his devotees as the famous Paramahamsa.

Darśan: a peep at the Divine or a vision of the Divine.

Dom: a member of the sweeper caste considered "untouchable."

Gurubhāi: "brother monk" or a monastic cohort—disciple of the same guru or spiritual master.

Hanuman: known also as Mahavīra (the Great Hero) is the fabled simian factotum of Lord Rama of the *Rāmāyana*. Considered as a model devotee and servant of God.

Hookah: a wooden tobacco pipe with a water bowl and a clay container of charcoal fire attached to it. It is so constructed as to draw the smoke through a hole in the water bowl.

Īśvarakoti: literally means "of the level of god." Ramakrishna used the word to designate his favorite young devotee a "divine being" born on earth to carry out God's plan for mankind.

Jagajjananī: "Mother of the Universe," an appellation of Goddess Kali.

Jagannath: "Lord of the World," an appellation of Vishnu and a popular deity of Orissa and West Bengal. He is represented as an unfinished idol with a masklike face.

Kali: also known as *Jagajjananī,* Kali (literally meaning a black female) represents *Shakti* or Energy and is worshipped as Shiva's consort. She also manifests, like Shiva, a dual nature: benign and bizarre.

Kamandulu: a brass water vessel usually belonging to a priest or a monk.

Kāminī: literally, a lusty female, generally designates woman.

Kāminī-kāncana: literally, woman and gold but standing as a metaphor for lust and lure. Ramakrishna popularized the phrase in his numerous sermons on the absolute necessity of shunning *kāminī-kāncana* on the part of a spiritual adept.

Karmayogī: an activist who believes in the *Karmayoga* as enunciated in the *Bhāgavadgītā*.

Kaupīna: a strip of loincloth worn by Hindu monks just for being in public.

Kīrtan: devotional; song (popularized by the Vaishnava sect of the Hindus) sung in chorus and often accompanied by dancing.

Krishna: an incarnation of Vishnu and one of the principal characters of the

Mahābhārata, most importantly, the inculcator of the wisdom embodied in the *Bhāgavadgītā.*

Kshatriya: next to the Brahmins, it is the second highest caste in Hindu society, comprising the warriors, princes, and statesmen.

Kundalinī: literally, "coiled," referring to the Divine Person lying dormant at the base of the spine in all individuals, until it is aroused and until it ascends through the *susumnā,* passing on its way through six centers of *cakras* within the body, ultimately merging in the *sahasrāra,* the thousand-petaled lotus located in the roof of the brain.

Lakshmi: the Hindu goddess of fortune, beauty, and well-being (reminiscent of the Egyptian Maat) and regarded as Vishnu's consort.

Lingam: phallic representation of Shiva, popularly worshiped throughout Hindu India.

Mādhukarī: holy begging, that is, a monk's begging from door to door like the bee gathering honey *(madhu)* from flower to flower.

Madhurbhāv: Bengali version of the Sanskrit *Madhura Bhāva,* meaning, literally, "sweet mood," represents the Vaishnava devotional practice in which the adept regards himself as a female lover of God, the Divine male.

Mahābhārata: one of the two Indian epics (the other and the earlier being the story of Rama or the *Rāmāyana*), composed perhaps throughout the first millennium B.C., though probably taking its final form between the fourth and the second century B.C.

Maharsi: meaning a great *(mahā)* sage *(ṛṣi)*—a respectable appellation for a religious leader of great learning.

Manikraja: literally, "Prince Manik," designates Maniklal Bandopadhyay, a property holder of Kamarpukur, Ramakrishna's native village.

Mantra: incantation or mystical words.

Mleccha: an alien, that is, a non-Hindu, usually designating the Europeans.

Moksha: liberation from the cycle of birth, that is, salvation.

Naisthika brahmacarinī: a female *brahmacārī* who has ritually taken the vows of renunciation and celibacy for life.

Nirvikalpa samādhi: undifferentiated *entasis,* which is considered the pinnacle of yogic experience, resulting in a sense of the unity of the self and the world. In Freudian phrase this state is called "oceanic feeling" *(Ewigkeitsgefühl).*

Nyangtā: a vulgar Bengali word, meaning "naked," designating a sect of Hindu monks who stay naked. In the book *nyangtā* refers to Ramakrishna's putative Vedanta teacher, Totapuri of Punjab, who belonged to this sect.

Ojas: according to the ancient Hindu medical science *(Ayurveda),* it stands for the seven vital fluids of the male body, including the semen.

Pākhwāj: a percussion instrument of the Hindu classical musical tradition.

Paṇḍit: a scholar or a pedant.

Paramahaṁsa: literally, "supreme swan," connoting the realization of discrimination between the Truth and the Untruth. In Hindu mythology the swan is seen as the great discriminator, who consumes only the milk substance leaving the water from liquid milk. From a Tantric viewpoint, a *paramahaṁsa* is someone who has attained success in the *haṁsamantra,* a symbolic *mantra* in the form of inhalation *(haṁ)* and exhalation *(saḥ)* of breath.

Rajas: denotes the quality of activity, one of the three *guṇas* or constitutive elements of phenomena.

Rāmāyaṇa: see *Mahābhārata.*

Rasagollā: cheese ball dipped in sugar syrup and reputedly the most famous of the Bengali sweets.

Sādhak: (sādhaka in Sanskrit) a spiritual adept.

Samādhi: statis or a superconscious state or an ecstatic state.

Sanātana dharma: traditional (literally "eternal") religious practices of the Hindus.

Sannyāsa/Sannyāsī: ascetic exercises and career of a monk or an ascetic who has renounced the world.

Saraswati: the Hindu Minerva—goddess of learning and speech.

Sattva: on of the three *guṇas,* the quality of tranquillity, purity, virtue, and enlightenment.

Shakti: the Mother Goddess, power, or energy, originating, perhaps, in the non-Aryan culture of the Indus Valley. Mythologically *Shakti* is equated with the Goddesses Kali, Parvati, and Durga, consorts of Shiva. The cult of *Shakti* flourished since the fifth century A.D.

Shiva: also known as Maheśvara or Mahādeva ("Great God" of Destruction), is one of the great Hindu Trinity, the other two being Brahma (the Creator) and Vishnu (the Sustainer). In the *Purāṇas,* Shiva is spoken of as a Supreme Being. Shiva is the benign aspect of Maheśvara or the Vedic god Rudra.

Shudra: the lowest caste in Hindu society, whose occupation is chiefly manual labor.

Shyambazar: an area of north Calcutta.

Śrutidhar: Bengali for *śrutidhara* in Sanskrit, means one who holds into memory whatever he hears, and thus the word designates a person of prodigious memory.

Syce: or *sahis,* meaning an assistant to the coachman of a horse-drawn carriage.

Tablā: a percussion instrument consisting of a pair of drums, belonging to the Indo-Persian musical tradition of northern India.

Tamas: one of the three *guṇas,* the quality of darkness, inertia, and ignorance.

Tantra: system of religious philosophy in which Shiva, Vishnu, or the Divine Mother is the Ultimate Reality, differentiated, respectively, as Shaiva, Vaishnava, and Shakta *tantras.* Also means the scriptures dealing with these philosophies.

Tantric: A practitioner of *tantra.*

Tapasyā: spiritual exercise, including *dhyāna* or meditation.

Upanishad: Hindu spiritual treatises, about one hundred twelve in number, the oldest of which were composed between 800 and 400 B.C. The central vision of the Upanishads is Brahman. The Upanishads provide a spiritual interpretation to the ideas and rituals of the Vedas.

Vaishnava: a Hindu sect worshipping Lord Vishnu and His other incarnational forms.

Vedanta: literally meaning, "the end or the epitome of the Vedas," Vedanta sprang from the Upanishads with its central Upanisadic doctrine of the Brahman. Its founder was Badrayana, the author of the *Brahmasūtra* (also known as *Uttara-mīmāṁsa*), and its greatest exponent was the eighth-century south Indian mystic Shankaracharya (or Shankara). The Vedanta designates a system of metaphysics comprising the *Brahmasūtra,* the *Bhāgavadgītā,* and the Upanishads.

Vishnu: see Shiva.

Virajā Hom: (or *Virajā Homa* in Sanskrit) is a Vedic rite for initiation of the monks.

Yātrā: open-air Bengali opera emphasizing mythological, religious, or didactic themes and stories as well as folk tales.

Yoga: one of the six Hindu philosophical systems, dealing with the problems of the realization of the Self through prescribed physical and mental discipline, ascribed to Patanjali—a semimythical figure supposed to have flourished in the second century B.C. and authored the *Yoga-sūtras.* Yoga, meaning, "yoke," aspires to unite the individual self with the Supreme Self, that is, God.

Bibliography

Primary Sources

Bengali

Abhedananda, Swami. *Āmār Jīvankathā*. Kalikātā: Ramakrishna-Vivekananda Math, 1964.

Abjajananda, Swami. *Swamijīr Padaprānte (Swami Vivekanander Sannyāsī-Śisyaganer Jīvancarit)*. 4th ed. Kalikātā: Udbodhan Kāryālay, 1398 B.E.

Akhandananda, Swami. *Smṛtikathā*. 4th ed. Kalikātā: Udbodhan Kāryālay, 1983.

Bandopadhyay, Brajendranath, and Sajanikanta Das, eds. *Samasāmayik Dṛstite Śrīramakrishna Paramahaṁsa*. 1359 B.E. 3d printing. Calcutta: General Printers & Publishers Pvt. Ltd., 1390 B.E.

Chakrabarti, Sharacchandra. *Swami-Śisya Saṁvād*. 9th ed. Kalikātā: Udbodhan Kāryālay, 1400 B.E.

Chattopadhyay, Chandrashekhar. *Śrīśrīlātumahārajer Smṛtikathā*. 5th ed. Kalikātā: Udbodhan Kāryālay, 1398 B.E.

Datta, Mahendranath. *Kāśīdhāme Swami Vivekananda*. 5th printing. Calcutta: Mahendra Publishing Committee, 1398 B.E.

———. *Londone Swami Vivekananda*. 3 vols. in 2 pts. 1338–45 B.E. Reprint. Calcutta: Mahendra Publishing Committee, 1391–92 B.E.

———. *Guruprāṇ Ramchandrer Anudhyān*. Calcutta: Mahendra Publishing Committee, 1958.

———. *Śrīmat Vivekananda Swamijir Jīvaner Ghaṭanāvalī*. 3 vols. 5th printing. Calcutta: Mahendra Publishing Committee, 1393–95 B.E.

———. *Śrīmat Saradananda Swamijir Jīvaner Ghaṭanāvalī*. Calcutta: Mahendra Publishing Committee, 1355 B.E.

———. *Śrīśrīramakrishner Anudhyān*. Edited by Dhirendranath Basu. 6th ed. Calcutta: Mahendra Publishing Committee, 1396 B.E.

———. *Swami Vivekanander Vālyajīvanī*. 4th ed. Calcutta: Mahendra Publishing Committee, 1397 B.E.

Datta, Ramchandra. *Śrīśrīramakrishna Paramahaṁsadever Jīvanvṛttānta*. 1297 B.E. 8th ed. Kalikātā: Udbodhan Kāryālay, 1402 B.E.

Gambhirananda, Swami. *Yuganāyak Vivekananda*. 3 vols. Kalikātā: Udbodhan Kāryālay, 1373 B.E.

Ghosh, Girishchandra. *Śrīramakrishna Śrīśrīma O Vivekananda*. 3d ed. Calcutta: J. N. Chakravarti & Co., 1993.

Gupta, Mahendranath (ŚrīM). *Śrīśrīramakrishnakathāmṛta*. 5 vols. 1902–32. Reprint. Kalikātā: Kathāmṛta Bhavan, 1987.

Hirananda, Swami, and Sannyasini Tapomayi Puri, comp. *Vivekanander Hindu Cetanā*. 3rd ed. Jadavpur: Calcutta: Śrīsatyānanda Devāyatan, 1990.

Jagadishwarananda, Swami, comp. and ed. *Śrīramakrishna Pārṣad-Prasaṅga*. 1357 B.E. Reprint. Belur: Śrīramakrishna Dharmachakra, 1398 B.E.

Majumdar, Rameshchandra. *Śrīramakrishner Ātmakathā*. Navabarakpur: Srisriramakrishna Trust, 1987.

Purnatmananda, Swami. *Smṛtir Āloy Swamiji*. 1396 B.E. Reprint. Kalikātā: Udbodhan Kāryālay, 1397 B.E.

Saradananda, Swami. *Śrīśrīramakrishnalīlāprasaṅga*, 5 pts. in 2 vols. Each part with separate pagination. Vol. I in 3 pts. (Pūrvakathā O Vālyajīvan, Sādhakbhāv, and Gurubhāv—Pūrvārdha); Vol. II in 2 pts. (Gurubhāv—Uttarārdha and Divyabhāv O Narendranath). Kalikātā: Udbodhan Kāryālay, 1398 B.E.

Saradeshananda, Swami. *Śrīśrīmāyer Smṛtikathā*. 2d ed. Kalikātā: Udbodhan Kāryālay, 1983.

Sen, Akshaykumar. *Śrīśrīramakrishnapunthi*. 10th ed. Kalikātā: Udbodhan Kāryālay, 1392 B.E.

Swami Vivekanander Vāṇī O Racanā Samkalan. 6 ed. Kalikātā: Udbodhan Kāryālay, 1400 B.E.

Vivekananda, Swami. *Patrāvalī*. 5th ed. Kalikātā: Udbodhan Kāryālay, 1394 B.E.

———. *Swamijir Vāṇī O Racanā*. 10 vols. 4th ed. Kalikātā: Udbodhan Kāryālay, 1383–84 B.E.

English

Basu, Sankari P., ed. *Letters of Sister Nivedita*. 2 vols. Calcutta: Navabharat Publishers, 1982.

Burke, Marie Louise (Sister Gargi). *Swami Vivekananda in the West: New Discoveries*. 6 pts. 3d ed. Calcutta: Advaita Ashrama, 1983–87): *His Prophetic Mission*, 2 pts. (1983–84); *The World Teacher*, 2 pts. (1985–86); *A New Gospel*, 2 pts. (1987). Cited with subtitles only.

His Eastern and Western Admirers. *Reminiscences of Swami Vivekananda* 3d ed. Calcutta: Advaita Ashrama, 1983.

Nikhilananda, Swami. *The Gospel of Sri Ramakrishna*. 7th printing. New York: Ramakrishna-Vivekananda Center, 1984.

Nivedita, Sister. *Notes of Some Wanderings with the Swami Vivekananda*, ed. Swami Saradananda. Authorized ed. Calcutta: Udbodhan Office, 1913.

Saradananda, Swami. *Sri Ramakrishna the Great Master*. Translated by Swami Jagadananda. 2 vols. 6th rev. ed. Mylapore: Sri Ramakrishna Math, 1983–84.

Swami Vivekananda and His Guru with Letters from Prominent Americans on the Alleged Progress of Vedantism in the United States. London and Madras: Christian Literature Society for India, 1897.

Vivekananda, Swami. *The Complete Works of Swami Vivekananda*, 8 vols. Mayavati Memorial ed. Calcutta: Advaita Ashrama, 1990.

———. *Inspired Talks: My Master and Other Writings*. Rev. paperback ed. New York: Ramakrishna-Vivekananda Center, 1987.

———. *Letters of Swami Vivekananda*. 6th impression. Calcutta: Advaita Ashrama, 1986.

————. *Swami Vivekananda on Himself.* Calcutta: Vivekananda Centenary, 1963.

————. *Vedanta: Voice of Freedom.* Edited by Swami Chetanananda. St. Louis: Vedanta Society of St. Louis, 1990.

————. *The Yogas and Other Works.* Comp. by Swami Nikhilananda. Rev. ed. New York: Ramakrishna-Vivekananda Center, 1984.

Secondary Sources

Bengali

Bagchi, Mani. *Nivedita.* 2d ed. Calcutta: Presidency Library, n.d..

————. *Sannyāsī Vivekananda.* 2d ed. Kalikātā: Jijñāsā, 1976.

Bandyopadhyay, Asitkumar, Shankariprasad Basu, and Shankar, eds. *Viśvavivek.* Kalikātā: Vāk Sāhitya, 1963.

Basu, Nemaisadhan, ed. *Śāśvata Vivekananda.* Calcutta: Ananda Publishers Pvt. Ltd., 1992.

————. "Samasāmayik Pāścātyer Dṛstite Chicago Dharmamahāsammelan O Swami Vivekanander Bhūmikār Tātparyer Mūlyayan." *Udbodhan* 96, nos. 5 and 6 (Jyaistha and Āsāḍ, 1401 B.E.).

Basu, Pramathanath. *Swami Vivekananda,* 2 vols. Kalikātā: Udbodhan Kāryālay, 1369–70 B.E.

Basu, Shankariprasad. *Vivekananda O Samakālīn Bhāratvarṣa.* 7 vols. Calcutta: Mandal Book House, 1382–89 B.E.

————. *Nivedita Lokmātā,* 4 vols. Vol. I in 4 pts. Calcutta: Ananda Publishers Pvt. Ltd., 1375–1401 B.E.

————. *Sahāsya Vivekananda.* 5th ed. Calcutta: Navabharat Publishers, 1991.

Bhattacharya, Abhaychandra. *ŚrīMar Jīvan Darśan.* Jñānpur: Jagabandhu Prakāśan, 1397 B.E.

Budhananda, Swami. *Swamijir Śrīramakrishna Sādhanā.* 3d ed. Kalikātā: Udbodhan Kāryālay, 1392 B.E.

Chakravarti, Surath. "Chicago Dharmasabhā (1893): Kichhu 'Myth' O Apapracār." *Dharmatattva* (Baiśākh-Jyaistha 1399 B.E.—Baiśākh-Āsāḍ 1400 B.E.).

————. "Chicago Dharmasabhāy Pratapchandra Majumdar O Swami Vivekananda (Apapracārer Svarūp Udghātan)." *Dharmatattva* (Māgh 1400 B.E.).

————. *Śrīmat Ramakrishna Paramahaṁser Prāmānya Jīvanī Hisābe Grhita Kayekti Granther Samālocanā.* Calcutta: Navavidhan Publication Committee, 1362 B.E.

————. "Swami Vivekananda Banām Brahmo Narendranath O Chicago Dharmasabhā." *Tattvakaumudī* (16 Māgh 1400 B.E., 16 Jyaistha 1401 B.E., and 16 Āsāḍ 1401 B.E.).

Chattopadhyaya, Rajagopal. "1893 Ār 1993 Sāler Dui Chicago Dharmasabhā Evaṁ Tanmadhye Bhāratīya Priatinidhitva." *Saṁvād Vicitra,* New York (16 January 1994 and 1 February 1994).

————. "Chicago Dharmasabhāy Bharatīya Pratinidhi: Ek Tathyaninbhar Vyavacched," 2 pts. *Utsa Mānus* (May and June 1995).

————. "'Parivrājak' Vivekanander Bhārat Bhramaṇ 1886 Theke 1893." *Utsa Mānus* (September-October 1995).

Chaudhury, Devendradas. *Vivekanander Chātrajīvan*. Chittagong: Kohinoor Press, 1338 B.E.

Chitragupta. *Ādālate Vipanna Vivekananda*. Kalikātā: Yogmāyā Prakaśanī, 1993.

Datta, Bhupendranath. *Swami Vivekananda*. 1961. 3rd ed. Calcutta: Navabharat Publishers, 1400 B.E.

Dhar, Niranjan. *Vivekananda Anya Cokhe*. 1987. 3rd ed. Salt Lake, Calcutta: Utsa Manus, 1995.

Gambhirananda, Swami. *Śriśrīramakrishna Bhaktamālikā*, 2 vols. Vol. I. 8th ed. Vol. II. 7th ed. Kalikātā: Udbodhan Kāryālay, 1396–98 B.E.

Ghosal, Shailendranarayan. *Vaidic Bhārat*. Kalikātā: Anandamohan Ghosal, 1397 B.E.

Ghosh, Arabinda. *Prajjvalita Sūrya*. Calcutta: M. C. Sarkar & Sons Pvt. Ltd., 1993.

Lokeshwarananda, Swami, ed. *Cintānāyak Vivekananda*. 2d rev. ed. 1395 B.E. Reprint. Calcutta: Ramakrishna Mission Institute of Culture, 1397 B.E.

Mukhopadhyay, Sanat, and Manju Datta. *Vivekananda Parikar Kirancandra Datta O Tatkālīn Samāj (1876–1960)*. Kalikātā: Kiran Niketan, 1396 B.E.

Muktiprana, Pravrajika. *Bhaginī Nivedita*. 6th ed. Calcutta: Sister Nivedita Girls' School, 1992.

Prabhananda, Swami. *Śrīramakrihsner Antyalīlā*. 2 vols. 2d ed. Kalikātā: Udbodhan Kāryālay, 1396–1401 B.E.

Prajnanananda, Swami. *Saṅgītpratibhāy Swami Vivekananda*. Kalikātā: Śrīramakrishna Vedanta Math, 1397 B.E.

Prameyananda, Swami, ed. *Viśvacetanāy Śrīramakrishna*. Kalikātā: Udbodhan Kāryālay, 1987.

Purnatmananda, Swami. *Swami Vivekananda Evaṁ Bhārater Svādhinatā Saṅgram*. 2d ed. Kalikātā: Udbodhan Kāryālay, 1993.

Ray, Tamasranjan. *Bhārat-Bhaginī Nivedita*. Kalikātā: Kalikātā Pustakālay, *ca*. 1967.

Sen, Amulyabhusan. *Vivekanander Itihāscetanā*. Kalikātā: n.p., 1966.

Someshwarananda, Swami. *Itihāscetanāy Vivekananda*. 2d ed. Kalikātā: Śraddhā Prakasán, 1988.

Vedantaprana, Pravrajika, ed. *Mahimā Tava Udbhāsita: Dharmasabhā-Śatavarṣa Smārakgrantha*. 1994. 2nd printing. Dakshineshwar: Śrī Sarada Math, 1995.

Vivekananda Anya Cokhe: Ekti Samīkṣā—Āro Kichhu Vitarka. 1987. 3rd ed. Salt Lake: Utsa Mānus, 1995.

English

Atmaprana, Pravrajika. *Sister Nivedita of Ramakrishna-Vivekananda*. Calcutta: Sister Nivedita Girls' School, 1961.

Atulananda, Swami. *With the Swamis in America and India*. Edited by Pravrajika Brahmaprana. Calcutta: Advaita Ashrama, 1988.

Bainton, Ronald. *Here I Stand: A Life of Martin Luther*. 1950. Reprint. New York: American Library, 1977.

Banerji, G. C. *Keshab Chandra and Ramakrishna*. 2d ed. Calcutta: Navavidhan Publication Committee, 1942.

Baumer, Rachel Van M., ed. *Aspects of Bengali History and Society*. Honolulu: University Press of Hawaii, 1975.

Bhagavad Gita: The Song of God. Translated by Swami Prabhavananda and Christopher Isherwood. 4th ed. Hollywood: Vedanta Press, 1987.

Bharati, Agehananda. *Hindu Views and Ways and the Hindu-Muslim Interface: An Anthropological Assessment.* New Delhi: Munshiram Manoharlal Publishers Pvt. Ltd., 1981.

Biswas, Arun K. *Vivekananda and the Indian Quest for Socialism.* Calcutta: Firma KLM Pvt. Ltd., 1986.

Blichfeldt, Anders. "Tantra in the Ramakrishna Math and Mission." *Update* 6 (1982).

Bois, Jules. "The New Religions of America—Hindu Cults." *Forum* 77 (March 1927).

Bonney, Charles C. *World's Congress Addresses.* Chicago: Open Court Publishing Co., 1900.

Borg, Marcus J. *Jesus: A New Vision.* San Francisco: Harper & Row Publishers, 1987.

Borthwick, Meredith. *Keshub Chunder Sen: A Search for Cultural Synthesis.* Calcutta: Minerva Associates (Publishers) Pvt. Ltd., 1978.

Bose, Nemaisadhan, *Swami Vivekananda.* New Delhi: Sahitya Akademi, 1994.

Brahmaprana, Pravrajika. "Swamiji and His Western Women Disciples." *Prabuddha Bharata* (May 1989).

Bryson, Thomas L. "The Cyclonic Hindu: Swami Vivekananda." Paper presented at the American Academy of Religion Conference, Kansas City, 23–26 November 1991.

———. "The Hermeneutics of Religious Syncretism: Swami Vivekananda's Practical Vedanta." Ph.D. diss., University of Chicago, 1992.

Chakravarti, Surath. *Chicago Parliament of Religions (September 1893): A Short History.* Calcutta: Navavidhan Publication Committee, 1993.

———. *Vivekananda, Brahmo Samaj and Chicago Parliament, 1893.* Calcutta: Navavidhan Publication Committee, 1994.

Chatterjee, Partha. *The Nation and Its Fragments: Colonial and Postcolonial Histories.* Princeton: Princeton University Press, 1993.

Chattopadhyaya, Rajagopal. *Swami Vivekananda in the West.* Calcutta: K. P. Bagchi, 1994.

———. *World's Parliament of Religions, 1893: Participation from the Indian Subcontinent and the 1993 Parliament.* Calcutta: Minerva Associates (Publications) Pvt. Ltd., 1995.

Chetanananda, Swami. *They Lived with God: Life Story of Some Devotees of Sri Ramakrishna.* St. Louis, MO: Vedanta Society of St. Louis, 1989.

Choudhary, Kamakhya P.S. *Modern Indian Mysticism.* Delhi: Motilal Banarasidass, 1981.

Comans, Michael, "The Question of the Importance of *Samadhi* in Modern and Classical Advaita Vedanta." *Philosophy East and West* 43 1 (1993).

Dasgupta, Rabindra K., ed. *Swami Vivekananda: A Hundred Years since Chicago: A Commemorative Volume.* Belur: Ramakrishna Math & Mission, 1994.

Datta, Bhupendranath. *Swami Vivekananda Patriot-Prophet: A Study* (1954. 2d rev. ed. Calcutta: Navabharat Publishers, 1993. (The 1993 edition is much shorter than the first 1954 ed.)

Dhar, Niranjan. *Vedanta and Bengal Renaissance.* Calcutta: Minerva Associates (Publications) Pvt. Ltd., 1978.

Dhar, Shailendra N. *A Comprehensive Biography of Swami Vivekananda,* 3 vols. in 2 pts. Madras: Vivekananda Kendra Prakashan, 1975–76. 2nd ed. in 2 vols., 1990.

Dimock, Edward C. "On Impersonality and Bengali Religious Biography," M. Naga-tomi, B. K. Matilal, J. M. Masson, and E. Dimock, ed. *Sanskrit and Indian Studies.* Dordrecht: D. Reidel Co., 1979.

———. *The Place of the Hidden Moon: Erotic Mysticism in the Vaisnava Sahajiya Cult of Bengal.* New ed. with Foreword by Wendy Doniger. Chicago: University of Chicago Press, 1989.

Dutta, Abhijit. *Nineteenth Century Bengal Society and the Christian Missionaries.* Cal-cutta: Minerva Associates (Publications) Pvt. Ltd., 1992.

Ellwood, Robert S., ed. *Eastern Spirituality in America: Selected Writings.* New York: Paulist Press, 1987.

Erikson, Erik. *Young Man Luther: A Study in Psychoanalysis and History.* New York: W. W. Norton, 1958.

Farquhar, John N. *Modern Religious Movements in India.* 1915. Reprint. New Delhi: Munshiram Manoharlal, 1967.

Foxe, Barbara. *Long Journey Home: A Biography of Margaret Noble (Nivedita).* Lon-don: Rider & Co., 1975.

Gambhirananda, Swami. *History of Ramakrishna Math and Ramakrishna Mission.* 3d rev. ed. Calcutta: Advaita Ashrama, 1983.

Ganguly, Manomohan. *The Swami Vivekananda: A Study.* 2d printing. Calcutta: Contemporary Publishers, 1962.

Ghanananda, Swami, and Geoffrey Parrinder, eds. *Swami Vivekananda in East and West.* London: Ramakrishna Vedanta Centre, 1968.

Ghatak, Kamal K. *Hindu Revivalism in Bengal: Rammohan to Ramakrishna.* Calcutta: Minerva Associates (Publications) Pvt. Ltd., 1991.

Gupta, Harish C., ed. *Swami Vivekananda Studies in Soviet Union.* Calcutta: Ramak-rishna Mission Institute of Culture, *ca.* 1987.

Gupta, Krishna P. "Religious Evolution and Social Change in India: A Study of the Ramakrishna Mission Movement." *Contributions to Indian Sociology* n.s., no. 8 (1974).

———. "Swami Vivekananda: A Case Study of the Hindu Religious Tradition and the Modern Secular Ideal." *Quest* 80 (1973).

Hanson, J. W., ed. *The World's Congress of Religions: The Addresses and Papers Delivered Before the Parliament, and an Abstract of the Congresses Held in the Art Institute, Chicago, Illinois, U.S.A., August 25 to October 15, 1893, Under the Auspices of the World's Columbian Exposition.* Chicago: W. B. Conkey Co., 1894.

Hiriyanna, M. *Outlines of Indian Philosophy.* 1st Indian ed. Delhi: Motilal Banarsidass Publishers, 1993.

His Eastern and Western Disciples. *The Life of Swami Vivekananda,* 2 vols. 5th ed. Calcutta: Advaita Ashrama, 1979–81.

Hyman, Ronald. *Nietzsche: A Critical Life.* New York: Oxford University Press, 1980.

Jackson, Carl T. *The Orientalist Religions and American Thought: Nineteenth-Century Explorations.* Westport, Conn.: Greenwood Press, 1981.

———. *Vedanta for the West: The Ramakrishna Movement in the United States.* Bloomington: Indiana University Press, 1994.

Jensen, Timothy A. "Madness, Yearning, and Play: The Life of Sri Ramakrishna." Ph.D. diss., University of Chicago, 1976.

Jones, Jenkin L. *A Chorus of Faith as Heard in the Parliament of Religions Held in Chicago, Sept. 10–27, 1893.* Chicago: Unity Publishing Co., 1893.

Kakar, Sudhir. *The Analyst and the Mystic: Psychoanalytic Reflections on Religion and Mysticism.* New Delhi: Viking, 1991.

———. *The Inner World: A Psycho-Analytic Study of Childhood and Society in India.* Delhi: Oxford University Press, 1978.

Kapoor, Satish K. *Cultural Contact and Fusion: Swami Vivekananda the West (1893–96).* Jalandhar: ABS Publications, 1987.

King, Ursula. "Indian Spirituality, Western Materialism: An Image and Its Function in the Reinterpretation of Modern Hinduism." *Social Action* 28 (January-March 1978).

Kopf, David. *The Brahmo Samaj and the Shaping of the Modern Indian Mind.* Princeton: Princeton University Press, 1979.

———. *British Orientalism and the Bengal Renaissance: The Dynamics of Indian Modernization.* Berkeley: University of California Press, 1969.

Kripal, Jeffrey J. *Kālī's Child: The Mystical and the Erotic in the Life and Teachings of Ramakrishna.* Chicago: University of Chicago Press, 1995.

———. "Kālī's Tongue and Ramakrishna: 'Biting the Tongue' of the Tantric Tradition." *History of Religions* 34, no. 2 (1994).

———. "Vivekananda and Ram Chandra Datta: An Early Conflict over the Person and Message of Ramakrishna." Paper presented at the Fourth International Congress of Vedanta, Miami University, Oxford, Ohio, 2–5 April 1992.

Mahadevan, Telliaravam M. P. *Swami Vivekananda and the Indian Renaissance.* Coimbatore: Sri Ramakrishna Mission Vidyalaya Teachers College, 1967.

Majumdar, Ramesh C. *Swami Vivekananda: A Historical Review.* Calcutta: General Printers & Publishers, 1965.

———, ed. *Swami Vivekananda Centenary Memorial Volume.* Calcutta: Swami Vivekananda Centenary, 1963.

Matchett, Freda. "The Teaching of Ramakrishna in Relation to the Hindu Tradition and as Interpreted by Vivekananda." *Religion* 11 (1982).

Mazumdar, Sucheta. "Women, Culture and Politics: Engendering the Hindu Nation." *South Asia Bulletin* 12, no. 2 (Fall 1992).

McLean, Malcolm D. "Are Ramakrishnaites Hindus? Some Implications of Recent Litigation on the Question." *South Asia* 14, no. 2 (1991).

Meissner, W. W. *The Psychology of a Saint: Ignatius Loyola.* New Haven: Yale University Press, 1992.

Mercer, Rev. Lewis P. *Review of the World's Religious Congresses of the World's Congress Auxiliary of the World's Columbian Exposition. Chicago, 1893.* Chicago: Rand, McNally & Co., 1893.

Mital, S. S. *The Social and Political Ideas of Swami Vivekananda.* New Delhi: Metropolitan Book Co. Pvt. Ltd., 1979.

Mukherjee, Jayashree. "The Institution of Caste in the Eyes of Ramakrishna and Vivekananda." *Quarterly Review of Historical Studies* 27, no. 2 (1987).

Mukherjee, Prabhati. *Hindu Women: Normative Models.* New Delhi: Orient Longman Ltd., 1978.

Müller, Frederick Max. *Rāmakrishna: His Life and Sayings.* 1899. Reprint. New York: AMS Press, 1975.

"Myths About the Swami." *Sunday* (Calcutta), January 31–February 6, 1992 and February 7–13, 1993.

Nikhilananda, Swami. *Vivekananda: A Biography*. 2d ed. Calcutta: Advaita Ashrama, 1971.

Nivedita, Sister. *The Master as I Saw Him*. 12th ed. Calcutta: Udbodhan Office, 1977.

Panchapagesan, K. "A Stylistic Study of Swami Vivekananda's Speech." *Prabuddha Bharata* 90 (January 1985).

Pande, Govind C. *Life and Thought of Shankaracharya*. Delhi: Motilal Banarsidass Publishers, 1994.

Prabhananda, Swami. *First Meetings with Sri Ramakrishna*. Mylapore: Sri Ramakrishna Math, 1987.

———. *More About Ramakrishna*. Calcutta: Advaita Ashrama, 1993.

Prabhavananda, Swami, and Christopher Isherwood, trans. *Bhagavad Gita: The Song of God*. 1944. Reprint. Hollywood, Calif.: Vedanta Press, 1987.

Prabuddhaprana, Pravrajika. *The Life of Josephine MacLeod: Friend of Swami Vivekananda*. Dakshineshwar: Sri Sarada Math, 1990.

Rai Chaudhuri, Sanat K. *Swami Vivekananda: The Man and His Mission*. Calcutta: Scientific Book Agency, 1966.

Ramakrishnananda, Swami. *Sri Ramakrishna and His Mission*. Madras: Sri Ramakrishna Math, 1972.

Rambachan, Anantanand. *The Limits of Scripture: Vivekananda's Interpretation of the Vedas*. Honolulu: Hawaii University Press, 1994.

———. "The Place of Reason in the Quest for *Moksha*—Problems in Vivekananda's Conceptualization of *Jnanayoga*." *Religious Studies* 23, no. 2 (June 1987).

Rao, V. K. R. V. *Swami Vivekananda: The Prophet of Vedantic Socialism*. New Delhi: Ministry of Information & Broadcasting, 1979.

Raychaudhuri, Tapan. *Europe Reconsidered: Perception of the West in Nineteenth Century Bengal*. Delhi: Oxford University Press, 1988.

Reymond, Lizelle. *The Dedicated: A Biography of Nivedita*. New York: John Day Co., 1953.

Rolland, Romain. *Life of Vivekananda and the Universal Gospel*. Translated by E. F. Malcolm-Smith. 10th impression. Calcutta: Advaita Ashrama, 1984.

Roy, Benoy K. *Socio-Political Views of Vivekananda*. New Delhi: People's Publishing House, 1970.

Rudra, Rita. "Swami Vivekananda's Concept of Man." Ph.D. diss., Claremont Graduate School, 1974.

Sarma, D.S. *The Master and the Disciple*. Mylapore: Sri Ramakrishna Math, 1967.

Satprakashananda, Swami. *Swami Vivekananda's Contribution to Present Age*. St. Louis, Miss.: The Vedanta Society of St. Louis, 1978.

Schuon, Frithjob. "The Problem of Sexuality." *Studies in Comparative Religion* 2, no. 1 (Winter 1977).

Seal, Brajendranath. "An Early Stage of Vivekananda's Mental Development." *Prabuddha Bharata*, 12 (April 1907).

Sen, M. "Swami Vivekananda and Social Reform." *Calcutta Review*, vol. 170 (February 1964).

Sharma, Arvind. *Ramakrishna and Vivekananda: New Perspectives.* New Delhi: Sterling Publishers Pvt. Ltd., 1989.

Sharma, Beni S. *Swami Vivekananda: A Forgotten Chapter in His Life.* Calcutta: Oxford Book & Stationary Co., 1963.

Sil, Narasingha P. "Indian Religious Movements in the United States" in *Asian American Encyclopedia.* New York: Marshall Cavendish Corporation, 1994.

———. *Kauṭilya's Arthaśāstra: A Comparative Study.* 2nd rev. ed. Berne: Peter Lang Publishers, 1989.

———. "Luther, Erikson, and History: A Strange Encounter," *Quarterly Review of Historical Studies* 22, no. 3 (1982).

———. *Rāmakṛṣṇa Paramahaṁsa: A Psychological Profile.* Leiden: E. J. Brill, 1991.

———. "Saradamani the Holy Mother: The Making of a Madonna," *Asian Culture Quarterly* 21, no. 2 (1993).

———. "Swami Vivekananda in the West: The Legend Reinterpreted," *South Asia* 18, no. 1 (1995).

———. "Vivekānanda's Rāmakṛṣṇa: An Untold Story of Mythmaking and Propaganda," *Numen* 40 (1993).

Sinha, Mrilanini. *Colonial Masculinity: The "Manly Englishman" and the "Effeminate Bengali" in the Late Nineteenth Century.* Manchester: Manchester University Press, 1995.

Sivaramakrishna, M., and Sumita Roy, ed. *Perspectives on Ramakrishna-Vivekananda Vedanta Tradition.* New Delhi: Sterling Publishers Pvt. Ltd., 1991.

Smith, Bardwell L., ed. *Hinduism: New Essays in the History of Religion.* Leiden: E. J. Brill, 1976.

Southard, Barbara. "Neo-Hduism and Militant Politics in Bengal, 1875–1910." PhD. diss. University of Hawaii, 1971.

Stark, Claude A. "Swami Vivekananda as a Devotee." *The Journal of Religious Studies,* 4 (Spring 1972).

Sutherland, Sally J. "Sītā and Draupadī: Aggressive Behavior and Female Role-Models in the Sanskrit Epics," *Journal of the American Oriental Society,* 109, no. 1 (1989).

Swami Vivekananda and His Guru with Letters from Prominent Americans on the Alleged Progress of Vedantism in the United States. London and Madras: Christian Literature Society for India, 1897.

Thomas, Wendell. *Hinduism Invades America.* New York: The Beacon Press, Inc., 1930.

Veysey, Laurence. *The Communal Experience: Anarchist & Mystical Communities in Twentieth-Century America.* 1973. With new preface. Chicago: University of Chicago Press, 1978.

Wadley, Susan S. "Women and The Hindu Tradition," *Signs: Journal of Women in Culture and Society,* 3, no. 1 (1977).

White, Charles S. J. "Indian Developments: Sainthood in Hinduism," Richard Kieckheifer and George D. Bond, ed. *Sainthood: Its Manifestations in World Religions.* Berkeley: University of California Press, 1988.

———. "The Sāi Bābā Movement: Approaches to the Study of Indian Saints." *Journal of Asian Studies* 33, no. 4 (1972).

Williams, George M. *The Quest for the Meaning of Swami Vivekananda: A Study of Religious Change.* Chico, Calif.: New Horizon Press, 1974.

———. "Swami Vivekananda: Archetypal Hero or Doubting Saint?" Robert D. Baird, ed. *Religion in Modern India.* New Delhi: Manohar, 1981.

Wilson, Horace Hyman. *Essays and Lectures Chiefly on the Religion of the Hindus.* Edited by Reinhold Rost. 2 vols. London: Trübner, 1861.

Index